"A Strange Sort of Being"

"A Strange Sort of Being"

The Transgender Life of Lucy Ann / Joseph Israel Lobdell, 1829–1912

BAMBI L. LOBDELL

McFarland & Company, Inc., Publishers
Jefferson, North Carolina, and London

All photographs are courtesy Susan Crawson Shields.

LIBRARY OF CONGRESS CATALOGUING-IN-PUBLICATION DATA

Lobdell, Bambi L., 1956–
    A strange sort of being : the transgender life of Lucy Ann/ Joseph Israel Lobdell, 1829–1912 / Bambi L. Lobdell.
        p.   cm.
    Includes bibliographical references and index.

    ISBN 978-0-7864-4805-0
    softcover : acid free paper ∞

    1. Lobdell, Lucy Ann, b. 1829. 2. Transgender people — United States — Case studies. 3. Transsexuals — United States — Case studies. 4. Lesbians — United States — Case studies. 5. Gender identity — United States — Case studies. 6. Queer theory. I. Title.
HQ77.8.L63L63 2012
306.76'80973 — dc23   2011044559

BRITISH LIBRARY CATALOGUING DATA ARE AVAILABLE

© 2012 Bambi L. Lobdell. All rights reserved

No part of this book may be reproduced or transmitted in any form or by any means, electronic or mechanical, including photocopying or recording, or by any information storage and retrieval system, without permission in writing from the publisher.

Front cover: Lucy Ann Lobdell, circa 1854; background and frame © 2012 Shutterstock; rabbit deer and turkey © 2012 clipart.com

Manufactured in the United States of America

McFarland & Company, Inc., Publishers
  Box 611, Jefferson, North Carolina 28640
    www.mcfarlandpub.com

For Joe

Acknowledgments

I would like to thank my aunt, Eadie Lobdell, for placing Lucy's story in my hands and insisting that I read it, and my uncle, Doug Lobdell, Sr., who loved Lucy's spirit, strength, and determination. I am grateful to Susan Crawson Shields for her generous loan of family pictures, documents, and stories and her mutual love and admiration for Lucy, and to Mindy Desens for her scholarship that contributed Lobdell's previously unknown trip to Minnesota to the making of the complete story. I would like to also thank Susan Campbell Bartoletti for her unwavering support, advice, and friendship, all of which helped make this project possible for me. I also thank Lauren Floden, Nancy Pirro, and Sharon Smith, cheerleaders extraordinaire, whose belief in me kept me floating during times of self-doubt. I must acknowledge my "personal librarian," Kay Benjamin, for all her help with research as well as her strong friendship, not to mention her love for and interest in Lucy Ann/Joseph Israel. I also thank Karen Ylimaki, Gloria McCullough, Dale Haynes, and Shirley Hauck for their help in my research. Most especially, I would like to thank my daughter, Chelsea Lobdell, for her patience and love, and her absolute conviction that her mother can do anything she sets her mind to do.

Table of Contents

Acknowledgments — vi
Preface — 1
Introduction — 5

   One • "Some Do Call Me a Strange Sort of Being" — 25
   Two • The Singing Teacher of Bethany — 59
   Three • The Queer Couple — 90
   Four • "A Man in All That the Name Implies" — 124

Appendix A. Narrative of Lucy Ann Lobdell, the Female Hunter of Delaware and Sullivan Counties, N.Y. — 155
Appendix B. Lunacy Testimonials — 184
Appendix C. Wise's "Case of Sexual Perversion" — 199
Appendix D. Excerpt from The History of Meeker County — 203
Chapter Notes — 211
Bibliography — 224
Index — 229

Preface

WHILE WORKING ON MY DOCTORATE, my original plan to write a dissertation on some piece of medieval literature fell through. I wondered what else I could research and write about based on my fields of study. I was free-falling through the type of panic that keeps a person awake all night, keenly aware of my adolescent daughter watching me. I needed to find something to research and write about that would meet scholarly criteria, attract academic interest, and hopefully not bore me to tears. I wanted a project that would excite me as much as medieval romances, a topic that I could become passionate about, a subject I could explore and learn from. A search through my books and notes and papers, looking for the perfect dissertation project, left me empty-handed and even more frantic.

After a tiring, unproductive week, I took a break from fruitless nail-biting and enjoyed a visit with my Aunt Eadie, an event that seemed completely unconnected to my scholarly problem. She handed me a copy of a book that someone in our family—Lucy Ann Lobdell—had written over a century ago and insisted I read it. I politely took the book, thanked her, and laid it on my desk, where I promptly forgot about it. After all, I had a mission to accomplish—finding a dissertation topic.

Aunt Eadie called me a few times, interested to know what I thought of Lucy's book. Courteous excuses did not satisfy her; she was a real pest, insisting that she knew I would love this story. So, to avoid being nagged, I figured I had better just sit down and read it. After all, it was only about 50 pages long.

Aunt Eadie was right; the story was intriguing. So much so that I ran to the office of the apartment complex I lived in to share it with Sue Shields, who ran the office. Sue just smiled and agreed it was a good story. She was aware of it because she was Lucy's great-great-granddaughter. Did I want to see pictures of Lucy?

At this point, I realized my dissertation topic had found me. In fact, it possessed me. I began with the autobiography, the pictures, and the few documents that Sue gave me, and spent years searching census records and legal documents, reading microfilm copies of newspaper articles, finding old histories and psychological articles, and tracking down any other scrap of information I could find on Lucy Ann Lobdell. Lucy, rebellious and daring, was a colorful character (to say the least), and her story was compelling and entertaining.

I ended up with a collage of stories in all sorts of forms, from clinical doctors' reports to amusing folktales to outraged newspaper articles. I realized it would be a challenge to put together Lucy Ann's life from information coming from so many different perspectives. And it seemed there was something significant about that wide range of viewpoints. Some stories seemed to praise Lucy while others condemned her. Some stories were built around cherry-picked information suited to the judgment imparted by the storyteller. Still others were mostly fiction, which made me wonder what purpose they served for the writer or the audience. Rarely did any form of story include Lucy's words, leaving her perspective noticeably absent. It seemed many people felt it necessary to define, label, and judge Lobdell, without her permission or cooperation.

While studying this collection, it became obvious to me that stories have enormous power to create meaning about a person and that person's life, meaning subsequently accepted as truth, even though those stories rarely used the words of their subjects. In other words, storytellers seemed to create meaning about their subjects, layer it onto them, and present their fiction as truth. When compared to Lobdell's life and the few recorded words left behind, a breech appeared between the stories and Lobdell's perspective, which made it clear that dominant stories and storytellers had the power to define a subject and contain, or even erase, an identity found to be disruptive.

To make sense of the breech in meaning surrounding Lobdell's life, I set out to examine the importance of storytelling and its role in shaping our understanding of people and ordering society. From my obsessive examination of stories about Lucy I learned that forms of story are everywhere, whether as histories, newspaper articles, medical diagnoses, or legal judgments, and all these stories shape how we understand people, relationships, and society. I call these various narratives "cultural stories."

Preface

To better understand the significance of Lobdell's life, I had to study various aspects of nineteenth-century American history, including social concepts about (and expectations of) men and women, education, the field of sexology, and ideas about insanity. I also had to study gender and queer theory in order to tell the story from Lobdell's perspective. All cultural stories I had gathered, except for the autobiography, had been written from outside perspectives that defined, classified, and judged Lobdell according to dominant concepts, which she rejected and rebelled against. In other words, Lobdell's story had been seized by others who claimed the authority to define the truth about Lobdell.

Queer theory helped me to understand the conflict that surrounded Lobdell's life and body. While people writing about Lobdell during the nineteenth century framed their subject as disruptive, immoral, and dangerous because of masculine gender presentation, writers in the 20th and 21st centuries treat Lobdell's masculine appearance and activities as merely rebellious, and present Lobdell as a lesbian because of her relationship with Marie.

But something didn't seem to ring true to me. In all the stories about Lobdell, he presented as a man. He dressed like a man, acted like a man, did work that was generally reserved for men, went by the name Joseph (or La-Roi), and loved women, although doing so brought much trouble to his life. Lobdell seemed more than just rebellious to me, more than just clever in trying to use male clothes to gain entrance into spaces and jobs reserved for men. Even after being placed in an insane asylum for wearing men's clothes, Lobdell persisted in presenting as a man named Joe and actually told the doctor he was a man — repeatedly.

Even though this information was in an article read by numerous others, it seemed that no one paid attention to it or gave it any credence. People writing about Lobdell ignored or dismissed his words and assumed the authority to tell her story, which didn't seem accurate to me.

I re-read all the articles and histories and diagnoses I had gathered, but I started from the assumption that Lobdell actually was a man, as he claimed, and came to the conclusion that Lobdell was a transgender man. This greatly changed the story and made it feel more like the story Lobdell would tell if given the chance. Since he had not been given the chance, I felt it necessary to tell the story differently, granting authority to Lobdell to define himself. I realize this presentation will prompt debate and maybe even anger, but my hope is that my presentation will help create a much-needed legitimacy to transgender history, people, and lives. I see Joe as a transgender pioneer, one who bravely lived life as authentically as possible, even though it brought him harassment, ridicule, and incarceration, and I feel it necessary to present Lobdell's life from that perspective.

Introduction

CULTURAL STORIES ARE THE MEANING-MAKING vehicles that explain and order our world, the building blocks of the reality in which people live. Aside from the obvious stories found in literature and various forms of entertainment, stories are woven into our culture in forms such as newspaper articles and news programs, legal activities and laws, scientific and research findings, judicial decisions, religious sermons and teachings, voting outcomes, medical diagnoses, fashion and clothing, personal disclosures, gossip and oral stories, and historical accounts, as well as everyday interactions among people.

Cultural stories offer an important window into understanding how people define, organize, and make sense of the world around them. Hegemonic stories construct and reinforce dominant cultural concepts understood as truth, ordering people and regulating society in predictable ways. These stories are widely circulated; they work to shape perspectives claimed as universal and create patterns of normalcy. Such stories reinforce what is considered acceptable by patrolling elements that are unacceptable and presenting them as negative in some way, making certain behaviors obviously ones to avoid. Stories that offer a positive presentation of people and activities that do not fit normative paradigms are considered subversive, and thus are often silenced by not being recorded and circulated, demonized to cast those who transgress social norms as the unacceptable Other, or manipulated and revised in ways that reduce any social threat the marginalized or disenfranchised subject might have had.

Whether stories are meant to report and inform, entertain, denounce, define, classify, punish, or caution, every story told features a subject deemed important and worthy of attention and reveals the meaning that the storyteller has found about some aspect of the human condition.

Through a combination of characterization, event and detail selection, and conclusions drawn about these elements, the storyteller's judgment is manifested. Through these narrative technologies, the storyteller's value system, worldview, political views, religious beliefs, and understanding of reality and truth are presented in a form that audiences can consume and adopt, or reject, protest or dismiss.

One story told from multiple viewpoints is that of Lucy Ann Lobdell, commonly known as the Female Hunter of Delaware County. Lucy Ann has been the focus of fascination, admiration, derision, persecution, study, and varied interpretation for over 150 years. The wide range of stories told from various points of view obscure an authentic knowing of Lobdell. Storytellers from newspaper article writers to doctors to judges to folklorists and academics have viewed Lobdell through their own lenses with diverse understandings of identity and subjectivity, but Lobdell's own words are cherry-picked at best and often dismissed or ignored, leaving Lobdell mute. In this way, the management and containment that society deemed necessary while Lobdell was alive continued long past death, as even those who had good intentions seized control over the presentation of Lobdell's identity. This book aims to present Lobdell as authentically as possible using Lobdell's words and life presentation.

Lobdell's story is one of adventure, individuality, bravery, survival, romance, persecution, and tragedy, all the makings of a sensational story. Lobdell was alternately vilified and glorified by contemporaries, and mythologized from the 1860s to today. Lobdell enjoyed a reputation as an expert marksman and legendary hunter; helped to settle white American civilization on the Minnesotan frontier; was renowned as a singer, fiddle player, saw mill worker, and school teacher; and yet was continually persecuted and lived in extreme poverty. Despite the complexity of Lobdell's life, the issue of gender is always the centerpiece of these stories.

Lucy Ann Lobdell was not your average girl. Many people today think of Lobdell as a cultural hero, a feminist, a woman before her time. But people in the nineteenth century found Lobdell socially disruptive and dangerous — dangerous enough to be locked away in an insane asylum. Storytellers — from authors of newspaper articles to judges to doctors to academics — have been shaping the meaning around Lobdell, interpreting her life in ways that managed Lucy Ann and safely contained her. This book will explore the various stories about Lobdell, the meanings and messages they crafted, the reasons behind attempts to contain and shape the meaning around Lobdell, and the resulting effects of these stories on the ways Lobdell has been understood.

Lucy Ann was born in 1829 to a working-class family living in Albany County in New York State. When she was a young woman, her family moved to the then-wilderness of Long Eddy in upstate New York. Lucy was coerced into a marriage with George Washington Slater, but she managed to be so difficult to live with that her husband left. Because of her father's age and health problems, the family became impoverished, and so looked the other way when Lucy Ann donned her brother's clothes, did the farm chores, worked at her father's saw mill, and hunted the forests for food, becoming known locally as the Female Hunter of Delaware County. Despite the notoriety earned through her hunting skills, most of the neighbors in this wilderness community did not approve of a woman displaying such radical, masculine behavior. Lobdell explains in her autobiography, *The Narrative of Lucy Ann Lobdell, Female Hunter of Delaware and Sullivan Counties, N.Y.*, published in 1855 (and reprinted herein as Appendix A), that, having been abandoned by her husband, in order to earn enough money to support her child, she had to leave home in men's clothes to earn a decent living, for women were severely underpaid. With an attitude equal to the most radical voices of first-wave feminism, Lobdell demanded more job opportunities and equal pay for women and condemned a society that restricted women economically.

First-wave feminists of the nineteenth century challenged entrenched notions about women as they demanded more opportunities and legal rights. Lucy Ann Lobdell's autobiography is framed by these early feminist ideas and philosophies, and so many have identified Lobdell as an early feminist. And indeed Lobdell was. But Lobdell's story is more complicated than that.

After leaving the familial home, Lobdell lived as a man for the next 60 years, wearing men's clothes, doing men's work, and going by male names. Leaving home to avoid exposure, Lobdell lived and thrived first in Bethany, Pennsylvania, as a singing teacher, and then in Manannah, Minnesota, as a hired gun and jack of all trades. Both communities embraced Lobdell as a hard-working, likable, and upstanding young man, but after a short term of social and economic success in those towns, Lobdell was vehemently rejected and cast out when her female body was discovered. The harassment and persecution Lobdell experienced because of her female body escalated after Lobdell returned from Minnesota. Having adopted the name Joseph Israel, Lobdell married Marie Louise Perry around 1862 and spent the next 17 years living with her in the woods and on the outskirts of towns in an unsuccessful attempt to avoid persecution from society. Lobdell was frequently arrested on charges of vagrancy, while Marie, properly feminine in appearance and deportment, was not, even though she shared her husband's lifestyle and feminist views.

While nineteenth-century feminists were disliked and vilified for their political views, it was Lobdell's adoption of a male persona that the surrounding society viewed as socially dangerous and unnatural. Newspaper reports presented Lobdell as maniacal, crazy, and socially disruptive; the stories always included descriptions of Lobdell's masculinity, even when there was no mention of legal charges. The dominant theme in nineteenth-century newspaper reports and historical accounts was that women who claimed any expression of masculinity were unnatural and needed to be disciplined and managed. These stories reinforced rigid gender lines, protected traditional male privilege, and presented social and legal harassment of unruly women as acceptable, even as they presented Lobdell as a cultural sensation.

During the winter of 1877, Lobdell's brother helped his sister gain payment of a widow's pension to which Lobdell was entitled, since George Slater had died in the Civil War. In February 1878 Lobdell bought a small farm outside of Honesdale, Pennsylvania, and Lobdell and Marie Perry set up housekeeping like any other couple, making them even more dangerous to society because Lobdell could no longer be arrested for vagrancy and managed with legal methods. At this point, persecution of Lobdell went well beyond being bad-mouthed by the press or harassed by law officials.

In 1879, the brother who had helped gain the widow's pension had Lobdell declared legally insane for wearing men's clothes and "pretending" to love a woman. The story told by judicial decisions was that Lobdell was insane as evidenced by his masculine appearance, behavior, and tastes in personal relationships, and Lobdell was committed to an insane asylum. However, not even Marie knew of Lobdell's fate, as the family released false obituaries that were published in newspapers from the *New York Times* to the *Galveston Daily News*. The stories the obituaries told focused on Lobdell's early fame as a legendary hunter and were a bit less harsh and judgmental, but effectively killed Lobdell off, erasing a life that still existed behind locked doors.

Dr. P.M. Wise, a sexologist at the Willard Insane Asylum, performed brief examinations on and interviews with his patient, Lucy Ann Lobdell, and reported that Lucy insisted on wearing men's clothes and claimed to be a man. In his article, "A Case of Sexual Perversion" published in 1883 in *Alienist and Neurologist*, Wise relates a brief history of Lobdell's life, especially that time spent with Marie. He focuses on details of Lobdell's masculine appearance and behavior and lewd mannerisms with women, giving specifics on Lobdell's discussion of married life that claimed connubial bliss with Marie, but never George Slater, to whom Lobdell had been married. Because common thought in the nineteenth century held that women had no sexual desire, these tales stood as evidence of insanity, and Wise, declaring this form of insanity so rare as to never happen again, offers the story of this case only as a clinical curiosity. In other words, the story Wise tells is that a woman claiming to be a man, living as a man, and loving a woman is such a bizarre type of insanity as to be an anomaly. Lobdell was eventually moved to the Binghamton Insane Asylum, died there in 1912, and was buried in the pauper's graveyard with no newspaper notice to acknowledge the death.

Dr. Wise's reports fell into obscurity until records were salvaged from Willard by Ellen Dwyer.[1] They then became fodder for academic study during the time of second-wave feminism. Renowned scholars, such as Jonathan Katz and Lillian Faderman, presented Lucy Ann Lobdell as a nineteenth-century "passing woman," meaning a woman who passed as a man to obtain access to economic gain, social mobility, and sometimes intimate relations with other women. Dr. Wise's report stated that Lucy and Marie lived "in the quiet monotony of Lesbian love."[2] In scholarly books, Jonathan Katz, Lillian Faderman, and others latched onto that one phrase, used in its archaic sense, and classified Lobdell as a lesbian. Since then, numerous articles and websites have been created that present Lucy Ann/Joseph Israel Lobdell as a historical lesbian — even the first medicalized, American lesbian — holding up Joe's intimate life with Marie as evidence of lesbianism. In these stories of Lobdell as a lesbian, his gendered behavior is painted either as opportunistic transvestitism or is not discussed at all, and the focus becomes only same-sex partnership and sexuality, not gender. Ironically, while the storytellers in the nineteenth century created a negative identity for Lobdell based solely on their reading of gendered appearance and behavior, those in the twentieth and twenty-first centuries ignore gender altogether and create an identity for Lobdell based solely on hegemonic understandings of sexed bodies and sexualities to present Lobdell as a lesbian and passing woman. However, such a classification is inaccurate and presents epistemological problems for a few reasons.

In the autobiography, Lobdell claimed the desire for economic mobility was the reason for leaving home in men's clothes, the traditional motivation for a passing woman — a woman who dressed as a man to gain opportunities and freedoms granted to only men — which would seem to justify classification of Lobdell as such by twentieth-century scholars. However, Lobdell knew a great deal more poverty than even modest success. Lobdell's persistence in living as a man only brought him poverty and a lack of employment opportunities, a marginalized life outside of society, and persecution and incarceration by legal and psychiatric authorities. Reverting to female clothing would have solved most of the problems that plagued Lobdell's life. Something more than desire for work caused him to present as male, and many have argued that he also desired relationships with women, resulting in male presentation.

Sexuality is a social construct with various meanings and judgments given to sex acts and those who participate in them. Broader culture gives meaning to sex — both acts and participants — through medical, legal, and religious interpretations that create identities, and those concepts and forms of identity change through time and place, and often clash across cultural institutions. Before the second half of the nineteenth century, there was no concept of homosexuality as an identity that described a type of person. The binary understanding about sex at this time was not heterosexual/homosexual, but procreative and non-procreative sex acts, which, when viewed through a religious lens, declared people to be either in accordance with God's natural rules for people or sinners. Even cross-sexed sexual activities that held no potential for new life were deemed unnatural and sinful. So same-sex activities would have fallen into the same classification as oral sex or masturbation — sinful acts that could not produce new life. The authority that managed this understanding and disciplined the practice of people's sexuality was the church, and so sexual behavior was understood as either following God's laws or being sinful. People in the nineteenth century did not have the terms, categories, or concepts to understand gays and lesbians as types of people; there was no homosexual identity at this time.

Society determines the meaning and appropriateness of sexual activities and partnerships, and these determinations vary according to place and time. Sex is complicated because it involves human behavior that affects social order, either to stabilize it or disrupt it, according to the rules and meanings society proclaims about sex at any given time. By the middle of the nineteenth century, doctors in the new field of sexology, the precursor to modern-day psychology, had proclaimed themselves the rightful authorities to define, manage, and treat sexual disorders. Basically sexologists labeled any sexual behavior that could not result in producing new life a perversion, and, influenced by Darwin, they set out to classify and categorize every form of aberrant sex as forms of mental illness, thereby reinforcing the heterosexual, procreative imperative as the foundation for defining normal and natural sexual behavior.

One specific area of sexology focused on same-sex activity, which led to the medical development of the concept of a homosexual identity as a specific form of mental illness. Claiming to be a basis of authority, sexologists and their science moved intimate same-sex activities and partnerships out of the religious realm of sinful perversions and into the psychological world of forms of mental illness, but these concepts were first applied only to men. Since sexual desire was read as an active behavior, and active behaviors were gendered as masculine, it was believed only men possessed sexual urges. Women were believed to have no sexual desire and simply passively received male advances and pleased men for the sake of forming families. Even though Lobdell made it clear to Wise that sexual satisfaction was always found with Marie, Wise framed these statements as confused attempts at real sex. Women with unnatural gender presentation, including displaying desire for women, were labeled "inverts" by sexologists and believed to somehow have male brains ruling them and their sexual behavior. Such a condition was viewed as mental illness, not sexual orientation, and certainly not as a category of human identification. In *The History of Sexuality*, Michel Foucault argues that it was not until the latter half of the nineteenth century that people in Europe and the United States came to view their sexual desires and orientations as part of what constituted them as individuals, or types of people based on sexual activity.

It may be with good intentions that theorists look to the past to reclaim gays and lesbians as a way to prove that they have always existed and so should be acknowledged as legitimate identities. However, to project current concepts, terms, and classifications onto historic figures who did not have those same concepts, terms, and classifications is to seize control over the historic subject's identity and fashion it to suit current needs rather than accurately present subjects as they might have understood themselves—with concepts and terms from their own lifetimes. While same-sex desire and activities have been present for millennia, the concept of a homosexual identity has only existed in common thought for little more than a century. Lobdell would not have identified as a lesbian, not just for this technical linguistic reason, but also because of competing definitions and understandings of sexed bodies and the categories of male and female.

Modern theorists focus on the word "Lesbian" in Wise's article, layering current meanings onto the word, but completely ignore the three quotes in the same article where Lobdell "declared herself to be a man,"[3] believed "herself to possess virility and the coaptation of a male,"[4] and claimed that, he was "a man in all that the name implies."[5] While others tell stories that present Lobdell either as an insane woman or a beleaguered lesbian, Lobdell's own story about sex and gender is that he is a heterosexual man. He lived his entire adult life as a man, dressed in men's clothes, did men's work, and claimed male identity wherever he went, even though it brought him nothing but trouble. Even to Dr. Wise, the one person with the authority to release him from the insane asylum, he insisted he was a man.

Because of simplistic binaries used to identify people as either male or female based on their genitals, Western cultures have traditionally recognized only two sexes. The stories told in our culture have presented men and women and prescribed gender behavior appropriate to each as part of the normalizing, heterosexist discourse of sex, gender, and sexuality. Historically, there have also been stories about people who do not fit into rigid categories of sex and/or gender. These stories most often punish those who do not comply with social norms by ridiculing and shaming them, labeling them as abnormal or dangerous, or distorting the story to eliminate the aspects that do not align with social expectations, thereby treating those elements as if they never existed.

As just stated, Western culture only acknowledges two sexes (male and female) and two genders (masculine and feminine) and uses these categories to order and organize society, even if some people must be disciplined to conform and fit into those rigid classifications. But an intermediary category of being has existed throughout time, a third category of sex that has not been acknowledged, let alone accepted, in Western culture; it is known today as transgender. The word *transgender* is an umbrella term used in reference to people who do not neatly fit into rigid categories of male and female, from cross-dressers to transsexuals. The concept of transgender is just now filtering its way into the zeitgeist of common awareness in our culture through various stories, from sensational and often degrading talk shows to legislative bills that have the potential to become laws that will protect transgender people. Today we would understand someone like Lucy Ann/Joseph Israel Lobdell, living as a man in a female body, as a transgender person, although at the time Lobdell understood himself as a man and lived according to that understanding.

Stories do not just present views about their subjects; they also reveal things about their storytellers and prevalent cultural attitudes. Because of Lobdell's male presentation and interest in women, nineteenth-century storytellers based their stories on traditional gender expectations for men and women and presented Lobdell as an unacceptable spectacle, an outlaw, and an insane woman. Their stories were an effort to discipline Lobdell's refusal to conform to gendered social expectations, revealing societal fear of gender transgression. Twentieth-century academics based their stories on theories of sexuality and, dismissing Lobdell's gender presentation as unimportant, presented Lobdell as a heroic passing woman and/or a lesbian in an effort to craft a legitimate identity for feminists and lesbians. But their articles reveal selective research and a privileging of the ideas of the male authority, Dr. Wise, over the words of the very subject about which they are writing.

Nearly all who have commented on Lobdell — whether nineteenth-century news reporters, historians, or doctors, or twentieth- and twenty-first-century family members, small pockets of feminists, or scholars — have interpreted Lobdell and his life based on the assumption that he was a woman. Because of the binary way that sexed bodies have been categorized as male (men) or female (women) in Western culture, common wisdom holds that people with female bodies are women, and this notion has been reinforced by social, medical, and religious concepts of sex and gender that provide specific details for how female (and male) bodies should look and behave. Because of Lobdell's anatomy and the obscurity of Lobdell's words in Wise's article, it is understandable that writers from popular culture would frame Lobdell as a woman, and, thanks to traditional understandings of sexed bodies, many are still more comfortable with understanding Lobdell as a woman.

Even scholarly writers working from a position informed by gender and queer theories, where transgender has been discussed and argued over for decades, still insist on referring to Lobdell as a woman. To do so, they must privilege the statements of an authority from the field of sexology, a science now viewed as primitive, uninformed, and restricted by concepts of normalcy rooted in religious ideology. They also completely ignore Lobdell's own words and life. While concepts and terminology that exist today did not exist in the nineteenth century, Lobdell used the vocabulary available to him, and made it clear that he did not consider himself a woman.

While others have assumed the authority to present Lobdell's story from points of view grounded in normative classifications, I present and analyze the story from Joseph Lobdell's point of view. In an effort to honor Lobdell's understanding of himself and grant authority and legitimacy to the way he identified himself, this book begins by authorizing Lobdell's self-identification as a (transgender) man and analyzes how the various narrative constructions of Lobdell's identity highlight the tension between the performed and assigned meanings of the transgendered body, and how others' classification of Lobdell changed over 150 years.

Because Lobdell not only lived as a man and husband to Marie but also insisted to the legal authorities and doctors who held control over his freedom that he was a man "in all that the name implies,"[6] I am presenting Lobdell's story from a perspective informed by his own words and enactments. This book will frame Lobdell as a transgender man, meaning, in this case, a person who was born into a female body but who understood himself as a man. The concepts and vocabulary available for common usage in the English language are inadequate to discuss someone who does not fit neatly in one of the two sex categories, so discussing transgender can be confusing. While gender-neutral pronouns have existed for decades,[7] they are not commonly used, recognized, or understood, so I will not use them here. While my argument is always that Lobdell was a transgender man, in discussing his life I will use terms that reflect his presentation to those around him. When discussing Lobdell's youth and very young adult life as a woman, and when quoting others, I will use the name *Lucy* and female pronouns. When discussing Lobdell's adult life after leaving home, I will use the names *Joe*, *Joseph*, or *La-Roi* and male pronouns.

In contrast to judgments made and conclusions drawn about Lobdell based on snippets from Lucy's autobiography and one psychological diagnosis based on nineteenth-century understandings of women and sex, this book deposes earlier theoretical analyses and constructions of Lobdell and creates the biography of Lobdell's life from nineteenth-century cultural narratives about Lobdell, including Lucy's full autobiography, newspaper articles, local and family histories, legal reports, judicial decisions, lunacy testimonials, and medical diagnoses. These stories offer insight into how gender was defined, managed, policed, disciplined, and enforced and how gender nonconformity was labeled as deviance and punished. These nineteenth-century narratives trace the beginning and development of Lobdell's public life as a transgender man and the corresponding transphobic social reaction that ensued.

Introduction 15

The perspective of storytelling in the collection of narratives about Lobdell shifts depending on who is telling the story, what beliefs are of concern, and what time period the storytellers live in, revealing changing uses of narrative technologies of truth-making that all result in reinforcing heteronormative binaries of sex and gender. The story shifts, presenting Lobdell variously as a dangerous, immoral social deviant, a pathetically ill person who should be pitied, or a strong, tenacious, feminist hero who should be celebrated and imitated. While nineteenth-century cultural narratives insisted Lobdell was a woman and focus on his gender nonconformity to define him as a social deviant, twentieth- and twenty-first-century scholars persistently classify him as a woman and define him as a lesbian because of his erotic object choice (Marie). In their attempts to present stable and knowable identities that fit a lesbian classification, scholars writing about Lobdell in the last 30 years have reinforced normative classifications of sexed bodies as either male or female based on genitals only, rendering third genders and queer sexualities other than lesbianism invisible. Absent, too, from their stories is the disruptive power of Lobdell's transgender, as he is often framed as a victim of unforgiving social regulations rather than a powerful disrupter of restrictive social norms. Lobdell's postmortem story reveals how lesbian and transgender male history was conflated, obscuring any clear genesis of either category.

Cultural stories and narratives in all forms are powerful shapers of what Foucault calls truth regimes (which are then claimed as foundations for reality), but they do not manifest pathenogenically from thin air. They spring from the human imagination and the need to create a knowable order, resulting in hegemonic stories grounded in the heteronormative, patriarchal structures that form and inform Western culture. To emphasize the human element of textual construction of meaning, this book will examine the narrative technologies used to create the stories and their meanings, such as choice and judgment of subject, selection and judgment of events and actions, vocabulary, selective viewpoints of observers, and characterizations. Such an examination will analyze how writers and storytellers, positioned as socially acceptable authorities, use heteronormativity as a lens to define what is important, correct, normal, natural, and socially acceptable, and what is not. The dominant narratives about Lobdell interpret him as the social Other (whether vilified or celebrated) bolster normative binaries of sexed bodies, and enforce the balance of a social order constructed through rigid gender and sex opposition.

The story of Lobdell's life revolves around a series of conflicts concerning gender that resulted in either expulsion or incarceration away from society by people who judged his gender difference as unnatural, immoral, perverted, and/or insane. While this story may seem to be one about the power and triumph of institutions in maintaining social order, I prefer to emphasize the power of disruption enacted by Lobdell's unruly body and gender-outlaw life. While the social institutions of family, community, law, and medicine (psychiatry) worked to control and contain the disruption of Lobdell's transgender, they never succeeded in forcing Lobdell to conform; they could only lock him away and pretend he did not exist to maintain the illusion of a natural gender binary. Lobdell bore the burden of oppression in his determination to be himself at all costs and did not conform. Aware of the risks of living openly as a man, Lobdell refused to cooperate with hegemonic gender codes for female bodies and actively resisted erasure.

Chapter One familiarizes the reader with the zeitgeist of nineteenth-century America by presenting a social history of the ways men and women, the spaces they occupied, and the functions they served were defined after the Industrial Revolution. This history explains the historical tensions and attitudes about women that produced the separation of male public space from the private, and isolated, female space of home and family that was then deemed natural. This separation of the sexes was reinforced by the philosophy touted by nineteenth-century authorities—the Cult of True Womanhood, which demanded women be pure, pious, submissive, and domestic. Clothing played an important part in visibly coding the separate spheres and it was unacceptable in many places for women to wear pants, which were viewed as symbols of male power, masculinity, and privilege. This chapter analyzes Lucy Ann's book in light of nineteenth-century sensibilities concerning gender to explain why her attitudes, behaviors, and choice of clothing were dangerous for her, and threats to society.

Lucy's autobiography will be examined against the backdrop of historical understandings and expectations of gender. Her discussion not only reveals clear examples of constructions of gender and gendered spaces but also gives glimpses into the restrictions in everyday life for working-class women, as well as the dangers of nonconformity.

Lucy's writing presents gender as the core of essentializing ideas about men and women, and then challenges those concepts by rebelling against them. Her narrative highlights how she troubles traditional gender binaries by questioning the ideas that construct them and, more forcefully, by sharing with the reader her experiences in men's clothes and doing men's work, especially hunting and marksmanship, activities that proved the artificial constructedness of gender boundaries by crossing them. These and other anecdotes form the foundation of Lucy's resistance to the social construction of women, female bodies, and gendered activity and space, in addition to the public birth of his transgender.

Lobdell's concerns over leaving home dressed in men's clothes reveal an historic transphobia that Lucy confides has the power to question her sanity and sequester her, underscoring the lengths to which nineteenth-century society would go to preserve gender construction, roles, and social spaces in order to maintain order, and Lucy's determination to rebel against that very power. The very dangers Lobdell discusses make his commitment to transgendered identity and life clear. The entirety of Lobdell's autobiography is included in Appendix A at the end of this book.

Chapter Two introduces young Lobdell's entry into a transgendered life with discussion of newspaper articles and histories written about his activities after leaving home as a man named Joseph Israel Lobdell. Narratives that form the history of Lobdell's life in Bethany, Pennsylvania, and Manannah, Minnesota, show that people initially accepted Lobdell as a man because his enactment of a male identity was so authentic, even within the intimate spaces men occupied, that he enjoyed social status, community respect, modest financial success, and male camaraderie in these communities that embraced him as a good and worthy man. Female love interests were the cause of his outings in each town, and the public uproar that ensued spotlights gender as the center of conflict between Lobdell and society.

The social acceptance of Lobdell as a man starkly contrasts with the communities' treatment of him once people had knowledge of his female body. The moment of exposure acts as a toggle switch, what Judith Halberstam refers to as "queer time,"[8] causing community members to review their understanding of Lobdell; acceptance, respect, and affection transform into rage, rejection, and violence. Stories that begin by characterizing Lobdell as a beloved and respectable member of each society end by presenting him as a vile threat to the community, a social ill that must be punished and cast out to reestablish the respectable and predictable social order.

Lobdell's persistence in living as a man challenges gender and sex binaries; his gender nonconformity brings attention to notions of gender and sex, revealing them as social constructions that order people. His transgender highlights a third space between man and woman, male and female, that falls outside the socially constructed norms of gender and sex. It is this exposure of gender as a tool of organization and restriction (especially for women) that threatens the stability of social order, which elicits violent responses from the men in control of the communities in which Lobdell lives. These stories reveal the levels of anger evident in the transphobic responses of these communities toward Lobdell and the violence that attended the punishing of gender transgression. The fact that violence is considered an appropriate response for gender transgression reveals the level of fear inspired when social order is threatened by a gender outlaw, and the corresponding measures taken by these communities indicate the desperate need to stabilize society through the forced enactment of restrictive, heteronormative constructions of gender, sex, and sexuality, or the complete expulsion of the one who will not conform.

Reports from Bethany and Manannah build on the story of Lobdell's transgender evident in his autobiography and reinforce his placement in transgendered history. These same stories give those in authority the social power to punish gender transgressors also highlight the disruptive power of the unruly transgendered body. The threat of tarring and feathering by the residents of Bethany, Pennsylvania, indicates the physical dangers of transgender living. The experience of such a violent expulsion from one community highlights Lobdell's courage and willingness to risk social rejection, punishment, and physical danger in order to be himself and live as a man after moving to Minnesota, and later in Pennsylvania. This type of determination is based on much more than the rebellious desire to dress in men's clothes for the sake of gaining male privileges; it is evidence of how Lobdell understood himself as a man.

This chapter ends with a short history of the poorhouse, the precursor to the modern-day welfare system. This background sets the stage for the story of Lobdell's placement in the Delaware County poorhouse after he is returned to New York State, and helps to explain attitudes that persist today about the poor as dangerous to society.

Chapter Three offers and analyzes the nineteenth-century narratives from Pennsylvania and New York that focus on Lobdell's masculine appearance and behaviors, especially in conjunction with his relationship with Marie Louise Perry. These stories spotlight past assumptions and understandings of body and gender and reveal how constructions of gender were used to interpret and define normalcy and deviance. Along with the narratives in Chapter Two, the stories in this chapter feature gender presentation and performance as the identifying factor for concern over Lobdell.

Introduction 19

The newspaper articles and histories in this chapter parallel the earlier pattern of social acceptance of believable masculinity until the female body is revealed through some form of legal intervention, at which point writers characterize Lobdell as a deranged, vile, unsexed woman, displaying historic anxieties about gender transgression.

Another concern featured in this chapter is the role of economic status, poverty, and homelessness. Lobdell and Perry lived most often in the woods outside of settled society in huts that Lobdell built. They survived through Lobdell's hunting skills and trading, or by foraging, doing menial labor, and, occasionally, begging. Lobdell's poverty amplified the danger of living as a transgender man and provided local law officials with legitimate reasons to harass and imprison Lobdell through the use of vagrancy laws. Once Lobdell and Perry established themselves in the wilderness outside Honesdale, Pennsylvania, and became known to the community, only Lobdell was ever imprisoned. Marie, the traditionally pretty and feminine woman, was viewed with confusion but also with respect, and was not harassed by the law or local residents.

The stories about Joe and Marie reveal how they challenged traditional constructions of male/female relationships and marriage as a heterosexual institution. Nineteenth-century writers frame the Lobdell-Perry relationship as strange even as they quote the couple's use of the words *husband* and *wife*, which alternately reinforces and challenges definitions of traditional marriage, for it offers up an alternative pattern of partnership and domesticity for female-bodied persons. These same stories show an historic ignorance of intimate and erotic relationships between female bodies and confusion over how to view the couple.

From this field of confusion, writers present Marie Perry respectfully as a normal woman — feminine, beautiful, and well educated — and save their disapproval and anger for the noticeably different, rebellious, and disruptive Lobdell. By enlisting the help of readers presumed to also be normal, writers of nineteenth-century newspaper articles, histories, and legal reports attempt to regulate normalcy, contain deviance, and dismantle the threat of transgender through literary vehicles that redefine Lobdell's masculinity as a form of deviance that was later defined as insanity. The narratives presented in this chapter chronicle Lobdell's continued challenge to gender and sex binaries and the corresponding transphobic reactions of the society around him. Lobdell's transgender becomes all the more visible through this narrative defamation.

While a transgender analysis of Lobdell as a third body between genders and sex clearly reveals the fragility of constructions of gender and sex binaries, an analysis of the relationship between Lobdell and Perry using queer theory reveals a gap between constructions of heterosexuality and homosexuality. While the word *queer* has a history of being used as a pejorative word to insult gay men and lesbians, many LGBTQ or polyamorous people today use the word to describe their identity as not conforming to heteronormative mandates. In this book, *queer* will be used in its more academic sense as a verb that describes roles, enactments, presentations, and relationships that challenge or complicate predictable heteronormative classifications of people based on sex, gender, and sexuality. To queer something in this sense means to question or challenge hegemonic concepts of normalcy and/or to reveal concepts concerning sexed bodies, gender, and sexuality as human constructs used to impose a predictable and restrictive order on people, one that is not natural but rather human-made. In short, to queer something in an academic sense means to be non-normative, which Lobdell does to all those categories: sexed body, gender, and sexuality.

Lobdell's life in the gaps between man/woman, male/female, hetero-homosexuality also spotlights a lack of concepts and knowledge systems concerning anything outside those binaries, and the attending lack of vocabulary to express those subject positions between gender, sex, and sexuality polar opposites. Lobdell's embodiment of masculinity questions the assumption that masculinity is a natural essence of male bodies only and positions masculinity more as a set of qualities that create male privilege, one that must be continuously guarded and policed in order to present it as naturally belonging only to biological men. When considering Perry's desire for Lobdell, specific questions arise about female erotic desire for a partner who is masculine but not necessarily male-bodied. In this case, was it gender that inspired desire rather than physical attributes of the lover's body?

The collection of Lobdell's autobiography and subsequent nineteenth-century cultural narratives concerning him present the social boundaries and effects of nineteenth-century gender construction. By refusing to perform the behaviors and enactments expected of women, Lobdell's resistance to gendered expectations makes the social constructedness of gender all the more visible. The power of constructed gender roles and spaces to organize society into a male-privileged hierarchy is evident in the dangers stemming from Lobdell's refusal to enact female gender or remain in the female sphere, and also from his appropriation of male identity, mobility, freedom, and public space. The stories offered here describe tremendous hardship, courage, resilience, dignity, and integrity, as well as societal fear.

This chapter ends with the tragic story of Lobdell's removal from society. After an unexpected financial windfall enabled him to buy a farm and set up housekeeping with Perry, he was almost immediately betrayed by his brother, who requested a lunacy hearing for his sister. With the testimonies of twelve men, some of whom had never met Lobdell, Lucy Ann Lobdell was declared insane in 1879 for wearing men's clothes and pretending to love another woman, and then removed to an insane asylum. False obituaries leaked by the family to the press virtually killed Lobdell off, rendering him nonexistent to Marie and greater society.

This chapter also presents the background of the beginnings of psychiatry and the nineteenth-century sexological construction of sexual difference, offering a short history of the development of concepts concerning sexuality and insanity. It also discusses the invention of the homosexual as a type of man, and the parallel ignorance of female sexuality that was the core of the popular Victorian belief that women had no sexual desire. Dr. Wise, the doctor examining and diagnosing Lobdell, formed an opinion of mental disorder that was derived almost entirely from his interpretation of gender difference and an ignorance of female sexuality and desire that was commonplace in the nineteenth century.

Chapter Four analyzes the twentieth-century development of the story about Lobdell, especially in the ways those stories erase Lobdell's transgender by misreading it as sexual difference. Feminist scholars in the second half of the twentieth century discovered Lobdell's medical file from Willard Insane Asylum and the previously mentioned article written by Dr. Wise for an early psychiatric journal, and based their conclusions about Lobdell on those papers and an abbreviated version of his autobiography. By framing Lobdell's habit of dressing in men's clothes as the mere disguise of a passing woman, twentieth- and twenty-first-century writers treat Lobdell's transgender in ways that ignore and dismiss his words in the same Wise article, those that claim he was "a man in all that the name implies."[9]

This chapter traces the discursive development of Lobdell as an historic American lesbian by twentieth- and twenty-first-century scholars and essayists who were eager to fit Lobdell to a modern definition of lesbianism because of his erotic relationship with Marie. In so doing, they identify Lobdell and Perry in relation to erotic desire and object choice, reinforce anatomy of both participants as the sole determinants of sexuality, and frame difference as sexual. By forcing both Lobdell and Perry into lesbian classification, these writers render Lobdell's transgender, Perry's erotic desire for queer masculinity, and a queer form of heterosexuality invisible. However, Lobdell was not a lesbian but a transgendered man who challenged the rigid and artificial classification of erotic desire as either hetero- or homosexual, based on equally artificial and restrictive constructions of men and women.

The erasure of Lobdell as a transgendered man is indicative of the wrongful definition of historical transgendered male subjects as lesbians or passing women. Chapter Four ends with a call to revisit the stories, articles, reports, and diagnoses that have been used to create lesbian history to draw out transgendered subjects and reposition them in transgendered history. This project must include the partners of transgendered men who have also been forced into lesbian classification. The creation of this transgendered history would also require the examination of sexuality that is not same-sex, and yet not conventional heterosexuality.

When my favorite aunt put Lobdell's narrative in my hands, a completely obsessive search for more information took over my life, and for more than seven years I spent countless hours reading microfilm, visiting historical societies and cemeteries, scouring county records, and digging for any scrap of story I could find. Each subsequent piece I found simply made the story more fantastic. Turning it into a dissertation necessitated my immersion into queer and gender theories, which granted me a whole new understanding of Lobdell and his life. While my research was derived from interest in a compelling family member, my main reason for writing this book is to grant Lobdell the authority to name himself, hopefully moving his story into American transgender history and helping to validate transgender lives today.

Today, transgender is becoming more widely visible and discussed as more and more people express gender in ways that do not conform to traditional expectations, or transition to a sex and gender different from that assigned at birth. In the twenty-first century, Lobdell would be known as a transgender man, or transman, or F2M — female-to-male (or man) person. But transgender is not a new phenomenon that suddenly sprang up in the latter half of the twentieth century; it is not the result of an overly permissive society influenced by a radical feminism whose aim is to destroy traditional patterns of people and life, or a proliferation of chemicals and pollution that has infiltrated our genes and confused them. Sexes other than male and female, and genders other than feminine or masculine, have existed for millennia, and this last chapter offers a brief discussion of such subjects in other time periods and non–Western cultures.

Kate Bornstein states that transgendered people are powerful because they cannot be humiliated into conformity, much like the character of the Fool. Joseph Israel Lobdell is just one such powerful fool in American history. By granting Lobdell's voice the power to define himself, I aim to make his participation in such a gender revolution visible.

In this presentation and discussion of Lobdell, my goal is to place the authority to define and label Lobdell with him, validating his identity as a transgendered man, and moving him from lesbian to transgender history. Lobdell's voice, when granted authority, complicates lesbian definition and history, for it demands the recognition of transgender subjects. It is my hope that presenting Lobdell's story from a perspective closer to his own will help to make sense of, and celebrate, changing concepts of sex and gender. While this book is meant to inform, I also hope it evokes questions and sparks discussion and reevaluation.

By focusing on the details of the struggles during his lifetime, I aim to reinstate and reinforce Lobdell's view of himself as a man, dismantle the body of scholarly work that presents him as a woman, and use Lobdell's voice to challenge contemporary constructions of gender and sex that create artificial classifications and punish those who do not conform. In so doing I hope to position Lobdell as a nineteenth-century transgendered figure, an early participant in what Leslie Feinberg calls transliberation. Feinberg believes "it is vital to defend the right of individuals to express and define their sex and gender, and to control their bodies."[10] As a nineteenth-century combatant against gender oppression, Lobdell ran the risks and punishments for living openly as transgendered. Perhaps his experience will help to validate non-normative expressions of gender and embodiments of sex that exist between and/or outside of polar extremes, and assist in some measure to establish those third spaces in safety.

• ONE •

"Some Do Call Me a Strange Sort of Being"

THE NINETEENTH CENTURY WAS A time of great social upheaval in America. Society was fraught with tensions created by opportunities, advancements, and challenges. Rapidly developing social and technological changes threw traditional patterns of political, economic, and family structures into disarray, threatening the balance of existing forms of power and order in America and creating a sense of chaos and disorder. Time moved faster and distances grew shorter with the development of the railroad and the telegraph. Developments of steam power and electricity "turned everyone's life upside down" while the railway system "ruined everyone's nervous system."[1] American individualism encouraged men's passions for exploration and economic adventure; the move west to new territories and the Industrial Revolution created vast opportunities for ambitious men who wanted adventure or economic success. The Civil War, the development of alternative religions,[2] and the bachelorhood of adventurers disrupted traditional marital and family patterns,[3] which greatly added to the sense of societal disintegration. Mass immigration and emancipation threatened white male control over the economy and accumulation of wealth. It seemed the world was out of control.

This amalgamation of changes challenged traditional social patterns and created a sense of instability that fostered anxieties, especially in white men, who believed that social order was derived from the (white) masculine control of politics, education, business, and religion. Such perceived social fragmentation created an extreme need to establish a social order that would regulate social interactions and create a sense of calm that would benefit business and industry.[4]

Anxieties over the conflicts created when ordered reason collided with individualism, imagination, and ambition had been building since the seventeenth century. In its infancy America was founded on principles of democracy that positioned freedoms and opportunities in uncomfortable opposition to traditional European patriarchal family structures. Freedoms granted by the new system of democracy eroded long-standing European patterns of paternal power. The traditional control European fathers had had over their sons no longer existed in a democratic society where all men were free to design their own lives and pursue their own goals. However, the patriarch of the family, the father, could still find a sense of control and order through his guaranteed authority over his wife and daughters.

Quickly changing circumstances contributed to the erosion of traditional male identity, which became vulnerable as an atmosphere of tension and disorder developed. As often happens, as a way of creating the semblance of order, management and restrictions of individual bodies ensued. By projecting disorder onto the female body, disciplining man's disruptive tendencies was possible through controlling those bodies believed to be naturally weaker and inferior. According to G.J. Barker-Benfield, a sense of order was created by

> assimilating the female area of reproductive power to those other physical and psychological regions beneath the sway of the male will. Man's disciplining woman (society's heart) represented sexual and social order, and avoided the curtailment of man's own anarchistic tendencies. The discipline of women ... represented man's subordination of himself. Conversely, ungoverned woman represented man's loss of control over himself and society.[5]

A social order constructed on top of gender distinctions required the emphasis and exaggeration of dissimilarities between men and women, which were then linked to the most obvious physiological difference—genitals and reproductive functions. Coding certain characteristics and functions as either masculine or feminine, and then associating them directly with bodies in the forms of masculinity and femininity, widened the social gap between men and women, creating gendered social roles and two separate spheres of living that artificially, but securely, kept order and balance.

Feminist theories of the twentieth century define gender as a social construction used to create social order by organizing people, activities, functions, and spaces according to sex. Gender creates a type of language, first by interpreting and defining various symbols — behaviors, appearances, functions, mannerisms, and abilities — as either masculine or feminine, then assigning those coded elements to either a male or female body, and finally declaring those assignments natural and normal. Gender then becomes a performed language that indicates the category to which a body belongs.[6] This complex system of defining and organizing people according to gendered aspects is so embedded in a sense of reality that understanding it becomes second nature, and, as a language, it is then used to read bodies and decipher the maleness or femaleness of the body hidden under clothing. The particulars of this language system of gender fluctuate with time and place, and although various individual elements used to read gender change, the rigidity of the binary system holds solidly, so much so that any ambiguity or misperformed gender is immediately noticed.

But in the nineteenth century, gender was believed to be a naturally occurring essence of the body that produced it — that is, bodies naturally presented themselves and behaved in ways dictated by the biology of that sexed body. Women were weak, emotional, gentle, and nurturing and men were rational, ambitious, and intelligent because their bodies biologically dictated such attributes. "True woman and true man equated biological femaleness and maleness with those constellations and qualities collectively called 'femininity' and 'masculinity,' No basic distinction was made in this era between biological sex and culturally constructed womanhood and manhood."[7] With this clear system of organizing people into distinct groups, a sense of order was created.

Order in nineteenth-century American society became characterized by rigid constructions of gender roles, functions, and spaces. The Industrial Revolution resulted in much centralized production, moving work from homes into factories, eliminating a source of income for women who worked at home and contributing to the gendered division of work. Activities and work conducted in the public space were framed as masculine endeavors, requiring logic, reason, and physical strength. In contrast, the sphere of the home was defined as a safe space for women who were considered physically and intellectually weaker than men, in need of male protection, emotional yet loving, and naturally domestic. Feminized gender characteristics (such as nurturance, passivity, dependency, and affection), and the sex roles of wife and mother were constructed on top of the female body and then termed natural behaviors and functions for that body.

From the newly born fields of obstetrics and gynecology, male physicians declared that the reproductive system was the source of a woman's identity, and it made her naturally gentle, emotional, and dependent just as it dictated her personality, abilities, and social functions as wife and mother. When femininity, and all its corresponding weaknesses and dependencies, was locked into place, so was masculinity, along with its strengths, privileges, and powers. Masculinity was constructed in opposition to femininity, and the clear differences between the sexes "[were] the ultimate foundation of all culture. The ideal of masculinity was reaffirmed as an imperative of the modern age."[8]

Gender construction enhanced physiological differences and positioned men and women as opposites that required separate spaces, spaces that seemed to manifest naturally as male/public and female/private arenas. These spaces were completely antithetical and divided the interior of domestic space within the home from the public world of politics and business, successfully keeping women confined as support systems for men. The concept that women were inferior in all ways led to the belief that the female body could not endure hard or long labor. Men became the wage-earning members of the family who worked outside the home, participating in the male world of capitalism, while women stayed home doing work that was not acknowledged as work and relied on husbands for financial support. Social ideologies declared that the work women did within the home, managing the household and caring for the family, was done out of pure, natural feminine love for their families, a performance that emanated from their very reason for being. Ambition and a longing for economic gain were elements believed to be unnatural to women, and therefore unthinkable characteristics.[9]

The absence of a legitimate public platform from which to speak worked further to lock women and their opinions into the domestic sphere where they could not be heard, effectively containing their potential to disrupt society. Public speaking was a male activity aimed at male audiences in the male sphere. Because the male sphere was understood to be competitive, amoral, and dangerous to women, any woman who spoke publicly was seen as stepping beyond her appropriate sphere of the home. Such a barrier to a public platform kept women from being heard or publicly expressing views important to them.[10]

The nineteenth-century philosophy of the Cult of True Womanhood reinforced an artificial gender balance and bolstered male privilege, mobility, and power by continuously reminding everyone that real women — meaning women who were socially acceptable — were pure, pious, domestic, and submissive. However, the illusion of control and stability created by the social construction and enforcement of rigid gender roles and gender-segregated spaces was challenged by the demands of first-wave feminists as women fought for equal rights to education, politics, careers, and public space. The angry backlash that accompanied the works of first-wave feminists revealed the level of fear created by the thought of women breaking free of functions believed to be natural and demanding entry into spaces and activities viewed as belonging to men only. Anxious men accused many feminists of wanting to be men. Since working in public spaces, being involved in politics, gaining an education, wearing pants, and earning money were all believed to be natural endeavors of men, any woman wanting those things coded as male was viewed as unnatural, and a sure sign of the disintegration of society as it was intended to be.

One particular method of segregating the sexes was controlling forms of education. Only boys had access to academic training, and then only if their families could afford it, as schooling was not free then. "Boys needed arithmetic, reading, and writing, the skills necessary for commerce.... Girls, it was thought, needed to learn about household duties and rarely needed to go outside the home for additional training."[11] In the nineteenth century, education for girls consisted of training at home in the domestic arts in preparation for their future roles as wives and mothers. "[M]ost communities saw no point in educating women or in paying for their education because until the mid–1800s, most girls were destined to work inside the home."[12] People of that time believed that, like work, intellectual capability was dictated by sex, and only boys could handle academic training. "Many believed that the education boys received would be detrimental to females because it was overly rigorous and demanding of the mind. In addition, educating girls would waste the teacher's time."[13]

The largest objection to educating girls came from the hegemonic belief that girls and women were intellectually inferior to boys and men, and thus incapable of scholarly learning. Most people in the nineteenth century believed that intelligence and reasoning were physically determined traits found only in boys and men. Therefore girls were not biologically designed for academics, especially math and philosophy, so attempting to educate them was a complete waste of time, effort, and resources.

The nineteenth-century scientific belief of the closed-energy system theorized that people had a finite amount of energy to use during their lives, and they should use it for what their bodies were designed to do naturally. Since men were believed to be the rational, intellectual, reasoning beings, they were to make a habit of sending their energy to their brains so they could attend to what they should be responsible for — building society and running politics and business. Women were urged to focus their energy on their wombs since their life purpose was creating the next generation. The fear in the nineteenth century was that if women used their energy to become educated — an endeavor their bodies were not designed to do — their wombs would suffer and they would become incapable of bearing children. Such a state of womanhood would leave women unmarriageable, a condition that would lead to the destruction of the family, which would harm society and bring about the dismantling of civilization itself.[14]

Girls did not begin to attend public school in large numbers until after the Civil War, and even then, their curriculum was different from what the boys received. "Early in the century, the girls' curriculum was not the same as the boys'. Boys in frontier schools were taught basic education, with a vocational emphasis on the trades and practical arts. Girls were educated for the private realm, emphasizing the skills needed to be a moral wife and mother."[15] Since education was not free and girls needed only education in domestic arts to prepare for their futures, most did not attend school. This gendered arrangement in education helped to reinforce the male public world as separate from the female domestic one.

Into this anxiously gendered zeitgeist, Lucy Ann Lobdell was born in Westerlo, Albany County, New York, on December 2, 1829, to James and Sarah Lobdell, and was the oldest of four children who survived.[16] Westerlo was a village south of Albany, somewhat rural but by no means a wilderness. Most of what little is known about Lucy's childhood comes from her autobiography, *Narrative of Lucy Ann Lobdell, the Female Hunter of Delaware and Sullivan Counties, N.Y.*, which was published in 1855. Lucy's narrative offers evidence that even in her youth, Lucy Ann was different from other girls.

Around 1839[17] young Lucy Ann Lobdell decided she wanted to go to school. Since schooling was not free in the nineteenth century, Lucy Ann struck a deal with her father to work to earn the money she needed for tuition and books.

> I was in my tenth or twelfth year when I had the charge of some hundred chickens, turkeys, and geese, that I used to raise and sell, and then I had half the money I made in that business and in tending the dairy; and so when I went to Coxsackie, I had money I had made in raising calves and poultry to pay for my schooling, and all the expenses I incurred in going to school.[18]

This business opportunity required more than merely tending to the animals and collecting eggs. A number of natural predators eat chicks, goslings, eggs, and full-grown fowl; others like to make meals out of grain and cracked corn — the food meant for the livestock. To protect her inventory of fowl and feed, and thus ensure the income needed to pay for her education, Lucy Ann borrowed her father's rifle and "learned to shoot the hawk, the weasel, the mink, and even down to the rat."[19] In 1840, a girl determined to get an education would have been viewed at best as unusual or odd, especially one who used the traditionally male activity of shooting guns to achieve that goal. Lucy Ann would have been among the first working-class girls to get a full education.

Lucy Ann was successful in gaining enough skill with a gun to protect her little business, and therefore her means of becoming educated to the point where she herself became a schoolteacher,[20] a field just opening up to women in the mid–nineteenth century. The general nineteenth-century attitude held that "the two styles of life, male and female, be separate, but that women should remain subordinate, and in the home."[21] However, the one job men willingly handed over to women was that of teaching, since it lacked the competitive edge of other occupations in the masculine world. The transformation from schoolmaster to schoolmarm was aided by the attitude that women were more naturally suited to a job so confining, sedentary, and focused on the nurturing of children. Permitting women to teach school allowed more men to enjoy the adventure and profits of more manly endeavors.[22] Lucy Ann would have been among the earliest women to teach public school.

Lucy also had a love for the wilderness that was somewhat unusual for a girl of her time. Lucy Ann's first memory recorded in her autobiography was of wandering in the nearby forest as a very young child. "When care was a stranger, I was ofttimes strolling the little wood that was but a short distance from my home." She roamed the woods so often that her distressed mother finally secured a bell to her to make it easier to find the young girl.[23] Her love of the outdoors, her ambition to be educated, and her willingness to learn to shoot are just the earliest recorded instances of her tenacious foray into spaces and activities that had previously been reserved for males. As Lucy Ann grew to womanhood, her skill with guns would be honed to a degree that would earn her the nickname of "the Sure Shot."[24] This skill, combined with her love of being in the woods, enabled Lucy Ann to find sanctuary in the wilderness years later.

Lucy Ann begins her narrative with seemingly innocent accounts of adolescent love, the common sort of thing girls would be interested in. These tales clearly demonstrate her awareness of social expectations of gendered behavior and heteronormative relationships. After young William Smith walks her home from school a number of times, Lucy states, her father orders her to stop seeing him. While giving the appearance of obeying her father's command, Lucy and William exchange letters secretly. This clandestine love affair seems to please Lucy until her sisters discover the secret love letters and feel sorry for her, something Lucy cannot tolerate. "My sisters deeply sympathized with and pitied me, which roused my pride; and the result was I got sick of the idea of loving Mr. Smith."[25] When, a few days later, she hears that Mr. Smith has been telling people that she and he are to be married, she declares the news to be mistaken and does not speak to William again. Curiously, the details surrounding this romance focus more on the conflict between Lucy and her father than any actual content of the affair. Her discussion offers more dialogue exchange with her father than with her love interest, and Lucy's excitement seems to come more from challenging her father's authority than inspiring love in a boy.

Oddly, no details of appearance, character, or even activities and conversations are given when Lucy next discusses Mr. St. John, yet after he dies of consumption she claims, quite dramatically, that he is the only man she will ever truly love. "My heart had found its kindred spirit, but that spirit had soared away and found its mansion on high."[26] It seems from Lucy's account that the man best suited to her is one who is not around.

Lucy's next recorded love affair is with George Washington Slater. She claims that she found him "an innocent sort of boy; and as he was quite agreeable, I kept his company for some five or six months,"[27] until, according to Lucy, her father demands that she not associate with him. After she informs George that she must stop seeing him, Lucy paints a picture of herself as desirable to men by revealing that George "pressed me to his heaving bosom, and imprinted a wild kiss on my brow, and told me a tale of how he loved; how he loved without one hope; how he had struggled to be free; and how vain was it for him to endeavor to forget me."[28]

Lucy's father declares George lovesick, and when George develops a fever, she becomes concerned and anxious about his well-being and decides to disobey her father and check on him during the night.

> Night came, and at nine o'clock, I retired to my bed-room, but not to sleep, for the God that made me gave me a tender heart, and nerved me with a daring spirit; I therefore waited till all was quiet, and then arose and dressed myself in my brother's clothes, stole out of my bed-room window, and went

to the stable, and took one of father's horses, and away rode to learn what had become of Mr. Slater."[29]

After arriving at the house where George was living, Lucy peeks in a window and finds a doctor caring for him. Reassured, she leaves, getting caught in a rainstorm on the journey home. Once home, she has to dry her brother's clothes by a fire so no one will know she used them. The next morning, upon looking in the mirror, she "learned how much an adventure added health and beauty to the cheek."[30] This is the first written account that links her activity in male clothes with adventure and freedom, and it reveals an excitement not found in her romances.

Lucy thrives on rebelling against her father's orders and declares that since George had no home and no one to take care of him, she pitied him and "resolved to be his friend, if I was driven from my father's house the next moment."[31] In fact, it seems rebellion against her father is more appealing than the actual relationship with George, about which Lucy has misgivings. "I felt I knew not how; but in other words, that I was forming an acquaintance with Mr. Slater that I might repent if not carefully looked after. I therefore made up my mind to leave home, and to go to school then in Coxsackie, Green County, N.Y."[32] When George arrives for a visit, she tells him she is "going to Coxsackie to school, and thought it would be best to break off all our keeping company together, for I felt that father was each day growing more bitter against him,"[33] making it appear that her father — not she — had a problem with George.

For a short time, Lucy Ann stayed with an aunt and went to school in Coxsackie. When her father offered to move the family to that town, Lucy Ann informed him of cheap land deals in Delaware County, New York, an area the government was encouraging white people to settle.[34] In 1851, when James Lobdell bought land below Hancock, New York, the Lobdell family became the first white settlers in that area, known locally as the Basket.[35] Lucy left Coxsackie and joined her family in their new home in Long Eddy, where her father built a saw mill and began clearing lumber from the land.

At this point it would seem that the relationship between George and Lucy is old history; however, a short time later, George also moves to the Basket with the intention of marrying Lucy. Lucy claims that "my design for coming into the woods was to avoid [George] ... as my heart had no joy in him, for my early love was no more ... [but] as George was a good workman, and an innocent boy, I had told him I would have him if I could get [father's] consent."[36] Despite the clear contradiction in the story here, "to cut the story short, we were married, and father and mother had given their consent,"[37] either late in 1851 or very early in 1852.

"My Early Love Was No More"

The circumstances surrounding Lucy's relationship with George and her father's part in it are confusing in her narrative, as she relates that her father first encouraged her to treat George well so that he would grow to be a respectable man, then demanded she break off the relationship, and then consented to the marriage. By creating a story of conflict with her father, her marriage to George appears to be her decision, an event in her control, and a victory over her father. But her interview decades later with Dr. P.M. Wise reveals that "it was after the earnest solicitation of her parents and friends that she consented to marry, in her twentieth year, a man for whom, she has repeatedly stated, she had no affection and from whom she never derived a moment's pleasure, although she endeavored to be a dutiful wife."[38]

In the nineteenth century, male and female spheres were separate but linked through the control device of marriage, which, for women, was inevitable. From girlhood, women were taught to submit themselves to marriage. Women were perceived as innately loving beings whose natural place was in the home taking care of a family. All women were potential wives, and women who expressed interest in husbandless lifestyles were considered rebellious, unnatural, and dangerous to the order of society. However, if girls proved to be difficult, marriage and a family were regarded as a cure. The "sedative quality of a home could be counted on to subdue even the most restless spirits."[39] So unruly women were often coerced into marriage.

Lucy withholds accounts of her wandering in the woods and hunting until after the story of life with George is laid out, giving the illusion that Lucy Ann was a normal woman whose sole focus in married life was performing wifely duties with integrity. But the neighbors' accounts and her own later remarks about marriage to Dr. Wise reveal her resistance to familial and social expectations, and if marriage was forced upon Lucy in an attempt to tame her, the endeavor failed. While Lucy's claim of wanting to marry George against her father's wishes is not accurate, the telling of the tale in this way frames Lucy as an independent, free-thinking woman who would not be controlled by an authoritative male figure, and that aspect of her character is very accurate, as details in anecdotes about her unhappy marriage to George reveal.

Considering Lucy's strong-willed personality, it is no surprise that married life does not go well and one is almost tempted to pity George. At this point in her narrative, the story of conflict with and rebellion against men shifts from her father to her husband and male ministers. Lucy had been teaching at a district school before she married, but left that position to stay home and be a wife.[40] The narrative here becomes a laundry list of every incident of George's disappointing and unreasonable behavior as a husband, surrounded by all the circumstances of each event, making her distaste for marriage and lack of affection for George clear, along with her refusal to submit to male authority.

Shortly after getting married, George informs Lucy Ann that they will be taking in Mr. Allen as a boarder, and although Lucy complains that the work involved will confine her to the home, she complies. After becoming acquainted with Mr. Allen, an educated minister, Lucy Ann plays music for him on her violin upon his request. However, when George comes home from work with half a dozen of his friends and demands that she play her violin to entertain his troupe, she refuses. "After a while I put my violin into the stove, for I had no relish for the society it was bringing. This did not suit Mr. Slater at all, and he said he would get another. I told him I would not play any more for a gang of card-players and swearers."[41]

One of the many differences between Lucy and her husband is George's illiteracy and lack of education, which, compared to Lucy's full education, seems to be a major source of conflict. Lucy describes George's conversation skills as vulgar and prefers to discuss religion with Mr. Allen. "Mr. Allen was a professor of religion, and we would converse together on some topic of a different character from the low one Mr. Slater had announced."[42] George becomes jealous and complains that Lucy spends more time talking to the boarder than to her own husband. Lucy replies that she will not enter "upon a subject I knew nothing about, as I had not been in the habit of talking on so unlearned a subject, [and] I should not practice the art before Mr. Allen."[43]

Because of this conflict, Lucy insists that "Mr. Allen must be dismissed in the morning, as I would board him no longer."[44] George orders her to wait until Mr. Allen's rental time is up so that the neighbors will not think it strange for the minister to go away suddenly. Unconcerned with public speculation or her husband's social standing, Lucy Ann does not obey.

> I know not what [Mr. Slater] thought, but I concluded he thought I would say nothing to Mr. Allen of his talk; but he was disappointed if he did, for I had told Mr. Allen previous to that night that I believed Mr. Slater was jealous of his being there, as I had learned by a great many unguarded remarks Mr. Slater had made; and now the actions of the preceding night spoke louder than words. Mr. Allen accordingly left boarding at our house right away.[45]

While Lucy's sharp responses appear provoked by her husband's behavior, they are more than harsh; they are often humiliating, condescending, challenging, and emasculating. Lucy refused to play the role of the meek, obedient, supportive wife. But George was not the only man to experience Lucy Ann's independent spirit and harsh tongue, for she also challenged the authority and learning of the male ministers who passed through Long Eddy.

Lucy was keenly interested in theological philosophies and she mentions her many long discussions with learned ministers, her own strong and nontraditional religious views, and the conflict that arises between her and the clergy. "As the ministers had visited our house frequently I had become quite a curious person for them to talk with, as my sentiments varied from theirs with regard to their belief very much."[46] One evening after such a discussion, "Dr. Hale remarked that I was going ahead of the preacher in speaking in meetings; and he said he thought I did wrong in speaking after nine o'clock in meetings."[47] Dr. Hale's remark is evidence of a boundary line that he was attempting to police, that of woman being subordinate to the socially accepted authority of men and thus remaining silent in order to avoid controversy. Lucy refuses to honor or even acknowledge that boundary line between the genders. Even though Dr. Hale apologizes to Lucy the next morning, she feels that his later incarceration in an insane asylum was God's punishment for abusing her.

> As I got up in the morning I saw that Mr. Hale was worried about something, and at last he came to me and asked me to forgive him, "for," said he, "I have slept but little all night, fearing I have wounded your feelings." I told him I could forgive him if my Heavenly Father could. But whether God has forgiven him or not is not in my power to say. But in a short time the news came to me that Doctor Hale was crazy, and soon after he was sent to the asylum at Utica. He appears to be quite rational at different times, but he is there now at the asylum, a poor crazy thing.[48]

By the fall of 1852, the marriage was in serious trouble. After Lucy ignores George's order and dismisses Mr. Allen from boarding at their house, George retaliates and tries to embarrass Lucy publicly by not showing up to escort her to a quilting bee. However, Lucy refuses to be humiliated, and instead makes the most of the opportunity; she plays the violin, calls out the dances for the event, and engages an escort for the walk home, making George the fool. When George confronts her with the gossip he has heard, Lucy offers a sharp response. "I told him that as he did not come, I had the right to engage an escort; and as I had been his tool for a fool, he could hardly make it appear I had done anything but what he had intended me to do."[49] George's angry reply prompts Lucy to go to her parents' house, claiming to be afraid to go home. After telling her family what has been going on, she decides to move back home permanently, even though her father commands her to return to her rightful place and stay with her husband. At this point George leaves her "in consequence, it is said, of their not living very agreeably together."[50]

Here the story devolves into a bitter narrative of who said what, complete with letters to and from relatives, and a painfully tedious detailing of financial accounts. Lucy Ann states that George has left her with only a bushel of potatoes, having sold their cow and taken the money for himself. She reveals that he was financially irresponsible throughout their marriage (a whole year at best), and that even at the beginning, she had had to pay the five-dollar marriage fee.[51]

The Cult of True Womanhood

Lucy's narrative is not just a tawdry soap-opera story of a bad marriage; it is also evidence of her refusal to fit herself to rigid and demanding social expectations for women in the nineteenth century. Along with the then-prevalent belief that marriage and motherhood were natural roles, certain characteristics, attitudes, and behaviors were expected of women. The idea that women were naturally domestic reinforced the expectation that women were to stay home, relying on husbands for physical and economic protection, in order to support the illusion of balance and stability in society. Housed within separate spheres, social order was further regulated by the philosophy of the Cult of True Womanhood, which declared that women belonged in the home as wives and mothers. Women were repeatedly reminded of what made them true women through sermons, articles in women's magazines, newspapers, and religious literature. "The discourse on the Cult of True Womanhood prevalent in the nineteenth century stressed the virtues of piety, purity, domesticity, and submissiveness and emphasized the home as women's proper place as homemaker and mother."[52]

Along with the strong mechanism of public opinion, writers of women's magazines, gift books, religious tracts, advice pamphlets, and even newspapers continuously reinforced nineteenth-century ideology about characteristics, abilities, and functions that were expected of women. Social authorities such as doctors, ministers, teachers, and publishers circulated stories that presented women as dependent and naturally domestic, locking them into the restrictive domestic sphere where they were expected to perform as wives and mothers. "Women who failed to comply courted condemnation."[53]

Piety was at the core of a woman's virtues and identified as the source of her strength, which she was to use to gently guide her children and husband toward moral and ethical behavior. Religion, believed to be a natural component of feminine identity, provided an outlet for women that did not remove them from their appropriate sphere of domesticity while curbing rebellious spirits.

Although Lucy was well versed in the Bible, religion did not tame her. In her autobiography, while Lucy considers herself extremely moral and religious, she does not adhere to doctrine and religious understandings that were passed down by any church.[54] In fact, she repeatedly admits to disagreeing with and arguing theological points with doctors of religion without apology, resists prescribed dogma, and insists on thinking independently and forming her own interpretations of God's word. She frames her moral superiority not through passive, obedient behavior expected of a nineteenth-century Christian woman, but through her belief that God punishes those who dare to disagree with her or interfere with her life. Besides expressing her belief that Dr. Hale's insanity is punishment from God for not treating her well, she believes God will curse Peter Smith, whom she suspects of encouraging jealousy in George.[55]

Through her rebellion against socially expected behavior for women, she highlights the established gendered boundary lines by her resistance to them. She rejects male teachings, she causes controversy by offering alternative theories on religion, she refuses to be silent when men expect her to not speak publicly, and she does not use religion to influence her husband to follow Christ. Lucy defends her refusal to conform to social expectations because she feels that she is the exact person God made her to be. She considers herself approved by God, a much higher authority than any person, so she dismisses societal disapproval. "And though some do call me a strange sort of being, I thank God, in whom I believe, and in whom I trust, and who is my defense, and I can praise Him, that He has given me a heart, that He will mould and fashion after His holy will."[56] Nor does she use religion as a tool to comfort herself through disappointments in married life, for she is not resigned to silently living in misery.

The second important component of the Cult of True Womanhood was submission, which all but guaranteed social stability in a male-dominated world. A woman's entire focus was to be on her husband and his needs and pleasures — never her own. "[W]omen were expected to work silently and obey their husbands to demonstrate their affection, nurturance, and their lack of personal ambition."[57] She was to be pleasing to her husband and repress her own passions, needs, and opinions for the sake of order. Wives were repeatedly reminded by those who wrote guidelines and advice for women to follow the rules that ensured domestic happiness, "to repress a harsh answer, to confess a fault, and to stop (right or wrong) in the midst of self-defense, in gentle submission."[58] For the sake of order, women were not to ever disagree or argue with their husbands. They were instead encouraged to be childlike and obedient. Clearly, Lucy has no reverence for this expectation or the concern over social order; she gives evidence in her autobiography, again and again, that she disobeys, argues with, and finds fault with men who try to claim authority over her.

The men in Lucy's narrative illuminate the socially constructed boundary lines of female space and behavior by scolding her for her unacceptable speech and actions. They also attempt to make life decisions for her and command her to behave as women were expected to behave. Their failure to correct and contain Lucy is evidence of her disregard for nineteenth-century social definitions and restrictions of women. Lucy's refusal to comply with expectations generated by the Cult of True Womanhood clearly shows those definitions and expectations of women to be human constructions; however, since the nineteenth-century mind viewed those expectations as natural, biological elements of women, people around Lucy view her as an uncontained, ungovernable woman: disruptive, disorderly, and unnatural.

In failing at "true" womanhood, Lucy presents that ideal as a cage, annoying and harmful to women, and shows herself as a strong survivor of it. She uses religion creatively to serve her own needs and refuses to be the silent support system for her husband's needs and desires. Lucy does not simply make George's failings and shortcomings known in her community; she lists them in her book for all to read. This first part of Lucy's narrative reveals a nature that resists the boundaries and expectations for nineteenth-century women. She is a rebellious daughter, an argumentative member of the religious community, and a disobedient, judgmental, vocal wife who shows little true concern or affection for her husband.

However, Lucy displays her awareness of social expectations of women in her writing, and uses those expectations to build a pathway to her true purpose. Her narrative opens with safe romantic tales, the type expected of girls, and positions herself as a normal woman who likes boys and wants to marry. Having established herself as a normal woman who tries to live by society's rules, she next offers a sharp critique of those social expectations and leads the reader to a place of female anger, resentment, and rebellion, as if these were the natural attributes of women living in the True Woman realm. There is no more pretense of affection for men at this point in the narrative, and her frustration and anger are no longer hidden. Aware that refusing to live with her husband and returning to the Lobdell family home is the most rebellious and disruptive act a woman could do to marriage in the nineteenth century, Lucy carefully presents her story, first claiming to demand marriage, and then painting marriage as insufferable and George as unreasonable, incapable, and vulgar; she herself becomes an upstanding woman who did her best. While the Cult of True Womanhood promises happiness to women who follow its guidelines, Lucy's narrative is a keen indictment of a flawed social system framed by a philosophy that restricts and harms women. The mood of the story now is one of irritation and disgust, the tone indignant and accusatory, the vocabulary insulting and demeaning.

The Female Hunter

In the second part of Lucy's narrative, she reveals even further not just her refusal to conform to social expectations of behavior but also her absolute disregard for gendered boundaries around space, work, and clothing. After explaining when and why she learned to shoot a rifle, she shares stories about hunting. "So after I had moved to father's, and Mr. Slater had gone away, I used often to go hunting to drive care and sorrow away; for when I was upon the mountain's brow, chasing the wild deer, it was exciting for me."[59] She quickly follows with the explanation that her father was decrepit and it was necessary for her to hunt to bring home food, but her love of the freedom and excitement of being outside in the wild precedes her practical, mundane reason.

The hunting stories are compelling, as any good storyteller will make them, and Lucy invites the reader to go with her: "I will now take the reader to an excursion on a cold winter morn."[60] In giving her reasons for hunting, she mentions pleasure before necessity, and it is this pleasure that infuses her hunting stories. After explaining that she appropriated her brother's clothes and her father's guns in order to hunt, she relates her first attempts at hunting larger game in oral storytelling fashion. Her account is rich in active verbs, giving enormous detail to tracking, watching, and chasing. The story is filled with sensory details of the sounds of thunder and deer snorting, the feel and quiet of the wilderness around her, and the tension of waiting and chasing game. But there is also something else that has not appeared in her narrative to this point: humor.

Lucy's hunting stories paint her as bumbling and incapable. She misses her targets often, gets lost repeatedly, dangerously misuses her rifle as a staff, loses animal tracks, and misplaces her shoes and socks.[61] But her stories reveal that she is no novice because of certain small details she includes. She understands the workings of guns and how to discover what causes problems with shooting; she knows that animals can smell her track as well as her presence if she is downwind; she knows what clearings the deer visit; she is capable of hunting in moonlight; she patiently observes the actions of the deer to learn their habits; and she knows how to track her prey.

While Lucy has justified her hunting activities as being necessary for the family's survival, the joy and delight in the freedom and excitement of a traditional male activity is the focus of her story, as she talks only about the hunt, not the meal on the dinner table. She engages the reader with minute details of observations, the thrill of chasing game while trying to outwit it, and the sense of accomplishment when she does finally bring down a fawn.

Lucy does not brag about her rifle skills, even though by this time she was so accomplished that she was known as the Female Hunter of Delaware County; she leaves that up to the voice of a man. She passes over "some hundred little hunting adventures, [to] give them a place in [her] next book,"[62] and offers a letter from a Mr. Talmage, which was published in many newspapers. "I will copy his work here, as I may make truth appear convincing as it regards my present occupation."[63] She knows that a male voice will carry more authority than her own concerning prowess in such a masculine activity.

The story she reproduces is from a newspaper in Bridgeport, Connecticut, revealing a fame and reputation that was more than local.[64] In Mr. Talmage's letter, Lucy is seen through the objective eyes of a man who does not know her, so the account is not influenced by personal feelings about Lucy. Talmage explains that he was traveling by foot in Sullivan County when he was overtaken by a young man with a rifle on his shoulder. After a bit of conversation, he realized it was actually a woman, who claimed she was out tracking a deer she had wounded that morning. For the first time, the reader learns how Lucy dressed herself to go hunting and just what skill she had with a gun:

> Although I can not give a very clear idea of her appearance, I will try to describe her dress. The only article of female apparel visible was a close-fitting hood upon her head, such as is often worn by deer hunters; next, an India-rubber over-coat. Her nether limbs were encased in a pair of snug-fitting corduroy pants, and a pair of Indian moccasins were upon her feet. She had a good looking rifle upon her shoulder, and a brace of double-barreled pistols in the side-pockets of her coat, while a most formidable hunting-knife hung suspended by her side. Wishing to witness her skill with her hunting instruments, I commenced bantering her in regard to shooting. She smiled ... and to convince me, took out her hunting-knife, and cut a ring, about four inches in diameter, on a tree, with a small spot in the center; then stepping back thirty yards, and drawing up one of her pistols, put both balls inside the ring. She then, at eighteen rods[65] from the tree, fired a ball from her rifle into the very center.[66]

Since dark was coming on, Lucy offered Mr. Talmage safe shelter for the night at her father's house, and now the reader learns more details about Lucy's everyday life at home.

> The maiden-hunter instead of setting down to rest as most hunters do when they get home, remarked that she had got the chores to do. So, out she went, and fed, watered, and stabled a pair of young horses, a yoke of oxen, and three cows. She then went to the saw-mill, and brought back a slab on her shoulder, that I should not liked to have carried, and with an axe and saw, she soon worked it up into stove-wood. Her next business was to change her dress, and get tea, which she did in a manner which would have been creditable to a more scientific cook. After tea, she finished up the usual housework, and then sat down and commenced plying her needle in the most lady-like manner.[67]

Mr. Talmage goes on to explain that Lucy's father had become lame the first winter the family moved there, so Lucy had taken charge of plowing, planting, and harvesting the farm and had "learned to chop wood, drive the team, and do all the necessary [outdoor] work." She boasts to Talmage that the game in the area was plentiful, and, as the family had need, she had shot a large quantity of small game. After chatting for a while, Lucy brings out her violin and plays a number of songs, singing along to some of them, to entertain her guest, who notes that she is quite an accomplished musician and singer. According to Talmage,

> [t]he next morning she was up at four o'clock, and before sunrise, had the breakfast out of the way, and her work out of doors and in the house done; and when I left, a few minutes after sunrise, she had got on her hunting-suit, and was loading her rifle for another chase after the deer.[68]

As an objective, admiring observer, Talmage presents Lucy's numerous talents, abilities, and skills through the authority of an approving and impressed male voice, giving her traits more veracity than her own words could have done. While Lucy's humorous presentation of her hunting trips makes light of her covertly seized male identity, Talmage's jovial voice portrays Lucy as a benign wonder rather than a threat.

Mr. Talmage reported an event that he and others found unusual because nineteenth-century modes of thinking separated male from female through differences, especially types of apparel and work. Lucy's domestic abilities prove she is accomplished in the female sphere, but her exceptional rifle skills and ability to do male outdoor work challenge beliefs about gendered capabilities. Talmage has witnessed and reported Lucy's untraditional and nonconforming ability to switch from one gender to another, and move smoothly from one gendered sphere to the other. While his report grants authority to Lucy's abilities, it also confirms to Lucy's demonstration that gender is fluid and social spheres are artificial constructions with permeable boundaries.

After revealing her competence as a hunter to her readers, the narrative quickly reverts back to her conflict with George, as his letter announces his intention to return to see his child, a child that has hitherto not been mentioned.

Westerlo, Oct. 5th, 1854

Miss Lucy A. Lobdell,
(As you call yourself, but which is Slater truly, but I address you as you call yourself to please you,) in truth, I wish it were as it was once — peace and harmony.[69]

The remainder of George's letter wishes Lucy well and bids her do what she thinks is best for her life, yet he states that he longs to see her and his child, a desire Lucy views as carrying the potential for further domestic restriction.

Contrary to social expectations, marriage does not sedate Lucy; it becomes her stage for rebellion. The influences of family, public opinion, religious leaders, and the Cult of True Womanhood are powerless to bring her in line, and as a disorderly body, she rejects the space defined as a woman's natural arena. Lucy's rejection of her married name in favor of her maiden name violently disrupts and threatens the norms and social order of the patriarchal society within which she lived, for the adoption of the husband's name, which replaced her own, was evidence of her subjugation to him, a subjugation Lucy never accepted.

The nineteenth-century belief that women lose their separate identity upon marriage is evident in this statement of Sir William Blackstone's: "By marriage, the husband and wife are one person in the law; that is, the very being and legal existence of the woman is suspended during the marriage, or at least is incorporated into that of her husband under whose wing, protection and cover she performs everything."[70] In other words, upon marriage a woman experienced a civil death, losing any rights as a citizen, including the right to own or bestow property, make contracts or sue for legal redress, hold custody of minor children, or keep any wages she earned.

The married title made it clear that a woman's husband had power over her life. Even the outspoken feminist of Lucy's day, Lucy Stone, graciously adopted the title "Mrs." as she rebelliously retained her own last name. The insertion of George's letter gives evidence that even her husband acknowledges her autonomy, for he uses her maiden name. By discarding the name Slater and returning to Lobdell, Lucy claims a former persona, one not restricted by a husband. Not only has Lucy refused to perform according to social expectations for women but she also has rejected the state of marriage and refused to let it confine her. She has, in effect, erased her marriage and rendered George invisible, nonexistent, powerless and of no consequence in her life, stripping him of a husband's power and revealing her intent to live outside the confines of marriage.

At this time in the nineteenth century, women were expected to create a home as a place of joy, rest, and comfort for their families, a home to which men would want to return rather than search for pleasure in other places. The demands and restrictions on women's movements and behaviors left no room for challenge or refusal because of beliefs about women and their functions. Marriage, childbearing, housekeeping, and religion were seen as the ultimate purposes of women's lives, and sources of comfort that calmed women and provided them with serenity. But Lucy was having none of that.

Here in the narrative Lucy is no longer concerned with the imagined male reader or the patriarchal system that grants him power over women, as evidenced by her seizure of authority to define herself. With open defiance of societal expectations, Lucy explains that she will leave her home and child, in male clothes, to appropriate the freedoms relegated to men only and thus escape the imprisonment of the female body.

As Lucy offers an explanation for why she is leaving home dressed in men's clothes, she presents a portrait of what real life for a working-class woman was like in just the work at home, which would still need to be done if the woman had an outside job. She claims that she could live at her father's house but she would have a life of endless work and little monetary compensation, certainly not enough to support her child. She lists some of the chores that made up the lives of working women, keeping them at work from sunrise until late at night.

> Again, she must be up at early dawn to get breakfast, and whilst the breakfast is cooking, she must wash and dress some half a dozen children. After finishing up the usual morning's house-work, such as washing dishes, making beds, and filing the kitchen-floor, then comes the dinner as usual. Then comes the husband — the puddings have been burned a trifle when mother was busy at something else; then come complaints in regard to the pudding. Well, mother was busy with Bridget or Patrick, settling some quarrel or blows, and now mother has made father a little out of taste with the dinner. And this is the way the world is jogging along.[71]

Lucy offers a realistic story of women's lives, one created with the authority of experience and observation: a life filled with sorrow, poverty, ceaseless chores and hard work, and an irritated, ungrateful husband. In contrast to cultural fictions reinforced by True Woman ideology where marriage, motherhood, and domesticity are the keys to happiness and husbands care for wives, keep them safe, and provide generously for them, Lucy presents that world as a dreary, maddening prison and states, "And this is the way the world is jogging along."[72]

That is the way life is: harsh, exhausting, and loveless. That is an honest representation of a woman's life, and it challenges and exposes the crafted lives presented in novels, sermons, and magazine stories — all the fictional patterns designed to guide real-life women. Lucy's version, constructed from observation rather than imagination, is not the safe, pleasant life promised for women who climb into the patriarchal mold of female identity and willingly fit themselves to a prescribed pattern of servitude and submission. Lucy's descriptions of working-class domestic life paint a clear, bleak picture of never-ending work for women and nonexistent appreciation or help from the husband, quite the opposite of the dominant cultural story that insisted life at home for women was less taxing physically and mentally than work outside the home.

Next she openly challenges men to do a better job at women's work, feeling that such an experience would prove that men could not do the job as well and therefore they should have compassion and understand that women are worthy of wages equal to those earned by men.

> And, now, I ask, if a man can do a woman's work any quicker or better than a woman herself; or could he collect his thoughts sufficiently to say his prayers with a clear idea? No; if he was confused and housed up with the children all day, he would not hesitate to take the burden off his children's shoulders, and allow woman's wages to be on an equality with those of the man. Is there one, indeed, who can look upon that little daughter, and feel that she soon will grow up to toil for the unequal sum allotted to compensate her toil[?][73]

Lucy's challenge to men to do women's work centers on their ignorance about the lives of women they define and dominate, and it sharpens the point she is trying to make about the hard existence many working-class women had, arguing that, with such experience, men would not hesitate to compensate women fairly. Lucy seems to feel that if men simply knew what real women's lives were like, fairness would prevail. She understands that the political power over wages is unfairly in the hands of men, and so the plea must be made to men. However, the suggestion that men and women trade places is tantamount to turning social order upside-down, a threatening concept, so Lucy's perspective and hope is naïve at best. This vision of an enclosed, restricted life of work without relief reveals a hidden dark side to women's lives, a life that Lucy cannot endure because it restricts women's abilities and opportunities while demanding obedience, silence, and performance. With firm resolve, she rejects those restrictions:

> I feel that I can not submit to see all the bondage with which woman is oppressed, and listen to the voice of fashion, and repose upon the bosom of death. I can not be reconciled to die, and feel my poor babe will be obliged to toil and feel the wrongs that are unjustly heaped upon her. I am a mother; I love my offspring even better than words can tell. I can not bear to die and leave that little one to struggle in every way to live as I have had to do.[74]

Lucy spotlights the boundary of the female sphere through the examples and descriptions of everyday life and work for working-class women, as well as the expected attitude of acquiescence and deference to the husband. Since Lucy is writing at the time of the Civil War, the use of the word "bondage" resonates with images of overworked slaves, abused and controlled by white male masters. Considering Lucy's close relationship with the Bible, the word also summons up images of the bondage of God's chosen people, a people God favored and led to freedom. Both images create the sense that bondage is created by men who abuse their power, and it is dissolved by righteousness.

Lucy's entire narrative works to vindicate her actions and build empathy in the reader. She goes to great lengths to present herself as a good woman mistreated by men, making her rebellion seem a natural and understandable outcome. She makes it clear that social expectations are oppressive to women, denying them the right to form themselves through their own imaginations, abilities, and ambitions. Lucy points out that the whole culture embraces the patriarchal formation of women with a societal mold created to reduce and entrap them in the women's powerless sphere of the home only. By labeling these expectations as the "voice of fashion," she positions gender roles as constructions instead of natural, essential behaviors. To Lucy, submissively fitting herself to this inferior identity would cause her to die, which she refuses to do. While popular literature and thought might paint a picture of domestic bliss, happiness, and satisfaction for women who play the role correctly, Lucy presents another raw glimpse of real life for the working-class woman in an even darker scenario of everyday life for women.

Lucy describes a scene of female life that requires marriage for the sake of obtaining a home. This life imprisons the wife in the domestic sphere, where work and poverty literally drain the life from her. The husband, however, gets to escape from the crying babes and tension in the home because he enjoys the freedom of going to the tavern.

> Thus we see the home that our child has found. Ah! she indeed has found a home — a habitation of care and sorrow! She indeed hugs the cords that bind her there. Again, the husband comes home a little the worse for wine or rum. The mother marks that staggering form as he wends his way to the bed whereon he goes to sleep and forget[s] the care he now throws away in the whirl of drunkenness.... We behold that the father has squandered all his living in drunkenness. He has become a drunkard; his home is now a hovel of wretchedness and misery.[75]

This scene continues until the mother actually dies and the babies are left to charity as orphans, clearly framing marriage as a dangerous trap for women.

In contrast to the description of home as a haven of pleasure and comfort created by the woman for the man, as described by the Cult of True Womanhood, Lucy's version of home is a "habitation of care and sorrow" for the woman because of behaviors the husband is socially permitted to have. Here is an image of man that is the polar opposite of that standard offered by nineteenth-century consensus reality, for he is not financially successful, he is not generous and protective, he does not have the best interests of his wife and children at heart, and he is making poor decisions. Father's drinking has reshaped the home as a "hovel of wretchedness and misery" that the mother's touch is powerless to correct no matter how "true" a woman she has been, or perhaps because she has been the perfect true woman. True womanhood is revealed to be a flawed construct, where men are not held to the same high standards and expectations that women are, and women suffer because of this inequality. Lucy presents such a restricted life as fatal to women and, rather than enabling women to keep society healthy through socially expected behaviors, it becomes a source of social ills that women cannot cure. In this way, she exposes the order created by gender roles and expectations as an illusion, and promotes the advancement of women into the public world of work as a way to gain equality, a pronouncement sure to be viewed as a threat to gendered social order.

Lucy positions herself as an agent for social change, making sacrifices and working on behalf of others. "I am among strangers penning this little book. I am not permitted to lay the pen aside and kiss the child of my bosom. No; I am far away, struggling with my pen to lift the veil that has so long shrouded the hearts of fathers and mothers as regards the future of their offspring."[76] Lucy's solution to the problems of restrictions and poverty for women is to allow them to work outside the home and pay them equal wages.

> Help, one and all, to aid woman, the weaker vessel. If she is willing to toil, give her wages equal with that of man. And as in sorrow she bears her own curse, (nay, indeed she helps to bear a man's burden also,) secure to her the rights, or permit her to wear the pants, and breathe the pure air of heaven, and you stay and be convinced at home with the children how pleasant a task it is to act the part that woman must act.[77]

Lucy's subversive demand that women be able to work outside the home for pay equal to men's is made even more threatening by her insistence that women should have the right to wear pants as well. In the nineteenth century, clothing was the clearest indicator of sexed identity, signifying the gendered roles the wearers should enact; the functions, attributes, and abilities that could be expected from them; and the spaces they could properly inhabit.

In societies such as nineteenth-century England and America, which differentiated greatly between the role of men and women, the clothing of the two sexes also diverged widely. The rather minimal differences between the physical anatomy of men and women were enormously exaggerated by clothed bodies. More than identifying each sex, clothing defined the role of each sex.[78]

Skirts and dresses obscured women's legs, hiding their sexuality from the male gaze as they hampered women's movements. Pants provided more than freedom of movement for men; they signified male authority and power considered appropriate to male bodies. Women who wore pants without male approval "posed a threat to the masculine 'right' to govern and command."[79]

Lucy further rejects the female role and sphere when she demands the freedom to escape the sphere of female domesticity altogether, especially the traditional role of mother. Motherhood was embedded into wifehood as a primary function and identity of women, and girls were trained from an early age in how to perform as mothers. More than a simple natural function of women, motherhood was linked to social order, for it served the "higher duty of protecting the transcendent good of social health, which could be maintained only through the continued production of healthy children."[80] Any woman who did not embrace this role and affectionately love her children was considered monstrous. Lucy disrupts the official social story of motherhood as a woman's source of power with a subversive tale of motherhood as debilitating. While Lucy claims to miss her daughter, her suggestion that the invisible male reader stay home and take care of the family emphasizes just how difficult and draining that work is.

The darkest element in Lucy's versions of domesticity is motherhood. Contrary to social constructions of motherhood as the joyful source of women's very existence and the natural outlet for their innate loving tendencies, Lucy presents the activity of motherhood as tedious drudgery and confusion, suffocating the mother to the point of death. She refers to motherhood and domesticity as an "act ... that women must act," a performance guided by tacitly prescribed rules, based on social expectations. While her explanation of leaving to become a good provider for her child may seem honorable, leaving and living as a man with all the freedoms granted to that sex relieves her of the numbing drudgery of the actual performed activity of motherhood. Lucy's broader hunt for autonomy includes escape from motherhood, female behavior considered unnatural by her society.

In abandoning motherhood and domesticity, she presents an alternative pattern of life for women, a subversive one without children or husbands.

While Lucy mentions her concern for her daughter's future, saying she does not want to see her suffer under the cultural conditions that have the power to shape and control women's lives, she makes it much clearer that she herself simply will not live under those conditions. Lucy firmly refuses to reinforce or help perpetuate the restrictive, normative paradigm of woman, not by living as a nonconforming woman, but by no longer living as a woman at all.

She again reiterates why she is wearing men's clothes, restating that she could not support a child and herself on a dollar a week. At this point, her narrative becomes an angry manifesto,[81] revealing a harsh life where women are expected to perform to gendered expectations in the restricted space allowed them. With words that smack of emancipatory politics, she demands change for women.

By this point in the autobiography, Lucy has completely attacked three of the four cornerstones of the Cult of True Womanhood. No one ever questions her purity. But rather than be submissive, she has offered herself up as a pattern of righteous disobedience and vocal self-expression, one that has total disregard for male authority. She has revealed a dark and potentially deadly side of domesticity that was never a part of the dominant stories, and demanded changes and opportunities for women. And she has dared to use religion to suit her own needs and purposes rather than meekly adopting the philosophies and rules handed to women.

As stated earlier, many forms of cultural stories, from newspaper articles to religious tracts to women's magazines, constantly reminded women that the stability of society depended on them cooperatively keeping their traditional place within it. Any woman who asked for more than marriage, home, and family was viewed as dangerous and unnatural, a threat to social order. "If anyone, male or female, dared to tamper with the complex virtues which made up the Cult of True Womanhood, he was damned immediately as an enemy of God, of civilization and of the Republic."[82] Lucy is more than disruptive at this point, for she refuses to be controlled at all. She is the ungoverned woman, evidence of the loss of male control. Her threat to social order and stability is further amplified when she abandons domesticity and motherhood, takes on a male identity, and enters the public sphere as a man.

In stepping outside the dominant pattern for women, Lucy reveals its artificial construction and offers a different pattern for female subjectivity, one that includes masculine elements, activities, spaces, and privileges. Lucy presents herself as a living example to the reader as someone who is more than capable in both male and female spheres, proving that those spheres are artificial constructs, not God-made natural spaces, and that the boundaries are permeable, the gap between them crossable. In other words, Lucy reveals that the social order around her is an illusion, created to maintain a gendered control over people.

In looking to the future, she also implies that change is necessary so her daughter, and other women, will not have to live with those same restrictions. Calling for social change that will allow all women to slip the bonds of domesticity and join her in forging a new path for women's lives makes her even more dangerous to her society, for she challenges the very foundation of a social order that makes male dominance possible. By insisting that any woman who so desires it receive the right to wear pants and do men's work, she is demanding that women be freed from women's sphere of the home, the familial space of female confinement and restriction, the nucleus of the building blocks of a patriarchal system. Her carefully worded plea is nothing short of mutiny and rebellion seeking to empower and enable women to live however they choose, not as mandated by society. Her encouragement to other women to refuse the traditional roles of wife and mother is disruptive and challenges male-only access to work in the public sphere, money, and mobility. Such a rebellion blurs the lines between male/public and female/domestic spaces and the distinctions between the sexes, along with carrying the potential for social chaos. Social stability relied on women's acceptance of their subordinate position, inferior characterizations, and willing incarceration in the female sphere while performing expected feminine roles. When women did not comply with their assigned position, or the behaviors and clothing related to it, social order was threatened. "A woman who did not play the narrow and predictable role converted a man's sanctuary into a bottomless pit of uncertainty, the more threatening in proportion to his previous certainty of predictability."[83]

Perhaps the most dangerous change that Lucy suggests is one where the men stay home with the children while women enter the public sphere of work and opportunity in the authoritative, powerful garb of pants. This scenario feeds into nineteenth-century male fears of women becoming men and leaving their powerless, subordinate positions for men to fill. The concept of dominance and power was so strongly linked to clothing that "numerous articles and essays charged that if women wore the [pants] then it would logically follow that men would assume the feminine characteristics of dependence,"[84] a frightening concept for men who fully understood the power dynamics of the gendered social structure. Such a reversal of roles and spheres does not just challenge male mobility, privilege, and power but also attacks the meaning and enactment of masculinity, offering that role to women and removing it from men. It likewise threatens the artificial construction of a social order and reality that positions men above women based on gender and genitals. Lucy's narrative does not merely demand equality and opportunity for women; it suggests men should relinquish some of the market they have cornered on public power and masculinity, threatening the very identity of men.

However, Lucy's main goal in her narrative is not for all women to be freed from the restrictive domestic sphere; it is rather to vindicate her actions and her claim of the right to live as a man. Knowing how radical this demand is, Lucy builds a bridge for the reader from the beginning of her narrative to the end. She lures the reader into the story with a traditional, feminine, safe romance, defends herself so as to make her angry diatribe and manifesto appear reasonable, and then positions her desire to dress as a man to gain employment opportunities as the only rational alternative, considering the absolute lack of opportunities for women. She carefully proves that she is capable of performing men's work, and more than willing to do so. Even though she offers logical reasons for her decision to leave dressed as a man, she knows that doing so will be viewed as irrational, dangerous, punishable behavior — even by her parents, who have depended on her masculine activities for their survival. "I did not dare to tell our folks my calculations, for I knew that they would say I was crazy, and tie me up, perhaps."[85]

Metamorphosis

As disruptive as nonconforming behaviors might be, people living in the wilderness tend to let them slide if they help maintain survival. But certain behaviors can be viewed as dangerous and unacceptable even where there seems to be no civilization. What Lucy has not included in her autobiography are her public experiences of living in men's clothes before leaving home, and her neighbors' reactions.

The local residents told stories of a Native American girl named Gelerama and assumed she was friends with Lucy Ann. The one photograph of Lucy in a buckskin dress, long pigtails, and feathers in her hair would seem to support this assertion. According to Miss Ellen O'Meara,

> In those days, Lucy Ann wore her dark hair in two long braids and must have resembled an Indian, tanned from exposure to sun and wind as she roamed over the forested hills and explored dark valleys as yet untouched by the pioneer's axe. She was an expert shot and often spent days at a time away from her home, following old hunter's paths made originally by the native Indians, finding shelter at night under some overhanging ledge. Deer, bear, panthers were plentiful then and wolf signs were not unusual.[86]

Lucy Ann Lobdell, circa 1853 (in buckskin dress with braids).

Evelyn Halsey recalled that "Lucy Ann had a most wonderful voice and was often heard singing in the forest or on some high point in the mountains. One of her favorite songs was, 'Captain Jinks of the Horse Marines.'"[87] Other neighbors claimed they would rush to get evening chores finished so they could sit on their porches and listen to the Female Hunter, whose voice would carry through the valley as she tramped through the woods and sang while the sun set.[88]

Leslie D. LaValley states that because of her love for hunting, Lucy was "nick-named, 'The Female Hunter' by her hard working, but good natured neighbors."[89] Perhaps not all the neighbors were good natured, for disapproval was evident even in the wilderness. "Since woman's place was in the home then, Lucy Ann's professional activities were frowned on by many good women and possibly as a gesture of defiance [Lucy] cropped her hair and started wearing man's attire."[90]

W.B. Guinnip recalled seeing the Female Hunter when he was a boy:

> One day when I was seven or eight years of age there was a rapping at the door. Then at Mother's invitation a man, to all appearances, entered the room carrying a satchel. From this case he took a book, handed it to Mother, and entered into a conversation in which I had no interest. It was not until he had left the house that I learned that this was the "Female Hunter," not a man but a woman. With wide open eyes I rushed to the window and watched him (her) depart. Her clothes were exactly of the style worn by men and of fine black cloth; on her head she wore what was then called "a stove-pipe hat." ... This male attire was adopted, she said, for purposes of occupation. She thought she could make more money working in the woods and hunting.[91]

While wearing men's work clothes in the remote wilderness might have been accepted by her family for the sake of survival, silk suits and stove-pipe hats are not hunting attire. Lucy wanted more than just life in the woods as a hunter and presented herself to the public as an educated gentleman, a dangerous thing for a woman to do publicly in 1855.

Accounts from neighbors reveal behaviors uncommon to women, even in the wilderness. Harry Walsh remembered meeting Lucy "in her father's saw mill sawing or attempting to saw. She was then dressed in men's clothes and particularly attracted my attention."[92] He also recalled that she would hunt in men's clothes. This observation, recorded with similar ones from eleven other men in lunacy testimonials, was meant to point out Lucy's abnormal behavior, as these statements were used to declare her insane decades later. The wearing of men's clothes by a woman was not viewed as mere rebellion but as proof of insanity, visible evidence of behavior perceived as unnatural. Lucy's remark about her family thinking she is crazy for entering the world as a man is prophetic, for cross-dressing is the first reason listed for confinement on her commitment papers to Willard Insane Asylum in 1880.

Lucy's experiences in Rock Valley make her very aware of the cultural subtext that defines the sexes through their differences, requiring the distinct separation of men and women through gender roles believed to be natural. She knows that presenting herself as a man and entering male spaces is willful disregard of gendered boundaries, behavior so dangerous that it was designated as irrational by those who were aware of the transgression. For her own safety, she must go where people will not recognize her, for while her family overlooked her behavior for the sake of survival, the general public will not tolerate her masculine appearance and behavior. So Lucy decides to leave home and family.

> I could not even kiss my little Helen, nor tell her how her mother was going to seek employment to get a little spot to live, and earn something for her as she grew up. So, I stole away with a heavy heart, for I knew that I was going among strangers, who did not know my circumstances, or see my heart, so broken, and know its struggles.[93]

Lucy leaves home in her hunting clothes, but en route to the train depot a close neighbor recognizes her and she slips into the woods to change clothes. From her hiding place in the forest, she sees people pass who seem to be searching for her. She decides to walk through the woods rather than on the road and reaches a friend's house, leaving the area very early the next morning.

Lucy Ann Lobdell, circa 1854 (with hair cut off).

Putting on men's clothing is an enacted point of resistance for Lucy, not just a literary one. Because the language of gender is such a pervasive method of culturally knowing people, visible appearance is taken to accurately reflect the interiority of the body in such a way that society may recognize it for what it is supposed to be. By exchanging her clothes for that of the other sex, Lucy is disregarding social expectations and refusing to perform the behavior required of them. She becomes an unruly body, resisting and challenging the heterogeneity of the social and political body. Refusing the restrictions imposed on her sexed body, Lucy seizes male freedom when she wears men's clothes, and erases her original self, or rather the Lucy Ann Lobdell known by others.

Lucy's writing deceptively attempts to position her as female and feminine in the beginning, but ends up highlighting her masculine tendencies, behaviors, and activities. She refuses the socially subordinate position for women and insists on thinking independently, speaking her mind, and

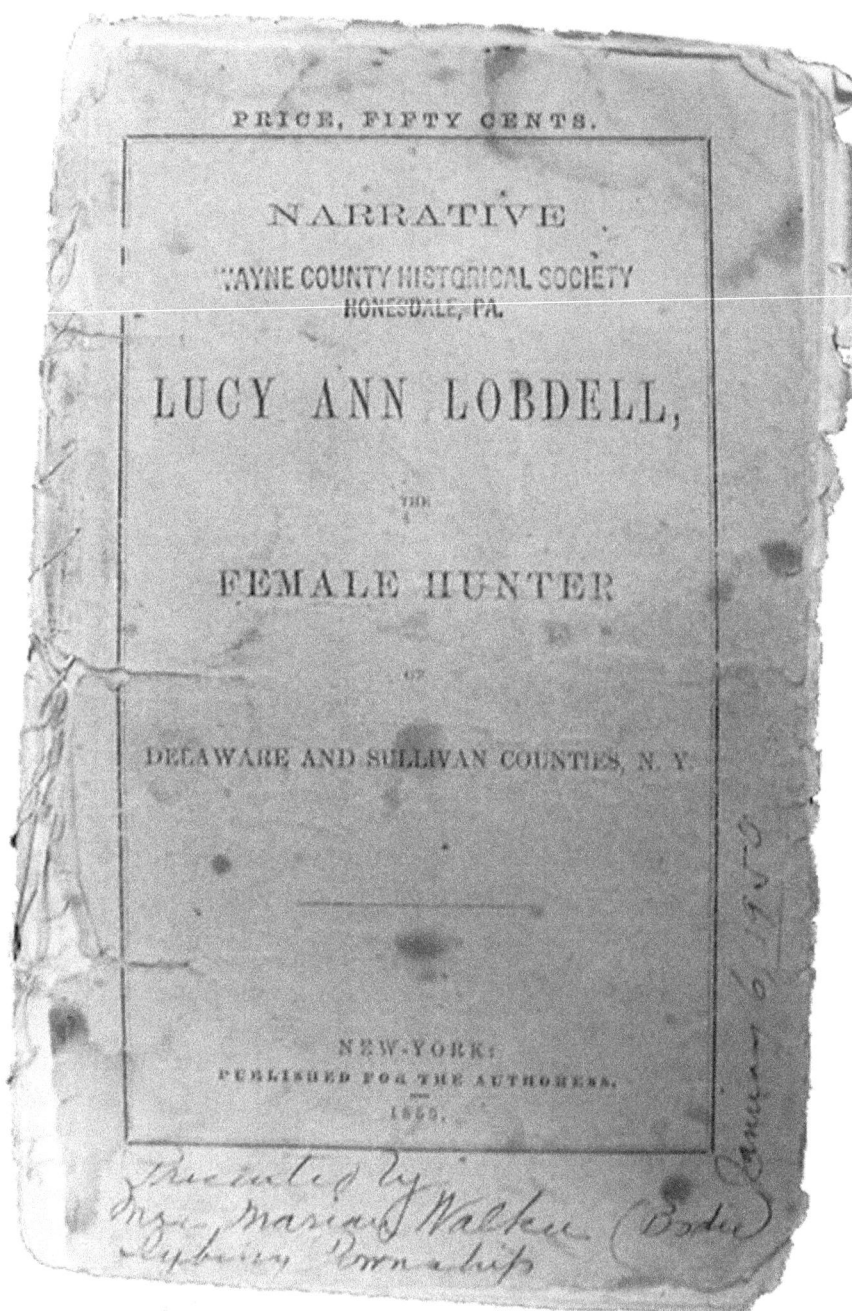

Lobdell's narrative, in the Wayne County Historical Society library collection in Honesdale, Pennsylvania.

making her own decisions. She views herself as equal to men intellectually, and feels her labors are equal in value to anything men do. Her superior shooting and hunting skills are admired by many, but those abilities, along with her exchange of home and family for the excitement of male privileges of mobility and economic opportunity, make her a dangerous threat to social stability and order.

When read in isolation, Lucy's narrative seems to be just a feminist manifesto. But Lucy's masculinity was more than a means to a more profitable life, more than good luck in hunting, more than a good male disguise. According to "A Case of Sexual Perversion," an article written by Dr. P.M. Wise, who was Lucy's doctor three decades later when she was incarcerated in the Willard Insane Asylum, "she was peculiar in girlhood, in that she preferred masculine sports and labor; had an aversion to attentions from young men and sought the society of her own sex."[94] This same article by Dr. Wise includes an explanation for her distaste for her first marriage in Lucy's own words, which ironically is dismissed as further evidence of her insanity. Lucy repeatedly tells Dr. Wise that she is a man, which was the core of the problem of being confined to a woman's body and life. "She states, however, that she did not refer to sexual causes to explain her conduct and mode of life at [the time of writing the autobiography], although she considered herself a man in all that the name implies."[95] Lucy identifies as a man, one who was not sexually attracted to men.

While Lucy does admit in her narrative that "some do call me a strange sort of being,"[96] she does not explain exactly what is strange about her. The female act of wearing men's clothes was considered transgressive behavior, but what Lucy does when she leaves home is even more subversive than appropriating male attire and freedoms. At the point of leaving home, Lobdell literally embodied the conflicts surrounding gender and class in the nineteenth century. While first-wave feminists posed a threat to traditional patriarchal power and structure, Lucy Ann Lobdell seemed to threaten the natural order of humankind as God had created it. As a gender outlaw who refused to follow social rules — even those believed to be grounded in biology — Lobdell created a threat that eventually necessitated incarceration in an attempt to protect the order of the surrounding nineteenth-century society.

Lobdell was a wrongful body, not just an unruly one, leaving home not merely dressed in the disguise of a man to gain male freedoms and privileges but also shedding femaleness altogether and entering the world as a man named Joseph Israel Lobdell. In abandoning the life of a woman, he rejected the female anatomy of his body, shedding the physiological shell of oppression and erasing a persona that had felt artificial and imposed to him.

Lobdell's narrative records the actual moment of change in his life, disowning and abandoning female identity and beginning life as a man, along with all the drama and danger involved in that moment of metamorphosis. Lobdell's life as a man challenged not only gender roles but also common understandings of sexed bodies, making life as a man with a female body dangerous for him. His story reveals what he is willing to give up, what he must give up, in order to be who he is; he must walk away from child, family, home, and all possessions except for a gun and go into the unknown world where there are no ready friends and family. "It takes so much courage [for transgender people] to live our lives that sometimes just leaving our homes in the morning and facing the world as who we really are is in itself an act of resistance."[97]

Erasure of the subordinated woman is in itself an act of resistance, but Lobdell completed the act of disappearance by changing his name again. Naming represents the ultimate power because it defines and creates a fixed knowing of someone. The one who names has the power to imagine and define identity. Having already claimed an identity free of forced subordination to a husband by reclaiming the surname Lobdell, he shed female identity by changing names once more. In October 1854, Lucy Ann Lobdell disappeared into the woods around Long Eddy, New York, a few days before Joseph Israel Lobdell entered Bethany, Pennsylvania.

• Two •

The Singing Teacher of Bethany

IN LATE OCTOBER 1854, Joseph Israel Lobdell entered the town of Bethany, Pennsylvania, about 35 miles south of Long Eddy, New York,[1] and opened a singing school. His talent with a violin and his understanding of music justified the title of "singing master" and led to a successful little business as nearly every young woman in town enrolled to study singing. Besides his musical ability, Joe brought other talents to Bethany, one of them being his hunting skill. In just a short time, everyone in town knew of Joe's superior hunting abilities, and if someone spotted a bear or a wolf, they would call upon Joe, who would grab his gun or an ax and not come back until the threatening animal was dead. Joe also enjoyed a reputation for being a good worker and could keep up his end on any saw and do every kind of work in the woods.[2]

Joseph Lobdell was also a bit of a ladies' man. He flirted with the girls and asked them all out. He was a tall, "dashing, good-looking young fellow ... [whose] manner and appearance captivated more than one backwoods lass in that community."[3] He was considered handsome even in his everyday work clothes, but when he put on his black suit made of beautiful material and his stove-pipe hat, and applied his charm, he became the center of attention among the young ladies.

> A handsome young man, giving the name of Joseph I. Lobdell, appeared in Bethany, Wayne County, Pa., and started a singing school. He soon had a large class of scholars, many of them young ladies of the best families of the village. One of these, now the wife of a prominent citizen of the county, living near Honesdale, fell in love with the teacher, and the affection apparently became mutual. Another lady, since married to a Boston millionaire also got up a flirtation with him, and, in fact, he was a general favorite among the girls.[4]

While Joe appreciated many young ladies, there was one special, unnamed woman, the daughter of a leading citizen of Bethany, who won his affections. The pair was engaged to be married in the spring of 1855, but nuptials were never performed. Just a day or two before the wedding was supposed to take place, a lumberman visiting Bethany from Long Eddy, New York, recognized the singing master as Lucy Ann Lobdell, who had been missing from that town for many months. This news passed through town, outraging some of the menfolk, who did not take kindly to a woman masquerading as a man and accessing those social positions and activities that were supposed to belong only to men. Anger led to the organization of a tar-and-feather crew for the purpose of punishing the imposter. Joe got wind of the impending danger, and fled town, thus escaping a violent punishment but losing his love.[5]

The story of the Bethany incident was reported years later in newspapers throughout New York and Pennsylvania, and made it as far as Galveston, Texas. These reports center on the drama created around Lobdell's gender expression, "the manifestation of an individual's fundamental sense of being either masculine or feminine through clothing, behavior, grooming, etc.," and gender identity, "the inner sense most of us have of being either male or female."[6] Joseph Lobdell's gender expression was an authentic performance of manhood, but — once alerted to his female body — the general public believed it was performed by a wrongful body. As stated earlier, nineteenth-century understanding believed gender was a natural essence of bodies that manifested in predictable ways, naturally separating and organizing people. Bethany's original acceptance of Joseph Israel Lobdell was based on the residents' reading of the signs apparent in Lobdell's masculinity — his mobility, his talents, his wooing of women — which led them to believe he was a traditional man. Of course, the most obvious sign of Joe's masculinity was his male clothing, and as Lobdell had feared before leaving home, a female-bodied person in men's clothes was courting danger.

In the nineteenth century, the most visible indicator of gender and the sexed body was clothing, as a person's place within society was clearly defined and visible through his or her style. The sex and sex role of each body was identified by the clothes it wore. Once the sex of the body was clearly known through gender expression, all other aspects of that body were assumed to align with the sex indicated by clothing: the space it could rightfully occupy, the attributes and qualities it should have, the roles it should fulfill, the functions it should perform, and the privileges and responsibilities it could claim.

Clothing styles became equated with the male and female spheres and their corresponding modes of work, functions, and social positions. "In the mid-nineteenth century, the ideology of separate 'spheres' for men and women dictated the nature of their activities and was both symbolized and reinforced by their clothing."[7] To emphasize the rather minimal difference between male and female bodies, clothing styles were greatly different. Two-legged garments, designed for men, signified masculinity and male authority and power; skirts and dresses announced women's subordination to men and their less privileged status. Gendered clothing styles resulted in the visual separation of the sexes and established clear guidelines for the corresponding gender roles and spheres assigned to men and women.

The dominant and powerful position of men and masculinity was made possible by female submission, and both positions in this power dynamic were symbolized through clothing. When men wore pants, they signaled their right to authority, dominance, mobility, and male privileges. When women wore dresses, they visibly signaled their agreement to defer to men and perform according to social definitions of womanhood.

When each sex dressed appropriately, a stable social order was visibly discernable, so the most obvious sign of disorder or chaos in society was a body in wrongful attire. Even the first-wave feminists who wanted dress reform simply to provide comfort and ease of activity in work for women were accused of wanting to be men because the simple two-legged design of their bloomers was considered an unnatural claim to male power and public space when worn by women. "Woman's outward appearance — her clothed body — had ties to gender and moral character. If a woman, through her apparel, transgressed the gender line (e.g., wore a 'male' garment), she constituted a threat to 'natural' order and produced near-hysterical reactions."[8] Women who challenged traditional dress codes were considered unnatural and threatening to society.

Whenever women appropriated pants, the symbol of male privilege and power, they were not viewed as merely desiring access to power, positions, mobility, and privileges that had been reserved for men; a woman wearing pants signaled the usurpation of all male roles, privileges, and opportunities, and the text of her clothing was read as her desire to actually be a man. Women's perceived desire to be men disrupted the natural relationships between men and women, since there would be a lack of those people who should take the subordinated position. "Since articles of clothing had been designated as masculine or feminine, to disregard these distinctions was to disregard the relationship between the sexes as it was ordained by God."[9]

Because balance in society hinged on the male-dominant/female-subordinate relationship, women wearing clothes equated to maleness were seen as deliberately stepping away from the dependent and subservient position that had been deemed natural for them, so such a visible act of defiance was extremely transgressive. Women's decision to wear pants, in any form, "initiated a subtle shift in perception of male and female power relations: the boundaries between the separate spheres began to crumble or at least to blur a bit."[10] Women's insistence on access to male spaces, activities, and garments confused the distinctions of gendered spaces and threatened the stability of social order, fostering fears about the ruination of the family and American civilization.[11]

Such behavior was also viewed as an attack on masculinity, for male clothing equaled male behavior, freedom, privilege, and power. Since there were only two gendered subject positions, men felt that "if woman was changing roles, she could only be becoming man,"[12] which meant she would begin behaving like a man, seeking social power and privilege, thus inverting gendered social order. So closely was an understanding of gender performance linked to clothing that opponents of dress reform believed that masculine clothes would automatically foster masculine behavior, which was dangerous to the natural relationship between men and women since pants meant authority and power, both of which were supposed to belong to men. Worse, because social order required a balance of both genders, men feared a complete gender reversal, and writers of "numerous articles and essays charged that if women wore the pantaloons then men would become feminine."[13]

Women in men's clothes, or even in clothes styled like men's, threatened the boundaries of male territory. When women appropriated pantaloons and other articles of male apparel, they directly challenged the binary gender system that required gender-distinctive dress. When rigid gender distinctions were blurred, observers reacted strongly, and many critics dealt with their anxiety over changing gender roles by attacking cross-dressers. The assaults on women dressed entirely, or partly, in masculine apparel were attempts to preserve the existing gender system by forcing women back into long dresses and, by implication, into their feminine roles. "For either women or men to question conventional gender distinctions — for women to grasp power, for men to relinquish it — would violate nature. Disease and death, social disarray, all would result within the elaborate physiological systems men had created. The gender violator emerged as 'unnatural' and 'perverted.'"[14] The gender transgressor had to be disciplined to contain potential social disorder. In other words, punishment awaited any female-bodied person who dressed in men's clothes.

In a society fearful of social chaos, normal and abnormal behaviors had to be clearly defined and locked into place for the sake of order. Deviance and unconventionality in the nineteenth century were viewed as social ills, dangerous not just to individual health but also to the health of the state and nation. Darwinism strengthened the view of the survival of the fittest that "necessitated a healthy national organism, free of hereditary disease and moral weakness."[15] One of the greatest perceived threats to social order and health were women who refused their inferior status and their domestic roles as wives and mothers. If they could not be persuaded to return to and submissively remain in social positions deemed natural for them, rebuke and punishment were justifiable.

Joe's disregard for the rules concerning the social construction of gender, its strict assignment to appropriate sexed bodies, and the expectations of its daily (rightful) enactment was the actual root of anxiety in Bethany. As Judith Butler has stated, gender is performative, meaning it is a performed language where particular appearances, attitudes, abilities, functions, movements, mannerisms, and interactions with others are coded as either feminine or masculine and belonging to women or men respectively.[16] The hegemonic understanding of sex and gender in the nineteenth century regulated the manifestations of sexed bodies by compelling those bodies to perform according to normalizing expectations, even as it believed those gendered performances were products of some natural, internal essential gender.[17] The materialization of cultural norms declares a body acceptable only if it continuously performs those enactments of gender assigned to it.

The daily presentation of gender in ways that feel natural to the performing body is a continuous process of experiencing and displaying the self in ways that will be read and understood as male or female, a process that becomes so mundane as to not be noticed. This enactment of gender is such a familiar part of everyday life that it goes unnoticed until gendered beliefs about how men and women should look and act are disrupted by a person who does not conform to the established expectations. Joe's presentation as male did more than go against the expectations of the people of Bethany; it went against their understanding of the natural world. Since nineteenth-century beliefs held that gender was a natural manifestation that corresponded to the genital sex of the body, willing transgression of gender boundaries was viewed as a sign of degeneracy and moral transgression, so Bethany residents read Joe's masculine performance as unnatural and dangerous, perverted, going against the laws of Nature. Such a form of deviance required containment or punishment in order to reestablish a stable social order.

The presentation of the body in clothes appropriate only to that type of body reinforced cultural beliefs in a natural hierarchy and order, enabling people to know those bodies as men or women. The simple act of a female body wearing pants would have been enough to arouse the ire of the folks of Bethany, especially the men, because in the nineteenth century, "the sight of a woman in pants provoked intense anger and hostility."[18] Lobdell, in his fine black suit and stove-pipe hat, exacerbated the situation by presenting himself not just as a woman in men's clothes, but as a man, assuming all the privileges of masculinity and maleness, behavior interpreted as going against God's natural order and dangerous to social stability, and so in an attempt to reestablish order and respectability for Bethany, a punishment suitable to the crime was prepared.

The conflict caused by Joe was more than the challenge of a gender outlaw looking to earn money in the male public sphere of business in Bethany. Many newspapers that reported on this story only say that the men of the town got into an uproar and formed a tar-and-feather crew and that Joe somehow got word of impending danger and fled town. But those sources publishing a more in-depth story give details that reveal how dangerous Joe's challenge was, not to just male public space, but also to the very construction of masculinity. Apparently another man had been interested in the same young woman to whom Joe was engaged. Joe's successful competition with a traditional male rival for a woman's affection created a threat to an intimate, foundational aspect of masculinity. Even more interesting is the tidbit that, after he was discovered, the bride herself warned Joe.

> He had been a rival of the music teacher for the hand of the young woman. He planned with others to seize the music teacher, tar and feather her, and turn her out of town. The young woman who was to have married the singing master was let into the secret, and she warned Lucy Ann of her danger, and she escaped.[19]

Even at a moment of extreme tension, the bride's loyalty was with Joe, not any other men in town.

The inclusion of a rival in this drama places Lobdell's masculinity on the level of maleness that has access to not only public spaces and male employment but also the private spaces of women's bodies and attentions. This sort of masculinity, the kind that could win the affections of "more than one lass,"[20] is more dangerous than the simple threat of a woman out of her rightful sphere because it directly challenges male masculinity, especially male entitlement to access to women.

While many Bethany residents were shocked and scandalized, Joe's masculinity was so authentic that some of the young women refused to believe that the singing teacher was not a man. Irma Kimble Simons' grandmother had an older sister who "got pretty sweet on [Joe]" and refused to believe Joe was a woman. "Grandma's sister said, 'I don't believe it. He is the nicest fella I ever went out with.' She wouldn't believe it and they had quite a time before they had her convinced it was a woman."[21]

News of Lobdell's female body did not just challenge the rival's need to maintain a sense of reality through a knowing and ordering of different bodies; it made it clear to him that the woman's rejection of him was based on a preference for a man who was not a traditional man, which must surely have threatened the rival's sense of masculinity. He did not simply give a sound beating to the unruly body who had invaded the male sphere; he called for others to join him in their effort to disarm the threat Lobdell presented. The violence of their intended punishment was personal and territorial. It sought to punish and eliminate Lobdell for successfully claiming something to which he had no entitlement, which shamed the man who did.

The revelation of Lobdell's female body created a paradox because of his believable masculinity. His crossing of gender categories disrupted the rigid, binary positions established as normal in society, exposed the constructedness of masculinity, and revealed it as an illusion that could be fabricated by a wrongful female body. Lobdell challenged the category of man by being someplace in between the polar opposites of man and woman, and outside both, which cast doubt on assumptions about men and women and the visible signs of apparel, behavior, and actions that were to correctly announce which was which. In refusing to participate in the continuous creative process necessary to sustain the illusion of maleness and its power by being the feminine foil to masculinity, Lobdell revealed that the subordinating order of male and female bodies could be manipulated, which threatened the balance of power in society.

The phenomenon of Joseph Israel Lobdell was completely unexpected by the good people of Bethany. News of Lobdell's female body created a disordering, disorienting shift in perception. Judith Halberstam refers to this flashback effect as an aspect of "queer time" and applies this re-viewing process to films, but the citizens of Bethany experienced something similar in a real-life phenomenological way. "The exposure of a trans character whom the audience has already accepted as male or female, causes the audience to reorient themselves in relation to the film's past in order to read the film's present and prepare themselves for the film's future."[22] Lobdell's exposure caused people to mentally rewind their history with the singing teacher and, after substituting a female body for the one believed to be male, revise their understanding of him as a woman. The result of this gendered wind-back and reevaluation of the subject was great public anxiety and outrage. The discomfort felt by the community over Joe's transgender is evident in the stories told about the event.

Cultural stories create meaning first by focusing on a subject deemed important enough to discuss, and then by telling the tale in ways that impart a particular kind of understanding of the event and the people involved. Nineteenth-century newspaper articles about the Bethany incident are remarkably free of mean-spirited, judgmental descriptions of any of the characters; they simply present what happened. Yet strongly evident in this basic story is the concept that it is unacceptable and wrong for people with female bodies to wear men's clothes and horn in on the potential loves of real men, and perfectly acceptable for the dominant group of people to use violence to punish such a gender transgressor.

All versions of the story detail an event that is successful in defending established gender categories and sex roles, thus reinforcing the boundaries of each and playing out like moral tales, depicting transgendered masculinity — not the extreme violence — as the unacceptable behavior. Tarring and feathering was a form of punishment used on people who had damaged the community somehow, and its purpose was to either make the offender conform or drive them out of the community. The violence of the chosen form of punishment reveals a sharp-edged fear of a transgender threat to social order, for tarring and feathering left serious burns and a visual effect that lasted for days, extending the humiliation of the one so treated. The writers of all versions of the Bethany story present this violent form of punishment as socially acceptable and proportional to the threat Lobdell represented to social order, making clear the dangers of transgendered living in a society that would not protect the lives of gender transgressors. Through these narratives, boundaries for gendered appearance and behavior are brought back to a place interpreted by the writers as correct, right, normal, and natural, and heteronormative order is reestablished.

Two • *The Singing Teacher of Bethany* 67

Accounts of the Bethany incident work to emasculate Joe by framing his masculinity as a mere disguise used by someone deliberately deceiving the public. Later accounts especially embellish and elaborate with fictitious details that paint Lobdell as a pathetic woman rather than a social danger. While Lobdell had obviously been a successful man — a thriving business and many love interests attest to this — articles about this incident work hard to strip him of that masculinity and reduce him to a fearful woman.

This version, representative of the way the story was presented, is found in the *Wayne County Herald*, which glances over the tale in its obituary for Lobdell in 1885.

> The deserted and destitute wife left her baby with her parents and was next known in this neighborhood as a singing schoolteacher by the name of Joseph Lobdell. Many stories are remembered of the flirtations and trials of the gay young singest, but the secret of her sex leaking out, she abandoned society and took to the forests bordering the upper Delaware as a hunter.[23]

Aside from the mention of some flirtations, this version completely strips Lobdell of all masculinity and presents a pathetic woman, deserted by her husband and consequently destitute, somewhat justifying a resourceful endeavor to earn money. It does not include the conflict, violence, or love story found in more detailed versions, making it seem as if Lobdell calmly chose to move on in his adventures once his secret was known. But even this weakened version clearly presents public knowledge of cross-gendered living as a legitimate reason for removing the gender outlaw from society.

The older versions that present Lobdell escaping from violent punishment aided by a woman who willingly aligned herself with the criminal, not the punisher, is not the one that gets circulated, and the character of the would-be bride is rewritten with fictional flare. Many decades after this incident, Frank Woodward assumed the authority to judge what is normal and correct in creating a narrative that includes the Bethany account situated within the larger context of a collection of tales about the Female Hunter, whom he labels "strange" from his opening sentence. Just as earlier newspaper accounts did, his narrative becomes the organizing mechanism that includes the reading public in a joint move to police constructed gender roles and defend masculinity by reinforcing the boundary lines for approved, gendered behavior. Woodward positions the residents of Bethany and the imagined readers of his article as normal, and characterizes Lobdell as a scandalous gender outlaw who disrupts the quiet order of the village and shocks and devastates the young bride. "The exposure of the identity of her supposed betrothed husband prostrated the girl, and for a long time her life was despaired of. She recovered, however, and a few years afterward married a prominent citizen of Wayne County, Pennsylvania."[24]

None of the oldest stories present the would-be bride as devastated or damaged by Joe's transgender; this detail is Woodward's interpretation and assumption, one that later stories will disprove, for this same woman befriended Joe again years later. However, Woodward's interpretation reestablishes the boundary line around heteronormative behavior as natural and correct and presents Lobdell's masculine performance as harmful and dangerous to the young woman, who was apparently cured of the shock by marrying the correct type of man. In light of such chaos, Lobdell is presented as deserving of public anger and ejection from society.

Woodward's words had a large audience and his story became part of the foundation of the mythology that grew up around Joseph Israel Lobdell and was perpetuated through the creation of other narratives. The legend eradicates the woman's loyalty to and love for Lobdell, while emphasizing the wrongness of a female body living as a man and the need for punishment that reestablishes correct boundaries and patterns for sex roles and gendered behavior.

Earlier versions of the Bethany incident showcase a betrayal between the bride and the rival. The knowledge of the planned punishment is "secret," implying a trust in confidence felt by the rival for the woman. The woman does not collapse in devastation, but runs to warn Joseph, revealing loyalty to the man she chose. Woodward revises the story to create betrayal between Lobdell and the bride, and a bride shattered by deception. Such a manipulation of the story eliminates the potential for successful romance between Joe and his bride. An examination of all the accounts of the Bethany incident written over the course of decades feature a woman pretending to be a man as the conflict of the story. To the authors, Lobdell is merely disguised as a man, so the conflict centers more on the usurpation of a public male presentation by a wrongful body than an inappropriate attachment formed between two female bodies.

The nineteenth-century mind believed female sexual desire was nonexistent, so, since women felt no desire for men other than creating babies with them, the notion of women desiring each other was inconceivable. The concept of same-sex desire between women did not exist in the cultural zeitgeist in 1855; lesbianism was not understood or acknowledged until after 1880, and then only in medical and theoretical circles. Common belief in the nineteenth century recognized only sex between men and women, understanding it to be so natural that no other forms of desire existed. The nineteenth century did not have the understanding developed later that divides sexuality into heterosexual expression and other styles.

> Back in Jefferson's day, if one did participate in a same-sex sex act, then one would be considered a transgressor of community standards — probably a sinner and even a criminal — but not as someone who had a sexual identity based on his or her conduct.[25]

Dominant nineteenth-century beliefs assumed that all people were heterosexual; anyone displaying desire for a person of his or her own sex was viewed as deviant and immoral, not as a person with an alternative sexuality. Whether the bride is presented as distraught or loyal after Lobdell's female body was revealed, there is no commentary on that relationship. Same-sex desire is nonexistent in these stories, even as they present an alternative lifestyle for women.

The Wild Woman of Manannah

Nineteenth-century accounts from newspapers in New York and Pennsylvania claim that Lobdell fled from Bethany and once again donned a hunting suit and spent the next six years wandering the woods, hunting and trapping and seeming to disappear from public view. This mysterious absence of any specific information about Lobdell is evidence of a common theme in narratives written about him: none of the authors formally interview Lobdell to gain their information, but instead rely on speculation and imagination to frame their stories.[26] The result is narratives formed around rumor, assumptions, a few eyewitness accounts of Lobdell's location and behaviors, and the interpretations of several observers and the writers themselves. Perhaps because Lobdell took to the safety and seclusion of the woods later in his life, newspaper writers assumed he did the same after leaving Bethany, and so his true adventures at that time are missing from virtually all eastern accounts of his life. Contrary to all these reports, Lobdell was busy trying to build his life elsewhere.

In the mid–1800s, the pioneer territory of Minnesota was an undeveloped frontier, and settlement was strongly encouraged by the government in order to bring civilization to the wilderness. The West was an open invitation for free, autonomous, ambitious white men who dreamed of profit and adventure. Male ambition and desire for financial success were viewed as normal and greatly encouraged, and expansion was accomplished mostly by single men: the mythic solitary hunter, entrepreneurial loner, and the self-reliant pioneer.[27]

Between 1854 and 1860, advertisements urging people to move to Minnesota, where great fortunes awaited adventurers, littered the weekly newspapers of Honesdale, Pennsylvania, a town near Lobdell's family home. Lobdell seems to vanish after the Bethany scandal,[28] but in the late spring of 1856 a young man named La-Roi Lobdell made his way to Albany, New York, and then passed west over central New York on the Hudson River Railroad toward Minnesota.[29] Along the way, he taught three different singing schools to fund his trip.[30] No one writing about Lobdell caught the use of the feminine article before the masculine French word for king, so perhaps that was La-Roi's private joke.

According to A.C. Smith in his *History of Meeker County*, in the summer of 1856, La-Roi[31] spent a short time in St. Paul, and then moved on to Minnetonka, where he met and befriended Edwin Gribble.

> Gribble had reason to know that [La-Roi] was somewhat eccentric, not only on account of the wildness of her tastes, but in the way she [was] dressed, her costume in the summer of 1856 having consisted of a pair of calico pants, a calico coat and a calico vest and hat. In this cool but rather odd suit of clothes, [La-Roi] hung around for some time waiting for a chance to make a strike.[32]

The man who had jumped the claim of land next to Gribble's had to leave temporarily, and he employed La-Roi as a hired gun to guard the property in his absence. As neighbors, "Gribble and [La-Roi] got pretty thick, tramping together through the woods in pursuit of game, and sleeping together under the same blanket when they wooed the gentle goddess of slumber under the umbrageous forest trees around Minnetonka."[33] Eventually La-Roi tired of waiting for the claim-jumper, who never returned, and decided to strike out on his own and go further into the wilderness. Gribble traded a $75 rifle for the quit-claim[34] deed La-Roi wrote out, and with a very fine gun over his shoulder, La-Roi made his way to Meeker County.[35]

La-Roi found employment, along with another man, guarding some land that speculators had purchased in hopes of building the capital there once Minnesota became a state. The two men spent the winter of 1856–1857 in a cabin on the site, but La-Roi's "companion ... never for a moment suspected that he was wintering with a woman."[36] In the summer of 1857, La-Roi moved to Manannah and, in exchange for room and board, was a jack-of-all-trades and did odd jobs. Though La-Roi had little money,

Those with whom she was acquainted seemed to enjoy her company — her male apparel often requiring her to sleep in close proximity with others of the male gender — but with no indiscretion and with no suspicion that she was other than what appeared on the surface....[37] [Lobdell] was a splendid hunter and was offensive to none ... was good company and a "hale fellow well met" with all the young people in the neighborhood, committing no sins or indiscretions.

Unfortunately, "in the summer of 1858, by accident, 'Satan, with the aid of original sin,' discovered and exposed her sex."[38] The blue code of Connecticut was consulted, and the law was invoked to purge the community of the scandal."[39]

Lobdell's second attempt to live as a man was successful in Manannah until his anatomical sex was revealed and he was arrested and imprisoned. Here, again, the social construction of gender and gendered spaces, and cultural patterns of power and dominance based on gender roles, were the source of Lobdell's troubles. Lobdell lived and earned a living in ways considered eccentric and rebellious for men by East Coast standards, so these activities were considered completely inappropriate for women. His distance from the safe core of female domesticity was even more exaggerated by his life in the frontier wilderness. Lobdell's female body was not secured within the institution of marriage, homebound and male governed, but rather had moved freely across the country into unknown territory and assumed male power and privilege in the life of a man. First as Joseph, then as La-Roi, Lobdell embodied the uncontained woman who threatened social order by wanting to be a man.

Adventures in nature, especially those designed to conquer nature in some way, were viewed as natural male activities. Nineteenth-century westward expansion was an activity that men were encouraged to pursue, and it went hand in hand with the quest for material gain. "Anthropologists Marilyn Strathern and Carol MacCormack have argued that nature/culture discourse regularly figures nature as female, in need of subordination by a culture that is invariably figured as male, active, and abstract."[40] The active role of physically crossing the passive land, taming the unpredictable wild, exploiting natural resources, and creating civilized order out of nature's chaos was believed to be the job of men. "The notion of the earth or land as female has a long tradition in the Western world. It derives from an understanding of nature as a female organism in contrast to human society as a male domain."[41] La-Roi's westward movement as a female body in men's clothes into wild, female territory seemed to go against the natural order as God ordained it. Because of his actions, his assumed male identity was seen as deviance.

As stated earlier, in the nineteenth century a person's place within the order of society was clearly defined and visible through the style of dress. Men's clothes were literally equivalent to masculinity and maleness, and, therefore, power. In his history, Smith connects pants to masculinity when he states that Lobdell's clothes required him to sleep in male quarters. La-Roi's outfits consisted of male garments such as pants, vest, and coat. They were made of calico, which seemed odd to Gribble, yet he merely passed the suit off as part of La-Roi's eccentric nature. Even in clothes that announce difference, La-Roi is accepted as a man by all who had dealings with him, especially those who actually lived and slept with him, because his masculinity was so authentic. For two years, La-Roi gained a reputation from men as a respected man for his exceptional rifle skills and ability to survive in the wilderness.

The male community accepted La-Roi as a man so completely that it welcomed him into that community, even its most intimate masculine spaces, as just another man. When his female anatomy was exposed, Smith feels a need to voice disclaimers to protect the reputations of the men of Minnesota from sexual scandal. Even before the trial and its outcome are discussed in Smith's history, he first clears the men who had dealings with La-Roi of any wrongdoing by making it clear none of them had sex with Lobdell. He repeatedly states that no sins or indiscretions took place, not so much defending Lobdell's virtue as defending that of the men who unwittingly came into contact with a female body. His defense of these men emphasizes Lobdell's masculinity — so authentic was it that the men who shared close quarters with him never suspected a female body next to them.

He speaks specifically on behalf of Gribble and assures the reader that if the man had known La-Roi was female, he would have been "less free with her." "But Gribble didn't dream that Lucy was a lone female, and hence he felt that his familiarity with her entitles him to a suspension of public opinion until he can prove his innocence of any evil intention."[42] Smith also defends the innocence of the unnamed man who spent the winter of 1856–1857 with Lobdell

> on the old Kandiyohi town-site on the north side of Kandiyohi lakes. The two were employed to reside on and thus hold possession of the new town-site, by the Minneapolis proprietors. Her companion spent the winter with her [in a small one-room cabin], but never for a moment suspected that he was wintering with a woman.[43]

Smith creates a clear caveat in rejecting any sexual improprieties between the men of Manannah and Mrs. Slater. He, as well as everyone else, thinks

Lobdell has merely pretended to be a man. Aligning the female body with feminine gender and working from heteronormative assumptions, he fears a heterosexual scandal involving a female body hidden within the male sphere.

As Riki Anne Wilchins points out, confusion occurs while reading gendered bodies, and specifically transgendered bodies, when the surface of those bodies is read as having an innate reality and meaning independent of the reading. "If gender is something composed of acts, both the act of performing gender and the action of reading that performance, then in each moment there is also the small possibility of change, of movement, of reading the map 'incorrectly.' There is the possibility of transgression and difference."[44] The people of Manannah and other Minnesotan towns read La-Roi and concluded Lobdell was a man because of the believable clues on the surface of his body.

However, because of the effects of queer time, as mentioned in the Bethany incident, the meaning of La-Roi's masculinity and male symbols

Sign in Meeker County, Minnesota, at site where Lobdell lived.

changes with the new information of the female body, which requires the citizens of Manannah to cycle back in time, and revise the meaning they constructed around La-Roi's body for two years. The belief that Lobdell was a man ran deeply and was uncontested. Reviewing the preceding two years, substituting a female body where a male one had been known, and revising their understanding of Lobdell created a rupture that confused the nineteenth-century understanding of male and female, man and woman, much as it still does today. The presentation of new information about Lobdell's body, coupled with assumptions based on nineteenth-century understandings of genders and spheres, indicated unnatural behavior and disorder to the citizens of Manannah.

As he did in Bethany, Lobdell confused the semiotic messages given off by appearance and behavior, challenging the naturalness of male and female bodies and their contingent expressions and behaviors, as well as destroying the certainty of the predictable body. He showed how easy it was to circumvent the rigid man-made structure of sexed bodies altogether by not being "what he appeared to be on the surface."[45] La-Roi's body became the site of social confusion and disorder, what Lisa Duggan calls the "locus of difference."[46] The clash in understanding formed between the meaning the experiencing body gave itself and the meaning observers gave to what they witnessed collided in a conflict at the skin level — the surface — of La-Roi. La-Roi's refusal to comply with gender system expectations disrupted categories of established binaries of man/woman, male/female, and masculine/feminine, thereby revealing the vulnerability of the synthetic constructedness of those categories.

Upon exposure, community members saw Lobdell as a deviant body that refused to fit any known system of meanings, a body "which escapes or exceeds the norm, as that which cannot be wholly defined or fixed by the repetitive labor of [the] norms."[47] He could not fit the category of woman and those around him could not see him as a man, and the displacement outside of normative sex and gender categories could not be tolerated by the confused public. While liminal spaces, such as frontiers, are often tolerant of marginal behavior, Lobdell's disidentification with regulatory norms of embodiment created a disruptive energy so dangerous it could not be accepted even in a space not completely civilized.

In both Bethany and Manannah, Lobdell presented a new category of being, outside of known classifications, seemingly uncontrolled by the laws of man or nature. Lobdell rejected the oppressive expectations and definitions of female bodies that offered only one pattern for life. By possessing and performing masculinity, he opened an alternative subject position and lifestyle for female-bodied persons, one open to male privileges of mobility, economic opportunities, and access to female bodies.

The focus of outrage centers on gender, rendering the element of sexuality nearly invisible amid all the proceedings in Manannah, and when it is mentioned it is dismissed as an "accident" that revealed Lobdell's "true" sex. The "accident," provoked by "Satan, with the aid of original sin," implies that sexual behavior of some kind was involved, but because the other party is not mentioned, we are left with a tantalizing mystery about what happened and who was involved. Since Smith puts so much effort into defending the ethics of the men in that community, and considering Lobdell's flirtations and love interests in Bethany, it is highly probable that the other person was a woman, perhaps one who did not appreciate the type of man La-Roi was. No accusations of improper behavior between two women are formed because "the legal evidence to prove the necessary fact could not be easily obtained, and was left in doubt."[48] Instead,

> The county attorney, Wm. Richards ... filed an information against Mrs. Slater before John Robson, Esq. J.P. ... alleging "that whereas, one Lobdell, being a woman, falsely impersonates a man, to the great scandal of the community, and against the peace and dignity of the State of Minnesota," and asked that she be dealt with according to the law, that so pernicious an example might not be repeated in this land of steady habits.[49]

Rigid gender roles and spheres were so entrenched that Lobdell's perceived impersonation of a man shocked even a frontier community, and they focused on the perceived immorality of his transgender behavior, not sexuality issues. Lobdell's behavior triggered transanxieties that drove the people of Manannah to try to contain the transgendered disorder he embodied. Lobdell was arrested and brought to trial with the expectation that the judge, under the power of the law, would punish Lobdell's transgressive behavior, protect society from unnatural behavior, and reestablish gendered boundaries of normalcy.

> It is unusual to find a nineteenth-century court case involving such explicit testimony [about sexual acts] because [female same-sex desire had not been imagined at this time and] there was no legal injunctions against sex between women. The indifference showed by law toward women has meant that there are few official records of same-sex eroticism. Any court cases that do exist tend to involve women who impersonated men.[50]

As in Bethany, the residents of Manannah believed social order relied on gender roles believed to be natural, so Lobdell's transgender was seen as a threat to social order that needed to be contained and punished to reestablish healthy order. And so an example was made of La-Roi to rechalk the line of normalcy.

The arrest of Lobdell was a transphobic reaction to nonconformity and the perceived threat of social instability, and it worked to define deviant behavior as it reinforced understandings and definitions of social norms and masculinity. According to Lisa Duggan, patterns of arrests, presented as "socially neutral enforcement of the law, actually constructed 'criminals' and the public perception of criminality in class-, race- and gender-specific ways.... The courtroom scenes following such arrests naturalized structures of social domination."[51] Lobdell's trial, and its publicity, enlisted those involved in the legal process — the sheriff, the judge, the attorneys — as well as all citizens familiar with the scandal, to guard public safety through commonly defining and policing gendered modes of female decency and normalcy.

As the judge was the ultimate legal authority in the territory, the people of Minnesota expected him to do his duty in ridding the community of a scandal so outrageous, so "pernicious," that it should not be "repeated in this land of steady habits."[52] The folks in Manannah expected the judge to find Lobdell guilty and pronounce punishment that would reestablish social order. But "the court, after taking the case under advisement, finally ruled that the right of females to 'wear the pants' had been recognized from the time of Justinian, and that the doctrine was too well settled to be upset by the case at bar, and Mrs. Slater was therefore discharged."[53]

While Justinian may have condoned women wearing men's pants and declared it legal if the woman was as capable as men were, La-Roi had not presented himself as a woman in men's clothes; he had presented himself as a man. As stated earlier, nineteenth-century men believed women would behave like men if they wore men's clothes, so forcing them back into women's clothes was meant to force them back into female sex roles. But Lobdell's transgender was an enactment only signaled by men's clothes, not reliant on them, and he was still transgendered in women's clothes. Because the judge focused narrowly on the letter of the law and the rather simple issue of gendered clothing styles and cross-dressing, he failed to reestablish normative gender boundaries and definitions or to contain Lobdell's transgendered disorder. Even though he declared Lobdell had not broken any laws, the local people believed he had broken a law of nature, and the violence of their transphobic rejection of Lobdell revealed a social fear of disrupted order and inverted power. Like the citizens of Bethany, they took the matter of punishment into their own hands. "This denouement had the effect to discredit her [Lobdell] in the settlement, subjecting her to insult from the vicious on every hand. She became deranged pending the proceedings, and, as it were, an outcast in society — an object of commiseration and sympathy, and soon thereafter a public charge."[54]

Lobdell did more than present a threat to social order by cross-dressing; he threatened the state of masculinity as an essence possessed only by men. Lobdell's masculinity was originally considered legitimate by the Manannah community, as it was in Bethany, even in the closest, most intimate male spaces where more than clothing would be needed to pass as male. Manannah accepted and respected La-Roi as a man because of his consistent and believable masculinity: his ability as a hunter, his marksmanship and ability to survive in the wilderness, his expensive gun, and his ability to live harmoniously with other men who enjoyed his company. Once La-Roi moved into town, he socialized with others on an everyday basis, becoming popular as a "hale fellow well met." Everyone he met accepted him as a man because his masculinity was authentic, and "if masculinity is not the social and cultural and indeed political expression of maleness, then what is it?"[55]

As witnessed by people in Minnesota and Bethany, Pennsylvania, as well as by the peddler Talmage in Long Eddy, Lobdell's embodiment was evidence that masculinity was not essentially male, and suggested it was a quality that female-bodied persons could also possess. Lobdell presented a threat to masculinity because he was no longer the female body that complemented and defined masculinity in men by being the feminine foil to it; his embodiment of masculinity challenged male-only ownership of it, frequently by surpassing other men's performance of masculinity.

Lobdell's challenge to male-only masculinity raises certain questions. The construction of masculinity comprises various strengths (physical, intellectual) and powers (political, economic), then positions them as natural attributes of men's bodies that only men are entitled to claim. By positioning masculinity as something only men can naturally possess, that quality that speaks of power is completely denied to women, implying that any trace of masculinity in women is not real masculinity. "In other words, female masculinities are framed as the rejected scraps of dominant masculinity in order that male masculinity may appear to be the real thing."[56] Masculinity, like male sexual access to female bodies, is just another form of entitlement, granted to the most powerful and superior men, and forbidden to female bodies all together.

Reacting to the double threat to social order and masculinity, the people of Manannah acted as what Kate Bornstein calls "Gender Defenders ... [people] who actively, or by knowing inaction, defend the status quo of the existing gender system, and thus perpetuate the violence of male privilege and all its social extension,"[57] and shunned Lobdell. Where the court failed, the people contained a subversive threat to social order. The reinforcement of acceptable sex and gender boundaries necessarily required the condemnation and containment of those bodies that did not comply with hegemonic definitions and expectations.

Public rejection of Lobdell accomplished the communal establishment of a boundary that defined normalcy by rendering him invisible through shunning and placing him outside that boundary in a space of deviance. Expulsion from society secured the borders of sex and gender while restoring the illusion of order, which required stable — if artificial — categories of sex and gender. With sex and gender binaries reinforced, social order was perceived to be restored.

Once restored, the gendered social order of Manannah was preserved through the policing and punishing actions of its citizens and the successful expulsion of a transgender threat, a success important enough to be recorded in its own chapter in A.C. Smith's *The History of Meeker County*. Through storytelling and the careful construction of character and plot, A.C. Smith reestablishes the order and power of a recognizable reality and rescues it from the two biggest threats presented by Lobdell: the unpredictable fluidity of meaning concerning gender and sexed bodies, and female-bodied trespass into the male sphere. His history includes the voices of male sheriffs, male lawyers, male judges, male witnesses, and his own male analysis of the events, and this interpretation presents actions and behaviors that reinforce traditional definitions for correct and acceptable behavior. His story also safely rescues masculinity and restores it to male-only ownership.

Smith uses narrative as the tool to fix the meaning of Lobdell's body and behavior and disempower the chaotic potential of a disorderly, wrongful body. Although Smith is Lobdell's counsel during the trial, he offers his own interpretations of Lobdell's behavior and motives rather than interviewing Lobdell for his perspective and explanations. In other words, Lobdell's voice is missing from the story; the men telling the story have usurped all the power to shape the meaning of La-Roi's identity and life in Manannah. By pinning Lobdell down as a woman, Smith reinforces the paradigm for acceptable gendered behavior through presenting

Lucy's usurpation of male identity as an act deserving punishment. He continues to drain disorderly power from Lobdell's masculinity first by passing along Lobdell's explanation for such a "disguise": "She claimed to have assumed this disguise, originally in order to better get away from home, without detection by a drunken husband,"[58] which would seem understandable. At this point, Lobdell had not publicly stated he was a man.

Rather than ask Lobdell for reasons behind his continued habit of wearing men's clothes after successfully escaping an abusive husband, Smith offers his own supposition. "[T]he difficulty that would naturally interpose in resuming, without loss of character, her natural and appropriate raiment probably induced her to continue the deception."[59] Smith's version implies Lobdell had not really found a natural place among men; he had merely painted himself into a corner from which he could not easily extract himself. Smith further anchors Lobdell as a woman by explaining that the name La-Roi had just been a prop, not part of an authentic identity. "For the purpose of completing her disguise she had assumed the name of La-Roi Lobdell."[60] By referring to La-Roi as "[t]he sorrowing wife, Mrs. Slater," he not only reimagined Lobdell's identity back to a pathetic and pitiable female but also secures him to the institution of marriage with the sentinel of the husband's last name.

Such an interpretation of Lobdell's need for male attire and a male name also reduces the threat of a female body within male spaces and activities, for it excises the interloper from them and reestablishes the borders of the separate male and female spheres. The focus on the utility of male clothing by a woman in distress reduces Lobdell's reasons for wearing them to a clever tactic, negating the believability of his masculine performance. Despite Lobdell's superior hunting and shooting skills and the wholehearted public inclusion of him as "one of the guys," this presentation works to feminize Lobdell and strip him of masculinity and return it to the rightful owners — men. A moral tale of crime and punishment is crafted through a narrative that checks female ambition in the male sphere. The warning to other women who might want to enter is clear, and in presenting Lobdell as a sad, pathetic form who deserves pity, the audience is distracted away from the social fear that demands he be presented as a threat.

The writers of narratives about Lobdell — Smith's history, the trial text, the newspaper articles about the Bethany incident — work in tandem with the gender defenders of Manannah and Bethany to characterize Lobdell as deviant, sanction punishments for that deviance, reinforce normative constructions of gender, clearly reestablish parameters for socially acceptable gendered behaviors, position Lobdell outside normal society in a xeno-transphobic act of Othering, and attack his masculinity. In narratives that attempt to emasculate Lobdell, his courage to be himself and seek a life he wants is obscured by the pot-banging and bell-ringing distraction of those whose fearful reactions reveal the fragility of a synthetic gendered order and a desperate need to protect it by containing a subversive subjectivity that carries the potential for liberation from rigid gender constructs. The very act of crafting these narratives reveals the importance of Lobdell's competing performed text, as it must be safely interpreted as deviant to negate the threat it presents.

Lobdell's embodiment, behaviors, and activities create a living text that contests cultural norms and hegemonic beliefs about what is real and natural, and that challenge is evident in the storytelling of writers who try to contain the disorder Lobdell represents. The contesting story Lobdell creates through performance states that female bodies are not innately weak, fragile, in need of protection, incapable, or feminine; some are strong, resourceful, ambitious, masculine, and capable of making decisions. Lobdell lived out his autobiographical refusal to be restrained, restricted, or dismissed, and with determination he created a life of mobility and possibility, even after the dangerous results in Bethany. And in Western culture, are not steadfast loyalty to a belief, resourcefulness, courage to be oneself, fearlessness, integrity, and risk-taking traits at the very core of the concept of masculinity? In contrast to the fear displayed by the people of Bethany and Manannah, Lobdell's bravery and masculinity become even more pronounced.

Lobdell's masculinity comes through no matter how the stories are told; diminishing or denying it only draws attention to it. Lobdell's masculinity is most directly linked to his ability to shoot and hunt, so stories developed in folkloric fashion that created a false mythology about Lobdell's methods and motivations for learning to shoot so well. In his report, Smith gives a history of Lucy Ann Lobdell that explains how she came by that masculine ability. He opens chapter ten—"A Wild Woman's History"—with a details and information gained from an 1876 Port Jervis newspaper article, rather than information gained directly from speaking with Lobdell. In other words, instead of interviewing Lobdell to learn about his life, he relies on stories told by other men, stories that were grossly inaccurate but effective in creating a mythology around Lobdell that was believed to be true, even when Lobdell was alive. This particular mythology grounds Lobdell's shooting skills in the efforts of men, thereby linking that masculine skill with men, not a young girl determined to go to school.

Smith's use of Sheriff Spencer's statements builds a safe foundation of male-centered power for his story. "'There' said Sheriff Spencer, as he pushed open the ponderous door of one of the cells of the county jail in his place, 'There is a woman with a history.'" From the very opening of Smith's narrative, Lobdell is presented as a woman and a troublemaker, one with a "history" of run-ins with the law.

> On a low chair in a cell in the jail at Honesdale, Pa., July 20th, 1876, sat a most singular looking person. A round, wrinkled, sun-burned face, small head crowned with thick, shaggy gray hair, that fell down over and almost concealed the blackest and sharpest of eyes; a slender body clothed in scant and shabby female garb, and the lower limbs encased in tattered trousers. This was the occupant of the cell — Lucy Ann Lobdell NEE Slater.[61]

The fact that Lobdell is still wearing men's trousers under female skirts is presented as less dangerous because they are tattered, revealing the harmlessness of the prisoner's poverty. Lobdell's masculinity has been watered down with skirts and feminized, yet the pants are still there, creating a mixed-gender look that would appear odd even today.

Much of Smith's history clearly comes from his Eastern sources, for it contains the same inaccurate information that Woodward's account and Pennsylvania newspapers also carried about Lobdell's early life. The story Smith presents of Lobdell's youth is the same one that becomes the core of the legend that builds around him, a legend that works to minimize his masculinity. Smith claims that Lobdell grew up in a wilderness cabin within a sparsely settled lumbering community in Delaware County, New York, where he learned and honed his rifle skills.

> From the time this child was old enough to walk she was a great favorite among the hardy woodchoppers and raftsmen. They often took her off to the logging camp and kept her there for days at a time, and she early became inured to the hardships of their life. The lumbermen in those days were all good hunters, and always carried their rifles with them. Before Lucy Ann was eight years old they had taught her the use of the rifle, and she soon became as good a shot as there was in the settlement. At the age of twelve she could out-shoot any of the men, and handled an ax with the ease of an old chopper. Before she had reached the age of sixteen she had killed numerous deer, and an absence of two or three days alone in the woods was for her not an uncommon thing.[62]

This story, which was widely circulated, is utter fiction. Its complete difference from Lobdell's actual youth erases the experience presented in the autobiography; the words of these male writers are privileged over Lobdell's own voice.

From 1871 to the present, nearly all histories and newspaper accounts of Lobdell recycle the old, inaccurate stories and give a version of the childhood described above, focusing on a practical backwoods tutorial with rifle and ax — even the newspapers written in Pennsylvania towns near where he lived.[63] Lobdell gained even more notoriety as a female hunter after returning home from the West, and in 1871, the *New York Times* published an article relating this same (false) story of his youth and claimed that, as a girl, "she was as wild as the deer and roamed the hills and learned to shoot a rifle early. At 19 she was acknowledged to be the equal of any man in cutting lumber or rafting, and the best shot in the entire settlement or any adjoining."[64]

This fictional tale of Lobdell's youth, wholly imagined by male authors, becomes the core of the legend, and while it seems to valorize a strong woman, it focuses on a skill that is decidedly masculine and reserved for men. The credit for this talent now lies with the lumbermen who took Lucy on as a pupil and taught her the arts of marksmanship and hunting. This displaced credit robs Lobdell of his motivation to learn how to shoot and his determination to get an education. His ambition becomes obscured as the desire to learn gets transformed into the act of men desiring to teach rifle skills to a child, apparently for their own entertainment, and the power of Lobdell's masculine endeavor is drained into masculine tutelage. Lobdell's accomplishments are made invisible as they become those of men, heightening the masculinity of the loggers.

> The way dominant culture contained the threat that the mannish woman represented to hegemonic masculinity was to absorb female masculinity into the dominant structures. Such an explanation assumes that manliness is built partly on the vigorous disavowal of female masculinity and partly on a simultaneous reconstruction of male masculinity it claims to have rejected.[65]

With credit given to men for Lobdell's rifle skills, his masculinity is rerouted, and he is robbed of agency and realigned in the patriarchal narrative, subordinate to men as their pupil.

Smith continues in his history of Meeker County by explaining that, although Lucy spent the majority of her time among men, she still possessed a necessary nineteenth-century quality of True Womanhood — purity — as well as many rural skills that made her an attractive candidate for a wife in the wilderness:

> Notwithstanding her masculine tastes Lucy Ann's name, as a girl and woman, was free from reproach. The breath of slander never reached her, and she could have had her choice of a husband from the most exemplary young men in the vicinity. But she had no inclination to marry and rejected all offers.
> A raftsman named Henry Slater came into the settlement about 1850. He formed the acquaintance of Lucy Ann and to the surprise of everybody, they were married. Slater proposed to Lucy Ann, and she told him that they would shoot at a mark with a rifle. If he beat her shots she would marry him, if not she would stay with her parents. The trial of skill took place and Slater was victorious.[66]

This fiction focuses on Lobdell's exceptional marksmanship, but not as a claim to fame. Here Lobdell's rifle skills betray him, apparently just this once, even though there are virtually no accounts of Slater ever using a gun. Lobdell's masculinity, evident in his talent with a gun, seems to falter when facing the institution of marriage's claim to a female body. Losing the marksmanship match grounds Lobdell's female masculinity and his rebelliousness to the institution of marriage is squashed. Yet glimpses of truth peek through from this myth. Lobdell did learn shooting and general survival skills at an early age; he was acknowledged as the best shot in the area; he did spend days at a time alone in the woods; he did kill a large number of animals; and he did reject the attentions of men.

In a 1931 retelling of previously compiled histories, Merle Potter gives a slightly altered and even more inaccurate version of the story in a chapter titled "Meeker County's Wild Woman," which shifts control of Lobdell's life to Slater and clearly identifies his misappropriated masculine ability with a rifle as the cause of his trouble.

> It was her skill with a rifle that was her undoing and sent her to Minnesota. A raftsman named Henry Slater came along one day and made her a sporting proposition. He offered to have a shooting match with her, and if he won she must become his bride. Confident that she could win (for she fancied the uncouth Henry very little), she accepted, but much to her discomfiture she lost the wager and was obliged to carry out her bad bargain.[67]

This later account is a reinterpretation of an already fictional, Atalanta-like contest that now places the origin, control, and requirements of the challenge with Slater, disempowering Lobdell even more. And while Lobdell's loss will clearly cost him his carefree, single status, there is no provision for him winning, as if such an outcome was unimaginable even though he was the best shot in the territory. His confidence in his skill is presented as overweening pride, leading him to foolishly accept the challenge.

In this version, Lobdell's loss of his "bachelor" freedom is his own fault. Not only is he practicing a masculine sport that is sure to bring about his "undoing" but he is also prideful about a skill designated as masculine. Misappropriated skill and inappropriate pride topple him from his lofty position as the "best shot" to a place automatically assigned to female bodies — wife.[68] With disempowering rhetoric, Potter shifts the placement of agency to Slater and eliminates any element that would suggest Lobdell might win. In an account that is fictional to begin with, Potter's interpretation has further weakened Lobdell, casting him as prideful and in need of taming through subordination to a man.

Writers relating this myth celebrate Lobdell's rifle skills because such masculine prowess must be celebrated. The combination of rifle skills, strength, and violence amount to survival, that primary and primal unconscious human priority. But hunting symbolizes masculine human domination and exploitation of a weaker, feminized nature and a rifle is a phallic symbol, so, necessarily, such a masculine accomplishment is destined to backfire on a woman, especially in nineteenth-century stories.

While most authors present inaccurate stories about Lobdell, one discounted the old myths. Leslie D. LaValley published his account of Lucy Ann Lobdell in *The Basket Letters* and made a point of declaring that the newspaper reports about Lobdell mixed fact with fiction; he also gave a more accurate account of Lobdell's youth. By the time LaValley's book was published, however, Lucy Ann was forgotten by all but a few and locked away along with other skeletons in the Lobdell family closet.

A close look at these fictional accounts of Lobdell's early life reveals a complete lack of Lobdell's own voice or the facts of his life. While many knew of Lobdell's autobiography, none seem aware of its contents, which negate these fictional accounts. What is clearly presented in newspaper stories and histories is a patriarchal discomfort with a female body not only performing as a man but also performing better than all the men around. Lobdell's attempts to gain an accomplished and dominant position in and over his own life results in either male-seized credit for his successes (via lumbermen) or male-driven violence to cage his disorder within the classification of woman and normative female gender behavior and roles. The presentation of Lobdell's life through male-crafted narratives virtually silences him, imprisons him in the female realm, and strips him of agency and masculinity, which are reassigned to men in his revised life.

Smith concludes the episode in Manannah by presenting Lobdell as a weak and pathetic character. Insulted and shunned by the people of Manannah, Lobdell becomes "deranged," but upon recovering from the mental shock, she expressed a willingness to return to her family and friends, but had no means save her rifle, and nobody in the settlement able to purchase that. Mrs. Slater was finally sent home at the expense of Meeker county, under the direction of Capt. A.D. Pierce, then of Manannah. Soon thereafter Capt. Pierce received a letter from Mrs. Slater's parents, thanking him and the county most heartily for their kindness in returning her to her friends. In 1859 she again appeared on her old stamping ground, "the basket," and still in male attire.[69]

Lobdell's first two attempts to live as a man built on the coming-out narrative in his autobiography, developed his story of resistance to social norms, and formed the documented foundation of the beginning of his adult transgendered life, a life story I offer up to the developing canon of historical American transgendered lives. While Lobdell's social and financial success in living as a man was not permanent either time, he continued to challenge traditional understandings of gender, space, masculinity, and femininity in more public ways than did his autobiography or life in the small village of Long Eddy, New York. His gender identity and expression, behavior, and actions were deconstructive acts that exposed the synthetic constructedness of gender categories and boundaries, exploded definitions of masculinity, and presented alternative patterns of female-bodied subjectivity. These early incidents in Lobdell's life illuminate gender expression and gender identity as the core of conflict between Lobdell and the society around him. Both defied cultural conceptions of normalcy and the battle line of this social conflict formed around competing meanings inscribed on his body. In *Female Masculinity*, Judith Halberstam argues that the idea of masculinity claiming a collection of qualities, attributes, and appearances that can only belong to male bodies is the result of the accretion of "myths and fantasies about masculinity that have endured that [claim] masculinity and maleness are profoundly difficult to pry apart."[70] Joseph Israel Lobdell can be added to the many examples Halberstam offers of female-bodied persons who debunk this myth about masculinity.

The inflexible classification of people as either male or female, masculine or feminine, in Western society refuses to acknowledge ambiguously gendered bodies; this refusal is "sustained by a conservative and protectionist attitude by men in general toward masculinity ... bolstered by a more general disbelief in female masculinity ... [even though] female-born people have been making convincing and powerful assaults on the coherence of male masculinity for well over a hundred years."[71] Disbelief in and reclassification of female masculinity shores up male masculinity, and the privileges and powers that attend it, as something only male bodies can claim. The two accounts of Lobdell's early life discussed in this chapter offer historic examples of female-bodied masculinity, here wedded to the claim of an alternative form of maleness, that challenge the myth of male-only masculinity by featuring a female-bodied person believed by entire communities to be a man. Lobdell's masculinity — his masculine appearance, talents, abilities, skills, and charms — was so believable that it was praised when thought performed by a traditional male body. Masculinity was only pried from Lobdell through various policing actions and narrative reinterpretations of his masculinity and transgender as either a deceptive disguise or something abnormal.

Transgender history is also the history of transphobia, and the narratives of both of these incidents give examples of historic nineteenth-century trans-anxieties and the fear-driven need to reestablish social order through policing the construction of gender, and male and female spheres, by punishing transgressive nonconformists. Both communities Lobdell lived in tried to contain his disordered body and behavior through arrest, legal action, public humiliation, shunning and banishment, in an effort to re-chalk the gendered boundary lines he smudged by transgressing them. Along with defining Lobdell from the privileged base of heteronormativity and classifying him as the abnormal, dangerous Other, these examples include the use of violence and the belief in its ability to bring society back to a recognizable balance; such a philosophy clearly outlines the historic dangers of transgender living.

The social commotion that followed Lobdell's exposure works to draw attention to the punishment of nonconformity, but Lobdell's original act of living as a man also presents alternative patterns of masculinity, gender, and lifestyles. These new patterns challenge gender and body binaries by presenting a space of possibilities outside restrictive either/or categories and definitions. The ungoverned, uncontainable freedom of this space generates fear in those who work to close it up, reestablish restrictive spaces for subjectivities, and punish the transgressor.

Analysis of the narrative technologies used to defend and reestablish heteronormative power structures concerning Lobdell's interaction with society exposes a historical unease with noncompliance to established gender roles. The newspaper articles and histories treating Lobdell's first two attempts to live as a man provide narrative examples of how gender was managed, policed, disciplined, and enforced, as well as how gender nonconformity was punished. These narratives trace the beginning of Lobdell's public life as a man and the corresponding public reaction.

Two • *The Singing Teacher of Bethany* 87

The historic narratives offered here reveal how Lobdell's masculine behaviors and activities were convincing enough for the society around him to assume that he was a man like all other men. Once exposed, the same masculine behaviors that earned him the position of respectable man became reclassified as anomalies that proved he was abnormal. The narrative redefining process included a social form of emasculation that stripped Lobdell of the masculinity that had formerly been respected, thereby policing masculinity as something only a traditional male body can claim. I include here a collection of narratives that work together to build a false mythology of Lobdell's youth contradicting the version from Lobdell's own book, and that either strip him of masculinity or attribute it to men around him. Through these narratives, masculinity is reestablished as belonging only to male-bodied men; the interloper is stripped of autonomy, freedom, and a masculinity perceived to be misappropriated, and recast as feminine, often more pathetic than dangerous.

Bethany and Manannah succeeded in ridding their communities of Lobdell and the threat he presented. For both incidents, writers of histories, newspaper articles, and legal narratives crafted literary vehicles that denied the validity of his masculinity and preserved that quality for men only. But neither attempt triumphed in permanently locking Lobdell back into the female sphere, women's clothes, or feminine gender roles. While Lobdell's experiences left him depressed upon his return home, they failed to change him. The security of gendered order created through the actions and writings of gender defenders was an illusion, as the threat Lobdell represented to social order still existed, evidenced by his life-long persistence in wearing men's clothes. However, the depression that resulted from being shunned in Manannah lingered with Lobdell and, combined with the rejection by Long Eddy neighbors who disapproved of his appearance and behaviors once he was back home, debilitated him to the point where he could not work at all. Not able to recover well enough to be financially independent, Lobdell became destitute. Without the financial support of a husband (which was tenuous at best when he was with Slater), Lobdell had few options for survival. According to an article in the *New York Times*[72] sometime after July 1860, Lobdell "applied to the Poor authorities of Delaware County, and asked to be placed in the Poor-house."[73]

One of the harsh side effects of nineteenth-century industrialization was the lack of paid work available for women, which forced many of them to either depend on men for financial security or live in poverty. When manufacturing moved textile production out of the home and into factories, "women lost an important source of supplementary income."[74] The very few jobs that were open to women did not even provide bare subsistence wages, and so many widows and single mothers entered poorhouses as a last resort.

As in all times, stigma was attached to extreme poverty in the nineteenth century. As an outgrowth of outdoor relief, which subsidized poor families with groceries, fuel, and other life necessities, the poorhouse was a precursor to the modern-day welfare system, and plagued by similar attitudes and failures. The dominant belief was that relief given to the poor made them dependent on the government and eroded their character, making poverty not simply a misfortune but also a moral failure.

Poorhouses were created to give compassionate relief of poverty with the intention of curbing the demand for that same relief, to check the threat of demoralization among the poor, and to inculcate a strong work ethic. In an era when the work ethic was part of the moral fiber on an individual and national level, belief in the myth of abundance and a job for every willing worker in America led to the assumption that poor people were lazy and immoral. In an effort to rehabilitate paupers, poorhouses demanded that all able bodies do work as a form of therapy and a way to help pay for the cost of keeping inmates. Other circumstances that were much crueler — such as inadequate food; lack of proper heating, sanitation and health care; the removal of children from their parents; and various abuses by those designated as caregivers — created an institution entered only by those in desperate situations.[75] Along with the social stigma of poverty, Lobdell would have had to submit to wearing women's clothes and doing only women's work because of his anatomy.

A year later and several states away, while Lobdell was enduring the poorhouse, Marie Louise Perry ran off with James Wilson.[76] She was the beautiful, intelligent, lady-like, and well-educated daughter of Thankful and Daniel Perry, a well-to-do couple in Abbington, Massachusetts. Marie's father had forbidden her to spend time with Wilson, but she disobeyed and eloped with the man. While on their honeymoon in Jersey City, Wilson proved to be untrustworthy and took off with the landlady's daughter. Marie was determined to track them down and took the Erie Rail Road train going to Buffalo, where she believed they were headed. Many miles before Buffalo, Marie ran out of money and was put off the train at Lordsville, a small town below Hancock, New York.

The authorities told Marie if she gave them her father's name, they would send her home, certain that her family would pay the ticket once their daughter was safely returned. Marie knew she could not look her mother in the face again, having disappointed her so badly, so she refused to name her father. Instead of returning home to safety and comfort, Marie chose instead to be taken to the poorhouse in Delhi. Her health was suffering by the time she got to the almshouse, and she was nursed by none other than Lucy Ann Lobdell.[77] Lobdell had been depressed while at the poorhouse, but after meeting Marie he "became full of life, and was the most cheerful person in the place."[78] From the time the two women met each other, they "formed a mutual affection so strong that they refused to be separated."[79]

And now, the plot thickens.

• THREE •

The Queer Couple

WRITERS IN THE LATTER HALF of the nineteenth century present Joseph Israel Lobdell, Marie Louise Perry and their relationship through the chronicling of their movements, activities, behaviors, and appearances. Stories about the couple are recorded in a collection of newspaper articles and editorials, first-hand accounts, arrest records, legal judgments, poorhouse and census records, medical diagnoses, lunacy testimonials, psychiatric evaluations, and (rarely) the words of the subjects themselves. These historical narratives about Lobdell and Perry shed light on past assumptions and understandings of bodies, genders, and desires, revealing how socially constructed concepts about gender were used by various nineteenth-century authorities to interpret and define normalcy and deviance. The body of narratives presented here highlights gendered presentation and performance as the focus of all identifying interpretations and definitions of Lobdell. It also contains historic examples of transphobia and consequences for gender transgressors in the nineteenth century.

Examining the types of narratives centered on Lobdell illuminates the importance of various writers who, being considered socially acceptable judges and authorities, interpreted the meanings of characters and events through heteronormative lenses; they then disseminated their conclusions as truths through the narratives they told to a larger audience. Close attention to vocabulary and characterization in articles, histories, and legal judgments reveals how writers constructed normalcy, deviance, respectability, immorality, and insanity. These narratives worked to reinforce traditional constructions and understandings of gender, spaces, relationships, and marriage, thereby strengthening the dominant heteronormative social order. They also reveal historical anxieties about non-normative gendered behavior and relationships outside the traditional constructions of marriage.

By positioning Lobdell and his relationship with Perry as strange, writers attempt to contain the power of difference within heteronormative language and classification. Offered as examples of deviance, stories about the couple were located within the frameworks of various institutions, which had the social power to name, define, contain, and remove that deviance in an attempt to ensure social safety and the continued balance of established power through enforcement of gender binaries.

Newspaper articles, histories, legal judgments, and medical diagnoses carried the weight of social authority and worked as literary controls to regulate normalcy and deviance, contain disorder, and dismantle the threat of transgender and queer behaviors and lifestyles (meaning those that did not align with heteronormative definitions and enactments). Writers enlisted the imagined readers, assumed to fit normative expectations and be in agreement, to aid the social utility of the narrative's regulation of gender. Conclusions, which were offered as natural truths, were constructed through the use of heteronormative assumptions, language and classifications in narratives. These conclusions proliferated through reader dissemination and shored up the traditional social constructions of sex, gender, heteronormative time and space, and relationships. Communal policing through the use of labels, containment, and punishment of transgender disorder maintained the perception of traditional (gendered) patriarchal order.

Combined with examples already discussed, these historic narratives give evidence that Lobdell, through his appearance, behavior, and lifestyle, queered traditional sex and gender binaries in addition to traditional gendered behaviors and spaces. When used as a verb, to *queer* something means to resist, trouble, or challenge heteronormative definitions and enactments of hegemonic understandings and classifications of sexed bodies, gender identity and presentation, and sexuality. These historic narratives also chronicle the transphobic reactions to Lobdell. Nineteenth-century transphobia is evident in the records of family and community members, article writers, sheriffs, deputies, judges, doctors, courts, and psychiatrists/sexologists who interpret Lobdell's transgender behavior and appearance as unnatural, immoral, and/or insane. The narratives presented here usually accompany reports on legal measures taken to bring Lobdell out of the wilderness and into society, where he could then be locked up and safely cordoned off from the larger community.

Nineteenth-century writers focus on gendered behavior as the core of criminal identification, which works to frame Lobdell's masculinity as deviant, or worse, ridiculous, and secures masculinity as an entitlement for male bodies only. While writers continue to mention Lobdell's hunting skills, any other accomplishments are not included; they only report on his disruptive behaviors and poverty. Through a process of literary emasculation, writers redefine Lobdell's masculine behaviors as socially disruptive, deviant acts.

The relationship between Lobdell and Perry is a nineteenth-century example of what Judith Halberstam calls a queer use of time and space; it follows none of the guidelines for traditional domesticity, marriage, or family structure. It also challenges the necessity for a union of differently sexed bodies as it queers conventional constructions and understandings of marriage and husband and wife. As a couple, Lobdell and Perry present an alternative pattern and spatial construction of domesticity and intimacy in a differently imagined lifestyle outside of traditional gendered spaces. Writers who discuss the Lobdell-Perry relationship present it as strange and abnormal, antithetical to traditional cross-sexed relationships. While intending to marginalize or even demonize this relationship, their presentation offers up the centerpiece of a different pattern for domestic partnership. Although framed as deviant, this alternative domestic relationship becomes visible in its challenge to tradition, often in romanticized ways.

Just as feminist theory reveals the constructedness of gender in Lobdell's enacted life/narrative, queer theories inform an analysis of Lobdell as a third body between sexes, genders, and desires. Such an analysis examines the constructedness of sex and sexuality and the failure of traditional heteronormative binaries and labels to create an accurate body of knowledge of possible human classifications, or even to succeed in forcing all people into categories defined as natural. The discourse surrounding Lobdell highlights the failure to acknowledge any gendered categories except the polar opposites used to define normalcy, placing anyone who does not comply with expectations of gendered behavior into a catch-all category of deviance even as it makes visible alternative patterns for bodies, living spaces, relationships, and lifestyles. Nineteenth-century narratives define him as deviant, disruptive, and dangerous, shaping him as an example of abnormality that reinforces the hegemonic bi-gendered definition of normalcy; they also simultaneously point out the fragility of that normalcy, which is easily challenged by Lobdell's disorderly body and life.

Lobdell and Perry lived a queer lifestyle in a third space outside of traditional gendered spheres and traditional marriages, and they physically resided in a third spatial category outside of the social space of civilization, a space neither rural nor urban, a space not settled at all. Lobdell and Perry lived much of their lives in the wilderness, a space symbolizing the dangerous and the unknown — wild, untamed, and uncontrolled by humans. By living in the wilderness, Lobdell and Perry removed themselves from social constructs of civilized space that demanded compliance with established social expectations and institutions. They shaped that undomesticated venue into a place free from social norms and mandates, and created a competing form of domesticity that was literally, as well as philosophically, outside social boundaries.

Nineteenth-century writers use the terms *wife*, *husband*, and *couple*, but they do not recognize the Lobdell-Perry marriage as legitimate, even as they present it as an alternative form of domestic arrangement. Nineteenth-century understanding of sexuality declared that women had no sexual desire, so the aspect of physical intimacy between Lobdell and Perry is nonexistent in these stories, as writers perceive the relationship as simply a "singular attachment" between two women. Because Perry looked and behaved like women were expected to — she was beautiful, lady-like, and educated — writers treat her more kindly. Confused by her loyal and persistent companionship with Lobdell, they present her as an enigma, not an immoral or deviant character, while masculine Lobdell is most often vilified. Because narratives focus mainly on Lobdell's visible difference, Perry's queerness is rendered invisible even though she also insists that she and Joseph Lobdell are husband and wife. The scant attention writers give to her as the normal woman frames her as a secondary character in the shadow of the more noticeably different and disruptive Lobdell.

Writers of newspaper articles, arrest records, first-hand accounts, testimonials, and histories present Lobdell's non-normative behaviors as deviance, which reinforced traditional understandings of normalcy and combined to create a consensus view of deviant queerness that contributed to a knowledge base then used to form and inform legal definitions of insanity. "The structure of the law, the discourse of psychiatry, and the needs and expectations of the 'respectable' white community — as constituted through the [nineteenth-century] newspapers — interacted, shaping and being shaped by their differing parameters" to categorize transgender and queer behaviors as insane.[1] Examination of social narratives about Lobdell shows how a confluence of similar interpretations formed by family, community members, and law officials identified him as an immoral, unnatural, outlaw; this consensus interpretation informed judges, medical doctors, psychiatrists, and early sexologists who then redefined queer behaviors as mental illness.

Treatment and characterization of Lobdell changes among authors depending on what information is used or rejected, how the information is interpreted, and what the authors' individual perspectives and belief systems might be, resulting in various classifications of Lobdell. To flesh out the body of knowledge about Lobdell, these same writers assume the authority to do so by using the myths that had already sprung up from storytellers who did not have accurate information, but who did have access to the legends already in the making about the Female Hunter. These writers literally created a fiction about Lobdell's youth that formed a mythology around him that relied on and enhanced his notoriety as a hunter and became the common, but inaccurate, knowledge base for their readers. Newspaper writers in areas surrounding Delhi, New York, and Honesdale, Pennsylvania, included a fictionalized history in nearly every article on Lobdell, the same mythologized account of Lobdell's youth that was used in the Meeker County history discussed in the previous chapter. This version presented young Lucy Ann Lobdell as a wild child, living in the wilderness among hardy, good-natured lumbermen who taught her how to shoot, hunt, and chop wood. She was "known far and wide for her wonderful skill with the rifle, not only in target-shooting, but in hunting deer and other game."[2] "She was acknowledged to be the equal of any man in cutting lumber or rafting, and the best shot in the entire settlement, or in any adjoining."[3]

Ignorance of Lobdell's actual life is evident in reports from New York and Pennsylvania due to the complete absence of any remarks about his life and adventures in Minnesota and the assumption that he had spent between four and six years hidden away in the wilderness. Writers explain away this time period by stating that Lobdell "made her appearance at the settlements only when in need of ammunition or supplies, exchanging skins and game for what she required."[4] While self-sufficiency is evident in a life that needs only occasional contact with others, that same life is blamed for destroying Lobdell. These article writers believed that women could not support themselves and suffered economically without the benefit of a husband who would take care of them. The next leap in logic for newspaper writers was that life as a huntress brought about Lobdell's downfall. "She had grown prematurely old, and was but a wreck of the former dashing backwoods favorite."[5]

Writers assumed that Lobdell's complete immersion into a hunter's life in the woods was a resourceful attempt to survive after Slater "deserted" his wife and child, "leaving them in destitute circumstances,"[6] not a choice made to seek mobility and wages equal to those of men. Slater, as the source of Lobdell's desperation, is credited as the reason for Lobdell's decision to live as a hunter in the woods, giving agency to Slater rather than Lobdell. Writers make it appear that, after Slater left, resorting to talent and skill was necessary, and Lobdell is referred to as the "unfortunate wife and mother."[7] In contrast to the strong, independent, and successful figure presented of Lucy as a young single woman, Lucy as a deserted wife is treated as a resourceful but pathetic woman, suffering without the company and financial support of a husband.

With no knowledge of the circumstances that caused Lobdell's depression in 1858, or of the fact that Lobdell was actually living with his parents and daughter in Long Eddy in 1860,[8] these same writers use their normative ideas about women to characterize Lobdell as weak and broken without a man's support. They attribute Lobdell's state of depression and inability to work to the accumulated damage suffered from being cast off by a husband and living a difficult life in the wilderness. "Her wild life was one of thrilling adventure and privation, and it was not until she was broken down in body and mind by its hardships that she returned to the haunts of civilization."[9]

Despite the many reports of Lobdell's hunting prowess that won him not only renown and fame but also a livelihood, writers present that same masculine behavior as the source of Lobdell's collapse. The masculine behavior of young, single Lobdell that was celebrated by lumbermen is here presented as dangerous activity for a grown woman. In contrast to the goals of living in men's clothes listed in Lobdell's autobiography, newspaper writers position his masculinity as the cause of his physical and economic breakdown. Female masculinity becomes a certain pathway to destitution for a woman who refuses to live as a woman, and writers present Lobdell's entry into the poorhouse as tragic, yet common for women with children and no husbands.

The truth offered by nineteenth-century writers is that a successful life as a hunter can lead men to fortune, but it leads women to destruction physically, emotionally, and economically, thereby reinforcing the dominant parameters for female behavior confined to traditional domesticity and a husband's management. Lobdell's misery in the poorhouse is read as the emotional and economic reaction to abandonment. Described as moody, sullen, and miserable while in the poorhouse, Lobdell is presented as a sad, pathetic woman who suffered poverty because of the desertion of her husband, not someone who suffered depression due to the gendered restrictions of his life. The freedom Lobdell enjoyed in the wilderness life of a hunter, described as a great joy in his autobiography, is grounded and negated by its connection to the humiliation of life in the Delaware County poorhouse. After meeting Marie and escaping back to the wilderness, reports on Lobdell reveal struggle, poverty, and harassment, but also freedom and companionship.

Sometime early in 1862, Lobdell and Perry ran away from the poorhouse in Delhi, and a short time later, Joseph Israel Lobdell and Marie Louise Perry were married by a justice of the peace in Wayne County, Pennsylvania.[10] The couple spent an unknown amount of time between 1862 and 1865 (possibly later) at the Lobdells' house in Long Eddy. Their relationship was noted by neighbors who came forth in 1880 as witnesses at Lobdell's lunacy hearing. Census records of Hancock in Delaware County, New York, also list the pair living there in June 1865.[11]

The couple wandered from place to place, living in the woods in caves or rude cabins built by Lobdell, and subsisting on game, fish, and whatever could be gathered from the surrounding environment.[12]

> In the summer of 1868 a party of fishermen discovered two strange persons living in a cave in Barrett township, Monroe County, Pa. They were a man and woman. Soon thereafter there appeared in one of the villages a tall, gaunt man, carrying a rifle and leading a half-grown bear cub by a string tied about his neck. The man was bare-headed and his clothing was torn and dirty. Accompanying him was a woman about twenty-five years old, shabbily dressed, but giving evidence of more intelligence than the man, who called himself the Rev. Joseph Lobdell, and said that the woman was his wife. As they walked about, the man delivered noisy and meaningless "sermons," declaring that he was a prophet of the new dispensation, and that the bear had been sent to him by the Lord to guard him in the wilderness. For two years these vagrants wandered about that portion of the country, living in caves, and subsisting on roots, berries, and the game killed by the man.[13]

In 1869 they were living in Canadensis, Jackson Township, Monroe County, Pennsylvania, and were arrested on charges of vagrancy. They were discharged after a short incarceration and wandered into Barrett Township.[14]

> In the spring of 1869 there appeared in the town of Barrett, in the western part of Monroe County, a couple calling themselves the Rev. Joseph Israel Lobdell and wife. The man was of medium height, dressed in tattered hunting garb, and carried a long single-barrel rifle. He wore no hat, and his head was covered with thick black curly hair, streaked with gray. The woman was

taller than the man, and was meanly clad. She was fine looking, wore spectacles, and her conversation showed that she was educated and intelligent. For two years the strange couple roamed about the township, living most of the time in the woods, but frequently making their appearance in the village, where the man would deliver wild and incoherent harangues on religion, and both would beg for food and shelter.[15]

By 1871, "they had become such a nuisance to the inhabitants that they were arrested on the charge of vagrancy and committed to jail in Stroudsburg."[16] Provoked by the villagers, the law was called upon to take care of the bothersome couple; because of vagrancy laws, anyone without a home could be arrested:

> The law requires all persons going from door to door, or placing themselves in streets, highways or other roads to beg or gather alms, and all persons wandering abroad and begging, who have no fixed place of residence in the township, ward or borough, to be arrested as vagrants, by the constable or other officers of the peace, upon notice to him by any inhabitant of the township, or in his own view.[17]

In the nineteenth century, troublemakers were dealt with by returning them to their hometown and having the officials there pay for the legal costs, so the sheriff at the jail in Stroudsburg, Pennsylvania, repeatedly asked the "couple of dilapidated specimens" where they were from, but did not get an immediate answer. After seizing and reading letters the couple possessed, officials suspected that Lobdell had a female body. "Suspicion having been excited as to the sex of the pretended husband, proper persons were deputed to examine the matter, when it was discovered that 'he' too was a woman."[18]

From Marie the sheriff learned that they had escaped from the poorhouse in Delaware County, New York, and the legal authorities of Monroe County arranged to return them there.[19] But first, "when the true sex of the woman was ascertained ... 'Joe' [was] furnished with women's clothes."[20] Via train, the poorhouse overseers of Barrett Township, Henry Schaller and Friend Schoch, first took the couple back to Lobdell's father's house in Long Eddy. When it became clear that James and Sarah Lobdell were in no condition to take their child in, as they were living off the charity of their neighbors, the men took Lobdell and Perry back to the poorhouse in Delhi, Delaware County, New York.

Removing a troublemaker from a community is an understandable legal act. But in this case, before legal officials did just that, they forced Lobdell to change clothes. Lobdell's outward presentation troubled the understanding of female bodies, and while he had broken no laws by his choice of clothing, transanxiety is evident in the law officials' attempts to restore Lobdell's appropriate feminine appearance by forcing articles of female clothing onto his body, even though they removed him from their community that same day. Law officials considered gender conformity necessary and of more immediate concern than transporting the law-breaker to where he belonged.

Joe and Marie did not stay long at the poorhouse and escaped easily, this time settling somewhat outside of Honesdale, Pennsylvania, possibly because Joe's daughter, Helen — now a grown woman — lived in Damascus, a nearby town. Joe and Marie wandered between the Lobdell family home in Long Eddy[21] and Honesdale for eight years, living off the land and doing odd jobs to get by. After the arrest at Stroudsburg the news about the Man-Woman and the odd couple had spread to other towns, and at this point, Lobdell's anatomy was public knowledge. The story of the Female Hunter and Marie made it into the *New York Times*,[22] solidifying the mythology that had built up around Lobdell as the sensational story and Joe's notoriety spread like wildfire. Lobdell persistently presented as a man and continued to live the life he and Marie had carved out for themselves, but with the secret of his anatomy exposed, he was known everywhere he went. His visits to town were regularly noted in newspapers, sometimes for the most trivial things.

On the first day of November, 1871, the Female Hunter caused a local stir in Honesdale:

> On Monday evening, the Rev. E.O. Ward of Bethany, discovered the strange creature on his front stoop, dancing and singing in a lively, wild, and reckless manner. He recognized her as the person that years ago taught singing lessons in Bethany, passing herself successfully before the public as one of the masculine gender. She remained in Bethany during Monday night, and was next seen by John Hacker, while on his way driving from Bethany to Honesdale on Tuesday morning. As he drove to where she was standing, she immediately jumped into the wagon, and instead of getting out again, commenced hugging bashful John in a free and easy style. Mr. Hacker drove to the prison in this town, and did not succeed in getting free from his female passenger in male attire, but by strategic reasons afterward, she consented to part with him.[23]

After parting from a very relieved John Hacker, Joe went to the public square in front of the courthouse, and before a crowd of onlookers, proceeded to climb the statue of the Civil War Soldier and "embraced and kissed him, and talked to him in a sympathetic strain."[24]

Trying to avoid the trouble and expense of returning Lobdell to

Delaware County again, the authorities simply took Lobdell to the outskirts of the nearby town of Narrowsburg and dropped him off so that community could deal with him. But Joseph appeared in Honesdale the very next day. He entered a schoolhouse just outside of town, insisted on running the school, and disciplined several schoolboys by cuffing them on the ears with a book, for which he was arrested.[25]

This incident was reported in a voyeuristic fashion by many observers from various viewpoints, who skipped over the reason for arrest and focused on Lobdell's "scandalous" refusal to cooperate with officials who tried to force him into women's clothes. Reports written by witnesses do not even mention the behavior that resulted in arrest but instead focus on Joe's behavior after the arrest, and while judgments differ in degree as to his morality, all narratives reveal transphobia about the Female Hunter as they focus on the lure of the deviant.

One writer, the editor of the *Wayne Citizen*, had a somewhat amused attitude toward the "irrepressible female known as the Female Hunter," and explained that

Stone jailhouse in Honesdale, Pennsylvania, where Lobdell visited frequently.

stone walls do not a prison make, and in this instance they failed to check her exuberant demonstrations. She had been in her cell but a short time before she stripped off all her clothes and tore them into rags, and served the straw bed in like manner. Her conduct became completely maniacal, and it was found impossible to keep anything on her.[26]

Other writers were not even regular newspaper reporters, but had gotten permission from Sheriff Dorin to visit the jail and watch "the sensation,"[27] and then reported their observations — and judgments — to the public. The writer of the *Evening Gazette* refers to Lobdell as "the Maniac Man-Woman," a "singular creature" who was wrapped in a blanket after ripping clothing and bedding to shreds in a fit of rage. This writer also reports on Lobdell's other behaviors. "At times she utters the most unearthly shrieks and performs the craziest antics imaginable."[28]

While the previous reporter equates gender ambiguity with animalistic behavior, another visiting witness offers an even more condemning perspective. This indignant writer[29] never mentions the reason for Lobdell's arrest but focuses solely on Lobdell's behavior in jail, making clothing and gendered behavior the issue instead of public misconduct. The writer first claims that Lobdell's actions and condition are disgusting and "not fit to print" and then proceeds to give explicit details and sarcastic commentary. The writer witnessed Lobdell "singing songs of vulgar words, and climbing the iron bars across her cell window; even the prisoners that were in the jail were made to blush at the sight, as she was perfectly naked, not a stitch of clothing could be kept on her person." This writer gives more insight into the reason for Lobdell's nakedness by explaining that the sheriff had

> tried to put a petticoat over her; but was not successful in the undertaking. Nothing could subdue the "Female Hunter" but a pair of pantaloons. Without any coaxing she consented to have pants, vest, boots and hat, and dressed in the garb of an anti–"Dickinson," she marched forth from her cell like a "bully boy" hanging on the arm of our handsome sheriff. She seemed docile as a lamb, and the sheriff took the responsibility to transfer her "lone handed" without a handcuff with him.

This writer's tone of indignation and choice of vocabulary characterizes Lobdell as an immoral wild woman, preferring nudity to wearing clothes appropriate to her gender, which is so indecent that even male criminals blush. At the same time, the writer makes it clear that when allowed to wear men's clothes, Lobdell became calm and cooperative. This account suggests that the attempt to force Lobdell into female clothes prompted his wild behavior, since the presentation of male attire subdued him. Lobdell's strong objection and refusal to wear any clothes except men's clothes was viewed as deviance because the common nineteenth-century belief was that women were supposed to, and wanted to, wear female clothes. The onlookers who report the incident do not understand Lobdell's transgendered nature and mistake his refusal to behave in normal ways as a form of derangement. But in presenting Lobdell's behavior as deviant, the writer also reveals his successful resistance to social mandates about gendered dress.

Through the use of sarcasm and the derogatory terms "bully boy" and "anti–Dickinson," this writer constructs an immoral, deviant subject and positions Lobdell as worthy of public disdain and disapproval. Such a presentation creates the subject as deviant, and simultaneously offers a transphobic response framed as appropriate. This literary construction of Lobdell as a deranged and immoral subject acts as a guideline for readers. The language used, which centers on Lobdell's behavior and gender ambiguity, is loaded with meaning that the reading community understands and accepts within the language of that community, and Joe's gender nonconformity is commonly viewed as insane.

Lobdell, along with his wife Marie, were returned to the Delhi poorhouse on November 14, 1871, from which they quickly escaped, returning quietly to the woods.[30] However, even when well-behaved, Lobdell was harassed by the law.

When Joe entered Honesdale in July 1876, "out of common decency she was arrested."[31] As a curious throng gathered to watch, Marie wrote a petition to have her husband released from jail and delivered it to the commissioners.

> After reading her petition Mr. Dimmick was introduced to [Marie]. In reply to a question addressed to her by him as to what she desired, she said that in the first place she "wanted to see Joe," but she did not want to go to the jail alone, as she was not treated respectfully the last time she was there to see "her husband."
>
> The Commissioners, their attorney, and the writer [of this newspaper article], accompanied her to the jail. Mrs. Lobdell took with her her writing board, the bouquet, and a tin pail which she carried on her arm. On entering the corridor she began hastily to inspect the several cells in their order with evident eagerness of finding "Joe." Finally she pulled open an iron door, and her face lit up as she discovered the object of her search lying at the further end of the cell. The female hunter seemed equally glad to see her "wife," and immediately stepped up to the grated door, and thrust her hand through it for the earnest grasp which it received.

According to this source, Marie brings Joe a few gifts of apples and lilacs and the two are given a bit of privacy to hold a conversation. The couple seems like such an ordinary couple that a bystander asks the sheriff if Joe really is a woman.

> "Woman! Why of course she is," replied he. "When we first brought her in the cell she was dressed in woman's clothes, but one day she tore every rag of clothing off of her, and we gave her a man's suit. Since then she behaves pretty decently."[32]

Once again, Joe acts violently toward women's clothes, but becomes calm and manageable once he is given men's clothes. Marie's petition is successful, and the prisoner is released to his wife to return to the woods. But the key to great change is hinted at by the writer who witnessed Marie's visit. "If 'Joe' had her rights she was entitled to a pension, her real husband having lost his life in the late war."[33]

For eight years, newspaper writers reported stories of Joseph Israel Lobdell and his wife Marie, combining the bare details of arrest reports with plotlines of their activities and descriptions of their appearance presented through judgmental tones and vocabularies. "The specific operations of newspapers — their economic underpinnings, their managed readerships, their generic conventions and taboos — shaped the meanings and material contexts that gave such narratives cultural and political force."[34] In the first reports about the couple, they were presented as socially unacceptable because of their extreme poverty.

Inside cell in stone jailhouse.

View 2 of cell.

The discovery of Lobdell's female body granted them status as deviants, making them a dangerous threat to society, one that required expulsion.

Arrest reports gave terse accounts of criminal behavior and consequential actions taken by law officials in sparse terms, almost laundry-list fashion, that simply stated the facts. But the narratives created by nineteenth-century newspaper writers and essayists used the strategy of characterization and constructed moral meaning through their interpretations of Lobdell and Perry, influencing public perceptions of the couple. These judgments were then attached to the bodies of Lobdell and Perry, who were identified first as criminals, then as strange. In this way, writers crafted stories that became meaning-making vehicles that established deviance and normalcy by presenting the disorder the couple embodied through a moral lens that examined, judged, and labeled socially unacceptable lives and bodies. These negative identifications of Lobdell and Perry created a border that delineated and reinforced what was not acceptable, and what was.

> These narratives ... helped define the parameters of the American "general public"—the readers of the newspapers whose moral fitness for citizenship, or for the domestic morality underwriting it, was assumed. They accomplished this through their construction of unfit "others," social types who negatively defined the normative characteristics of Americans.[35]

The resourceful lifestyle of the couple became the setting in stories about them, but was presented as extreme, pathetic poverty by newspaper writers. By law, Lobdell's lack of a traditional home enabled sheriffs to place him in prison whenever he came into town for business or any other purpose, and they often did so without formally arresting him. Lobdell was never arrested in Pennsylvania for wearing men's clothes, yet commentary on his appearance made up the bulk of everything written about him. Newspaper writers reporting short incarcerations in jail focused not on the illegality of vagrancy, but on Lobdell's gendered appearance and behavior.

The interconnected relationship between the construction of gender and the social hierarchy of power is reinforced by those writing the newspaper articles that circulated throughout New York and Pennsylvania between 1868 and 1885; Lobdell is presented alternately and simultaneously as a champion hunter and a deranged social danger, both constructions based on his masculine behaviors. Newspaper writers composed reports from arrest records, rumors, fictionalized histories, and a few eyewitness observations — rarely from interviews with the subject(s) — and filtered them through a heteronormative lens that constructed Lobdell as the unfit Other, going against Nature and posing a threat to gender-ordered society. Nineteenth-century newspaper writers were involved in "discursive production (which also sometimes have the function of prohibiting), of the production of power (which sometimes have the function of prohibiting), of the propagation of knowledge (which often cause mistaken beliefs of systematic misconceptions to circulate)," forming what Foucault refers to as "truth regimes."[36]

In contrast to writers' presentations of Joseph when he was the dashing, well-dressed singing teacher in Bethany in 1855, their transphobic depictions of him in later years create the image of an ugly, degraded, and indecent person. Writers often focus on Joseph's masculine appearance, sometimes simply stating that he wore men's clothes, at others listing the details of each separate item of clothing. He is shown in white pants, a dark coat, a dilapidated corduroy suit, a light hat, or no hat to cover his matted hair. Descriptions of his masculine looks frame him as deviant and are bolstered by negative remarks about the loss of all traces of femininity in appearance. "[In youth] she was beautiful; now she is haggard."[37] "Looking at her now, one would never take her for one of the gentler sex; much less would one think that she was once a handsome girl, sought after for a wife by many worthy men; or that she was once a wife and mother."[38] Lobdell had "short, shaggy hair, and features in the main repulsive, but bearing traces of lost attractiveness."[39] Writers make it clear that Lobdell has fallen from womanhood and that abnormal masculine life in the wilderness has "driven every feminine feature from her face,"[40] even as they repeatedly reinforce the fact that he passed "herself successfully before the public as one of the masculine gender."[41] Lobdell's obvious masculinity troubles definitions of female bodies and is presented as dangerous to natural femininity. His appearance is described as ugliness, a characterization meant to punish Lobdell's presentation, yet it ironically further reinforces his masculinity.

Newspaper writers relied on information gathered from eyewitness and second-hand accounts that focused on what was peculiar and odd — but not illegal — about the couple to craft stories that spanned the years before and after the arrest in 1871. Relying on observations rather than interviews with the arrested subjects, the writers focused first on appearances. Descriptions detailed the couple's tattered and dirty clothes, but the major focus was on Lobdell's more unusual appearance and behavior.

Lobdell troubled the binaries of masculine/feminine and man/woman, refusing to fit the label assigned to his body — woman — as society denied the label he chose for himself— man. The separation of sex and gender was obvious in his transgender body, which revealed the constructedness of both. Public transanxiety and confusion over his sex and gender is evident in article titles, labels applied to him, and treatment of his name. With literary authority to define, writers create terms meant to be derogatory but that also give evidence that he fit on neither side of the sex or gender binary. The article titled "The Lady in Pantaloons: She (or He) Has Gone Away" reveals the author's anxiety and confusion over Lobdell's masculine behavior and appearance, as the writer attempts to categorize ambiguous sex and gender by offering a choice of gendered pronouns. Other article titles display that same transanxiety and language deficiency in classifying Lobdell, such as "The Man-Woman: Lucy Ann Lobdell in Town," and "Maniac Man-Woman Lobdell."[42]

Lobdell's name and terms used to depict sex come into play in nearly all written accounts. The conflict in meaning-making between Lobdell and those in authority to write social narratives is evident in those stories. In Western culture, only two sexes and genders are acknowledged, which reduces the choices to either man or woman. Lobdell, who did not identify as a woman, selected the only other terms available for a legitimate identity: man and husband. "For the marginal or powerless to challenge the dominant discourse, they must frame their challenge in a language meaningful within the hegemonic discourse."[43] In his effort to define himself as the man Joseph Israel, the husband of Marie, Lobdell fused a masculine self to a female body, simultaneously assenting to and challenging constructed sex and gender categories.

But writers observing Lobdell create meaning through heteronormative assumptions that fuse gender to genitals, and normalizing language that denies the meaning Lobdell gave himself. He is frequently referred to as Joseph Israel Lobdell until it is revealed that he is actually a woman named Lucy; at that point the name *Joe*, as well as the terms *he* and *husband*, are placed in quotation marks. In later accounts where Lobdell's identity is no longer secret and readers already know the person as Lucy Ann, the Female Hunter, writers still use quotation marks around gendered terms but state that to the public Lobdell was known locally as Joseph Israel Lobdell, "as she insisted on being called."[44] This literary treatment presents an alternative form of identity for female bodies, although it denies this identity's legitimacy.

The sharpest derogatory treatment of Lobdell's sex is found in a sidebar article devoted solely to chronicling a sighting of the Female Hunter leaving jail—here Lobdell is first offered both sexes, and then denied any sex at all: "Lucy Ann Lobdell, the would be gentleman-woman, has left the Spencer House[45] in company of its wife, Louise Perry."[46] This focus and treatment of name and pronoun usage means to ridicule Lobdell's gendered presentation; however, it highlights Lobdell's ambiguous gender and offers an alternative category of identification. This example treats Lobdell's sex with literary violence and contempt, yet ironically reinforces his relationship with Marie as a marriage.

Transphobia and disapproval concerning Lobdell's refusal to comply with cultural expectations of female appearance, behavior, and place in society are further developed by writers through inclusion of adjectives and details in their narratives that are completely unfounded and often fictional. Even though Woodward admits that "this strange creature was proficient in playing the violin," he refers to Lobdell as "uncouth" and a "crazy, filthy, diseased fellow-being" even though Lobdell had no documented disease or serious illness. Lobdell is reported as being "insane [and] wandering the country like a beast," reducing him to a less-than-human being.[47] Lobdell's life is repeatedly referred to as a "singular history," emphasizing the odd nature of his appearance, behaviors, and lifestyle. Although Lobdell was well educated for the times and actually taught school before marrying George Slater, writers say he was "rough and uncouth in manner and language," and that he "had always belonged to the lower order of humanity."[48] Success as a hunter is given cursory attention as the focus becomes the moral condemnation of "an insane, foul, and unsexed woman."[49]

Without ever interviewing Lobdell, writers of newspaper articles funnel first- and second-hand observations through heteronormative lenses that zero in on appearance, successfully shifting the focus from petty legal infractions to poverty and immoral behavior. Lobdell is stripped of subjectivity and reduced to an imagined object because "any time we are looked at, the observer takes control of interpreting us and what we mean, how we are defined and known — the meaning of our displays and performances."[50] By repeatedly presenting Lobdell as deviant, writers define his behavior and appearance as wrong, incorrect, unnatural, and harmful, and Lobdell is continually marginalized as a liminal character even as he becomes the focus of the community every time he enters town. Gender boundaries are repeatedly reinforced as Lobdell's alternative transgender is condemned through the cultural labor of the narratives created by article writers. Readers interact with writers to confirm the knowledge created and presented in stories as truths. "Newspapers thus operate at the boundaries of public and private, political and cultural, working to define the meanings of such binaries for a national reading public."[51] However, these stories also showcase Lobdell's constant contestation of gender boundaries.

In contrast to the narratives told by history and newspaper writers, Lobdell's silent, enacted text told his story of defiance through the way he lived, his earlier written words becoming deeds. Lobdell literally enacted the manifesto from his autobiography and refused to submit to society's oppression of women, or to participate in any way with the established classification and performance of women. Lobdell's life as a man was an absolute rejection of any female identity and rebellion against cultural imaginings, definitions, and expectations of women. Newspaper writers focused on Lobdell's gender rebellion, making gender boundaries the framework of articles about his behavior. As they connected his poverty and his whereabouts to his gendered presentation, writers defined Lobdell as the deviant, counter-social Other. "Such stories defined a dangerous 'outside' to respectable domesticity and enshrined a vision of the protections provided to virtuous women by the properly maintained white home. Of course, they also advertised the possibility, even the adventure and allure, of undomesticated lives for some women."[52]

Although Lobdell claimed orally and in writing to others that he was adopting men's clothes to gain employment and economic advantage,[53] which was an understandable motive, he did not acquire any wealth or live a comfortable lifestyle. Nor did his transgender secure anonymity. Life as a man brought about a large degree of community disdain and name-calling, along with feeble attempts by law officials to discipline his appearance. Despite poverty, legal harassment, and public derision, he continued to wear men's clothes and to insist that he was, in fact, a man named Joseph Israel Lobdell.

Halberstam portrays "[t]he transgender person who risks his life by passing in a small town," living in a queer time and space, as an anachronism because of his gender inversion.[54] Lobdell's queer space was figuratively outside public understanding, and literally outside of society, in the wilderness, a space that symbolized the dangers of the untamed, unmanaged, unknown that threatened the safety and order of society. His life in the wilderness was a lived rejection of the structures, rules, and expectations of society. Beyond dismissing social expectations for women, he also made it clear he chose a life free from any of the goals prescribed as normal: traditional marriage, family, long life, and accumulation of wealth and property. Lobdell further queered expected norms by using the familiar social institution and language of marriage in such a creative way that others could not understand the expansion that Lobdell and Perry gave to the meaning of the term. In turning their backs on rigid social patterns, he and Marie created their own alternative society, without boundaries, and with their own rules.

Within this third space of wilderness and unrecognizable marriage, Lobdell lived in the third space of a body that would not fit into the tidy man/woman binary. Lobdell's constant embodiment as a man first troubled sex and gender binaries by revealing the obvious construction of them, and then by not fitting into either half. He was masculine and insisted he was a man, but because "the biological body, transformed by the human mind into a cultural construct, undergoes a … metamorphosis, emerging as the symbolic representation of the social forces that created it,"[55] society saw his female body and insisted he was a woman. Halberstam states that "[a]mbiguous gender, when and where it does appear, is inevitably transformed into deviance, thirdness, or a blurred version of either male or female."[56] The quality of thirdness evident in Lobdell's body and life made him an anomaly to his surrounding society, which placed him on the outside of the established gender boundaries that it patrolled, resulting in the derogatory terms presented earlier, such as "man-woman" and "it," created by writers intending to demean his sex and gender. Yet these same terms freed him from binary constraints as they acknowledged a space between the opposing poles.

While Gagne, Tewksbury, and McGaughey claim that transgenderists "live in a social region for which there [is] no idiom,"[57] Judith Butler refers to this third place as the "zone of inhabitability [which] constitute[s] the defining limit of the subject's domain; it will constitute that site of dreaded identification against which — and by virtue of which — the domain of the subject will circumscribe its own claim to autonomy and to life."[58] Lobdell did gain a certain degree of autonomy temporarily while living freely in the woods with the partner of his choice, outside of traditional domestic arrangements and expectations, but, like Kate Bornstein, he learned that "the in-between place itself was the truth [he] was made aware of: the existence of a place that lies outside the borders of what's culturally acceptable."[59] The space that is viewed as uninhabitable is the sociological space of the ostracized Other.

Lobdell's persistence in living as a man married to a woman created a point of conflict that challenged culturally constructed understandings of natural bodies and sex, which makes him dangerous to society.

> The person between categories is perceived as outside categories, institutions, and values. As such he embodies all the chaotic power of formlessness and disorder. The stage of being in between categories and the power inherent in that process have been designated by anthropologists as liminality.[60]

It was not just Lobdell's strength and determination to break out of the bonds created for women in the nineteenth century that made him so powerful; his resiliency to incarceration and public ridicule made him even more formidable because he could not be controlled by the usual vehicle of public shame used to bring a person into conformity and acceptable behavior.

Despite harassment and ridicule, Lobdell stubbornly lived by his declaration that he was a man. "Humiliation is a whip of the defenders of gender. Humiliation is sanctioned at virtually every level of the culture: people can laugh at a transgendered person; but when there's no fear of being humiliated for one's portrayal of gender, there's less opportunity for the culture to exert control."[61] Treatment as a public spectacle, name-calling, and incarceration failed to make Lobdell wear women's clothes, return to life in society, or exchange Marie for a husband. Lobdell simply did not care what the public thought of him, and often voluntarily played the clown for the amusement of others. It was this absolute lack of fear of humiliation that made Lobdell dangerous.

> Cross-culturally, the individuals who have freed themselves from the fear of humiliation are clowns, fools, jesters, and tricksters. [As fools] they don't play by the rules, they laugh at most rules, and they encourage us to laugh at ourselves. Their pranks of substituting one thing for another create instability and uncertainty, making visible the lies imbedded in a culture.[62]

Lobdell substituted manhood for his female body, exposing the constructions of concepts about bodies and the inadequacy of gender construction to fully define or contain people. He substituted his role as a wife for that of husband, and a traditional life of restricted domesticity for one of boundless freedoms and mobility, thereby presenting a new pattern and method for living one's life outside known paradigms.

Lobdell lived the role of the archetypal Trickster character, described by Carrol Smith-Rosenberg as a disorderly figure, of indeterminate sex and changeable gender, that embodies the disorder and creative power associated with liminality, breaking taboos, violating categories, and defying structure.[63] As the Trickster character, Lobdell challenged institutions and categories, revealing the fragility of social traditions, definitions, and order. But he suffered the results of his rebellion.

The Female Hunter's Wife

In contrast to the treatment Lobdell received, writers present Marie Louise Perry in more kindly terms. Her feminine looks and behavior fit gender expectations of women and do not challenge understandings of normalcy, so "when she is with Lobdell, as the 'normal' woman in the bigendered relationship, descriptions of her 'femininity' take over. Hence, she is always described as being in a dress, as attractive, and as having grown into graceful womanhood."[64] Reports of her appearance combined with gossip about her family history seem to be the sole basis for the interpretation given by the mostly male newspaper article writers, and while there is much consternation and confusion about her reasons for voluntarily living a life of poverty with Lobdell, she is characterized as a virtuous, intelligent, and attractive woman. Woodward notes that upon arriving in Long Eddy, Marie was "well dressed and ladylike." In later years, despite being "scantily dressed" in clothes "dirty and torn by brush and briers,"[65] she is frequently described as "attractive," "handsome," and "good-looking despite her rags."[66]

As stated earlier, during this time period, Victorian sexual ideology declared that women had no desire except to become mothers, so thoughts of sexual impropriety among women keeping company with each other were nonexistent. On the contrary, people in the nineteenth century considered romantic friendships between women natural and socially acceptable; they did not think passionate devotion between two women was disturbing or deviant. Without sexual desire, women had no sexual identity to express and the idea that women might desire each other had not yet formed in the public (male) imagination.

Newspaper writers do not judge Marie harshly, as they do Joseph, because she conformed more closely to gendered expectations of women's appearances and behaviors. But they clearly do not understand why Marie would not want to return to her father's home of perceived comfort, safety, and good society. After poorhouse authorities learned her father's name and contacted him to come and retrieve his daughter, they expressed consternation when, instead of going home, she ran away with Lobdell.[67] Writers are puzzled by Marie, "now a voluntary outcast and associate of an insane, foul, and unsexed woman, [as she] is highly educated, and capable of adorning the best circles."[68] There is general confusion over why she chose to live an impoverished, homeless life with a person who was not her social equal, and writers often imply that Lobdell, painted as low class, uneducated, and dangerously deviant, was responsible for Marie's fall into a dubious lifestyle and acquaintance.

Economic status and class, rather than female relationships, become the focus of writers' curiosity. Emphasis is placed on Marie's middle-class background and assumptions are made about her education and upbringing. Woodward claims she was "an educated woman who had been reared in refinement ... used to refined influences."[69] Drawing mostly on their imaginations, writers present her as the "daughter of a well-to-do Massachusetts family, a graduate of the Boston school,"[70] with "more than average intelligence, and to all appearances, respectable."[71] While incarcerated in the Stroudsburg jail with Joe in the summer of 1871, Marie wrote a letter to Joe's mother. Officials who confiscated the letter highlighted Marie's education, as the focus of the resulting report was that the letter was a superb piece of composition, "every word spelled correctly, perfect punctuation, and in an excellent hand."[72] Regrettably, the report does not discuss the contents of the letter.

The mystery of Marie's "strange attachment" to Lobdell became the theme of one article title in the April 8, 1877, edition of the *New York Times*: "A Mountain Romance: Strange Life of Unhappy Women — A Singular Family History — The Female Huntress of Long Eddy — Strange Love of Two Women — An Accomplished Boston Girl, A Voluntary Outcast — An Unfortunate Daughter." Ironically, contained within this same article and others that express confusion over Marie's association with Lobdell is the explanation offered repeatedly by the couple themselves: they are husband and wife. Woodward writes of them as "a couple, both women, who lived together as man and wife. The one who claimed to be and was accepted by the other as husband had been married and bore a child.... And the one who declared herself the wife was an educated woman who had been reared in refinement."[73] Public confusion about Marie's voluntary association with Joseph lies in the class and educational differences between the two. Despite her agreement with Lobdell's statement that he was her husband, her difference is not acknowledged and her queerness is always invisible.

Lobdell and Perry consistently presented themselves as man and woman, insisting they were husband and wife, and publicly acknowledged each other as such. Yet, when these terms were used by article writers, they were generally set off in quotation marks, negating the validity of the pair's view of themselves, even as writers presented them as a couple. At this time, marriage was acknowledged and understood as the intimate union of one man and one woman, with procreative desire as the natural bond between them, since no other desire was imagined for women. Nineteenth-century writers did not understand that Joseph and Marie saw themselves as fitting that normative paradigm, yet they presented them as a traditional married couple nonetheless, echoing the same perception the couple has of themselves. One writer notes "last winter [Lobdell] passed through our borough, in male attire, accompanied by a female whom she called her wife. They stopped at the dental office of Dr. Kessler where the 'wife' had a tooth extracted — the operation being paid for by the 'husband.'"[74] Although this report denies validity to the terms *wife* and *husband* by using quotation marks, it nonetheless positions Joseph as the traditional breadwinning husband who takes financial responsibility for his wife.

Curiously, despite public consternation, writers always present Marie in ways that represent the traditional role of wife. Background information in many articles clearly positions Marie as the dependent wife supported by her husband's hunting and survival skills and wilderness resources. When the Reverend Joseph Israel Lobdell led a tamed bear into Waymart, Pennsylvania, and began to preach a "gospel of new dispensation," Marie was beside him, quietly supportive and ready to pass the hat for donations.[75] Whenever Joseph was returned to the poorhouse in Delaware County, she accompanied him and was accepted by the authorities there. And when Joseph was jailed for vagrancy, she visited him, brought him food, and, on more than one occasion, petitioned for his release.

Newspaper writers link Marie's most noble act of loyalty with her superior education and writing skills. In 1876, Joseph and Marie gained permission to build a bark hut on the edge of a farm in Aldenville, Pennsylvania. When the man who owned the property learned that his wife, "who had been particularly charitable to the couple,"[76] had nearly married Joseph years before when he was the singing teacher in nearby Bethany, he remembered that Lobdell had a female body and had him arrested for vagrancy. While Joseph was in jail, Marie displayed her devotion in her attempt to free her husband:

> Marie Louise Perry, still showing in her manner traces of culture strangely antagonistic to this pariah life she had led for so many years, hovered constantly about the jail, beseeching the authorities to release her "husband." When court met she presented a petition, which covered two pages of foolscap paper, and which she had written with a split stick as a pen, and pokeberry juice for ink, praying for the release of her "dear husband, Joseph Israel Lobdell." This document was preserved among the court records until the bodiless ink faded and disappeared. It was strikingly neat in chirography, choice in diction, and ingenious in argument, showing the accomplishments of its author, who yet yearned for the companionship of a crazy, filthy, diseased fellow-being and the life of an outcast.[77]

Half a dozen newspaper writers present this evidence of Marie's superior intellect and status, describing her writing as "flawless, clear, correct argumentative English — a really superior piece of composition,"[78] and "a model of clear and correct English and powerful in its argument."[79] The petition, asking for the "release of her 'husband' because of 'his' failing health," was successful and the prisoner was delivered to Marie's safekeeping.[80] Marie's femininity, education, and class are positioned in opposition to Lobdell's transgender, poverty, and homelessness, dividing the two into the good-domestic-feminine woman and the bad-abnormal-masculine one.

Paradoxically, while writers present the relationship between Lobdell and Perry as strange and unexplainable, their constancy to one another is frequently noted as a laudable trait. "Their consistency to each other in every trial and hardship enlisted much sympathy [from the town's people]."[81] One writer, Mr. Ham, writes very kindly about the Female Hunter and her wife, perhaps because of his personal acquaintance with Marie. He admits that the community has never seen anything as strange as the relationship between the two women, yet urges the public to be kind to two who seek in

> earnestness a living in the few avenues left open to them, although always consistent, always true to each another in trials and adversity, their strange conduct may well excite more than a passing interest. Old age is creeping upon them yet they resist its ravages as stoutly and as successfully as the most favored. Always gentle, always quiet, defrauding no one, striving in humble yet honest ways to care for and protect themselves they may well be left alone to work out their own "problem of life."[82]

The relationship between Lobdell and Perry is presented as a rare, one-of-a-kind oddity that defies explanation because it queers conventional definitions of marriage.

> Stranger, even, than the story of Murray H. Hall, the Tammanyite who for thirty years concealed her sex and passed as a man in active business and social life, is the account of a couple, both women, who lived together as man and wife.... Here is the story without embellishment of fancy. Has it a parallel in this or any other country?[83]

Lobdell and Perry used an existing paradigm to define their relationship as husband and wife because no other patterns or vocabulary had been imagined at that time, and the words they used reflected their understanding of their bodies, genders, and relationship. However, the terms *husband* and *wife* made no sense to Lobdell's contemporaries because the couple troubled the man/woman binary, the belief in only procreative desire, and the institution of God-ordained, heteronormative marriage.

Even though Marie shared Joseph's lifestyle, living space, claim to marriage, and belief that he was a man, her queerness is rendered invisible. Writers focus more on Lobdell's masculine behaviors and transgender, making it the hypervisible, deviant centerpiece of most narratives, while they cast Marie as a normal—although somewhat out of place—woman because of her more traditional and feminine behavior, appearance and attitude. She seems normal—just not in a normal space. She is viewed more as an enigma than a deviant and is treated with gentle, respectful confusion by writers and law officials, while Joseph is treated generally with contempt and violence. Although given much less attention by article writers, when Marie is discussed, they present her in positive terms. Portrayed as attractive, well mannered, educated, and refined, Marie becomes the perfect foil to highlight the perceived unnaturalness of Lobdell's masculine appearance, traits, talents, and behaviors. While Marie is refined, beautiful, mannerly, and intelligent, Lobdell is uncouth, repulsive, ignorant, and wild; he is perceived as a dangerous influence on Marie. Despite their shared life, Lobdell is viewed as the one who is a threat to society because his challenge to established binaries and social order is obvious in his gendered presentation, making him the dangerous one.

Joseph and Marie practiced what Judith Halberstam calls a "queer use of time and space," which develops "at least in part, in opposition to the institutions of family, heterosexuality, and reproduction. They also develop according to other logics of location, movement, and identification."[84] Halberstam explains that when queerness is seen as "an outcome of strange temporalities, imaginative lifestyles, and eccentric economic practices," it moves from being associated with sexuality to being a way of life, "willfully eccentric modes of being," that, according to Foucault, threaten established social arrangements and lifestyles. "In Foucault's radical formulation, queer friendships, queer networks, and the existence of these relations in space and in relation to the use of time mark out the particularity and indeed the perceived menace of homosexual life."[85]

The historical spatial construction for women's lives was domesticity, the literal and psychological space of subordination, the approved space of home and family. Lobdell and Perry challenged the boundaries of female space not by inserting themselves into the male space of mobility and economics for which Lobdell had expressed a desire in the autobiography, but by abandoning civilized space altogether and disrupting the binary of male and female spheres. They exchanged the stationary and restrictive space of the house for unrestrained mobility in a third, undelineated, wild space outside of, and opposed to, civilization and society.

By inhabiting the third space of the wilderness, free from traditional domestic and economic structures, Lobdell and Perry escaped the mandates of socially defined bodies and behaviors. Physically outside of civilization, the couple used this third space to assert power over their lifestyle, bodies, and relationship by rejecting social constructions of and expectations for men, women, marriage, and domesticity. Their queer reconstruction of these same categories produced a differently imagined space of domesticity and patterns for bodies and relationships. This made them very dangerous to society.

While the communities around Lobdell and Perry were oblivious to the erotic component of their relationship, what the couple clearly presented was an alternative domesticity that queered the common definition of female bodies and marriage and refused to comply, in any aspect, with social expectations for women. To the public, it appeared that two women were living by themselves independent of male support, guardianship, or guidance. They had escaped the traditional female sphere of housekeeping, marriage, motherhood, and family altogether, and in fact wandered freely from one community to another, unrestricted by a cumbersome house or family. At times, Lobdell and Perry settled and worked at odd jobs, but more often the couple's resourcefulness and ability to survive off the land granted them unheard-of mobility, and enabled them to disregard the economic necessity of acquiring financial support from male husbands with traditional careers. Lobdell and Perry lived without boundaries, especially in the wilderness, which symbolized their abandonment of society and all its rules.

They also lived outside what Halberstam calls "family time," referring to "normative scheduling of daily lives that goes hand in hand with raising families, governed by an imagined set of needs that children have."[86] Lobdell rejected the demands and expectations of motherhood and devoted his life to living free of traditional marriage and family mandates; Perry did likewise. Neither dealt with the demands of raising children. There were no pregnant times, nursing times, feeding times, bedtimes, sick times, or time devoted to family for making clothes, religious education, disciplinary measures, or routine household chores. None of their time, mobility, or scant economic resources were hampered by children.

Without children, husbands, or homes, they were able to avoid those institutions and demands that repressed women because "[r]eproductive time and family time are, above all, heteronormative time/space constructs."[87] According to Halberstam, this time/space construct also includes those who elect to live "outside the logic of capital accumulation," choosing to live without homes or steady jobs and not making longevity or wealth the central focus of life. Lobdell and Perry lived in this queer space, preferring the freedom, and difficulties, of homelessness and poverty to the constraints of the traditional life women were expected to desire and achieve. Their ability to imagine, choose, and create a life outside conventional constructions of women's lives made their relationship and lifestyle a dangerous example of alternative domesticity, despite its hardships.

Lobdell and Perry presented a clear alternative to traditional relationships and lifestyles, which challenged the dominant understanding and expectations of women and their roles and functions. While their life together succeeded in providing freedom from social constraints on their thoughts, desires, goals, mobility, resources, and time, it was repeatedly treated as deviant, shameful, and dangerous even as it was presented as a compelling adventure.

Lobdell and Perry persistently lived in the woods and rural areas as man and wife for well over a decade, landing in and out of jails and newspapers until Joseph purchased a small farm outside of Honesdale, Pennsylvania, in 1878.[88] So newsworthy was this event that it made the local papers. The *Wayne County Herald* reports that after a few years of living near the road to Damascus "where the couple have found employment in picking whortleberries which were shipped from Narrowsburg to New York, and in gathering wintergreen leaves which were sold to a German named Yeddo, who has a still in that region for manufacture of wintergreen oil," Lobdell became a landowner. The writer was present at the transaction and noted that Lobdell "pulled a roll of bills out of her vest pocket" and that "Lucy was dressed in her usual style, and looked fully competent to manage a farm, including the chopping of a fallow or the swinging of a scythe."[89] Along with the farm, Lobdell purchased a horse, a wagon, a fiddle, and a watch.[90] The writer notes that, surprisingly, Lobdell had the deed recorded under the name of Lucy Slater rather than the more familiar name of Joseph Lobdell. In this and other articles, Lobdell is comfortable discussing the land purchase and his personal life and openly talks about his marriage. "On being asked how long she had been married, she answered, 'About thirteen years to this woman.'"[91]

While newspaper writers seem to celebrate Lobdell's purchase of land and home as a sign of the Female Hunter settling down, the acquisition of a farm actually made Lobdell even more dangerous to society. With money and a home, Lobdell no longer lived in homeless poverty, so he could not be arrested on charges of vagrancy. The legal tool created by the law, which enabled officials to incarcerate Lobdell with no more provocation than his entry into town, was no longer effective, leaving sheriffs powerless to contain his transgendered, disruptive energy or safely remove it from society. The legitimizing space of the farm granted a form of protection to Lobdell's gender nonconformity, which now had full opportunity to openly challenge heteronormative patterns and definitions and cause limitless social upheaval.

The second part of Lobdell's queer threat to society is evident in this newspaper article — his queer relationship is directly linked to the protection of a legitimate space, and his mention of his long-standing marriage to Marie gives notice that their queerness is enduring. Moving from the wilderness into a space acknowledged socially as domestic granted legitimacy to Lobdell and his relationship with Perry. By bringing Lobdell's third sex and gender and the alternative domesticity of a queer relationship with them, the farm acted as a foundation that granted protection to patterns for identities, relationships, and lifestyles created by Lobdell and Perry that challenged heteronormative constructions of bodies and marriage. With the legitimacy of land and home, Lobdell and Perry's relationship and lifestyle now more closely resembled traditional married life, except with a few queer twists. Living like normal folk suggested permanence to their challenge to heteronormative order.

With the simple acquisition of land, Lobdell gained a form of protection through his connection to a legitimate space. The thirdness that surrounded him while he lived in the wilderness, his third sex and gender and his marriage to Marie, was now housed in a secure, civilized space that held the potential to help new patterns of sex, gender, and marriage take root and flourish.

Lobdell, as Trickster, was supposed to be a "comic character, a joke" whose chaotic power "momentarily turns the world upside down" because the power of disorder is "transitory, rather than suggestive of an alternative order."[92] Having become a landowner, Lobdell could now claim legitimacy, making his challenge to constructions and classifications of gender and gendered spaces even more threatening.

However, this social disruption was short lived. Lobdell died mysteriously and unexpectedly and his death was reported in October 1879. The *New York Times* reported "Death of a Modern Diana: The Female Hunter of Long Eddy" on page 2 of the October 7 edition, a week before the obituary hit the hometown newspaper of Hancock, New York. Lobdell's death was also news for the October 23, 1879, edition of *Forest and Stream*, a men's journal devoted to hunting and outdoor life, which simply praised Lobdell's "wonderful skill with the rifle."[93] The October 25, 1879, edition of the *National Police Gazette*, a newspaper of dubious character that focused on the sensational, also reported Lobdell's death: "A Curious Career: Remarkable Adventures of Lucy Ann Lobdell, an Eccentric Female

Character who Figured Successfully as Hermit, Hunter, Music Teacher, Author and 'Female Husband.'" All four obituaries treated Lobdell more kindly than stories written prior to 1879, yet the newspapers still focused on the sensation of his transgendered appearance and lifestyle, and left the circumstances of his death a mystery, stating simply that he died after a brief illness.

According to Dr. P.M. Wise, after a relatively quiet life on the farm, Lobdell had "a maniacal attack"[94] and was taken to the poorhouse in Delhi, New York.[95] Although that institution had always accepted Marie Perry before when Lobdell was taken there, this time when she demanded companionship with her husband, the authorities refused to provide further for her. When she inquired about her husband, she was informed that he had died. Returning to the area she had known as home, Marie continued her nomadic life in the woods around Honesdale, Pennsylvania.

> [One day] Maria Perry appeared saying her husband, Joe, was dead. Maria picked berries to sell and slept during the summer wherever night overtook her. The people of the locality were kind to her and she did not find it hard to find someone to "take her in" when winter came. Her baggage for a long time she kept at the home of Reuben Comfort; and she has stayed for as long as a week at a time at our house.[96]

The fate of the farm that Lobdell owned is unclear, but what is evident is that Marie did not continue to live on the property. Although newspaper writers still viewed her more as a curiosity than a threat, she continued to live in that third space of mobile poverty, to queer definitions of marriage, and to defend nontraditional relationships between women. Mr. Ham, the editor of the *Wayne County Herald*, received a private letter from Marie, which followed a discussion that had begun on a street corner in town, and decided to publish it on June 15, 1882.[97] In this letter, even as Marie thanks Mr. Ham for his kind words about her and her husband, she sets the record straight about a number of things that newspaper writers have either neglected or presented inaccurately for years. She explains that even though she did receive a good education, she "paid [her] own tuition, board, clothes, etc., while at school apart from the common public schools" and that she had never been seen in Pennsylvania in her "proper dress" because doing so was dangerous.

While all other depictions of Marie by writers of histories, personal accounts, and articles for newspapers and medical journals present her as a harmless and passive sidekick to Lobdell, in this letter Marie makes her politics very clear, revealing a subversive attitude that sheds light on her connection to Lobdell. In her discussion of a woman's experience with poverty, she criticizes the lack of employment opportunities for women and points to political inequality and male negligence for the harsh situation that claimed many women:

> But, Mr. Ham, the abuse and injustice [woman] often has to endure, and which has such a crushing influence upon her existence, seems to be a wrong on the part of the administrators of the law and the voters who create them. If woman has no voice in the making of the laws of our country, she should as recompense, be granted sufficient other privileges to preserve her equality of rights.

With public focus finally on Marie, she challenges public perceptions of her and Lobdell, as well as traditional understandings of husbands and wives, as she makes her queerness visible:

> If, instead of styling me the "Female Hunter's Wife," you had said "his apparent widow," I think the expression would have been more correct. I do not know why the companionship of two women should be termed "strange." The opposite sex are often seen in close companionship and friendly conversation, and, Mr. Ham, my sex are not inferior to yours. "Not many may know the depth of true sisterly love." Is not this a remark from your own sex?

Marie's words emphasize the ambiguity of Lobdell's sex and challenge the social view of women. She first posits Joseph as male by declaring she is his widow, denying the public perception of Lobdell as female, then challenges public indictment of two women in close companionship, using that public perception of female bodies against the behaviors and ideologies of those who attacked Lobdell. After making it clear that she is that sex opposite to men, she denies men a superior position over her.

Ironically, even though Marie shared Lobdell's politics, views on marriage, and understanding of transgendered embodiment, because of her long-standing invisible queerness, she was never accosted by legal or medical authorities, and was allowed to roam freely in the area she and Lobdell had considered home. Not even her public acknowledgment of her marriage to her husband, Joe, aroused alarm or caused people to think of her as anything but a normal woman. One report states that Marie had white hair and poor health after her husband died,[98] and then she mysteriously disappeared from public sightings. Marie peddled wintergreen berries in Honesdale after her husband died, but after 1883, she was not seen in public and many speculated that she finally went home to her father's house in Massachusetts, although there is no proof of that.[99]

Tragically, Marie was not actually a widow. While the comic Trickster presented temporary challenges to established order, Lobdell's unflagging dedication to his lifestyle and gender were considered too dangerous to allow him to live freely in society, blazing a new pattern for an existence between sexes and genders that fractured the binaries that kept people locked in place socially. As a person who refused to conform to known categories, Lobdell disrupted order and prevented it from being cleanly reestablished by his very presence.

Lobdell, in fact, had not died in 1879. At the end of 1877, John Lobdell offered to help his sister, Lucy Ann. George Slater, Lobdell's husband, had died in the Civil War, and since Lobdell had never divorced him, he was entitled to a widow's pension under his legal name, Lucy Ann Slater. John Lobdell completed the paperwork so Lobdell could collect approximately fifteen years of back payments, resulting in thousands of dollars. Joseph Lobdell's first act after receiving this pension money was the purchase of a farm and home, along with items needed to work the farm.

But he was not permitted to live there long. Shortly after purchasing the farm he was moved back to Long Eddy, where he lived with his daughter, Helen Crawson, in a house owned by his brother, John Lobdell. The release of false obituaries from the family effectively erased his existence for the public in general, and Marie specifically. On May 31, 1880, John Lobdell petitioned the county court at Delhi, New York, to issue a writ de lunatico inquirendo to investigate the sanity of his sister, Lucy Ann Lobdell, whom he claimed to have supported for two years. The sheriff was commissioned to summon a jury, and John Lobdell was appointed to select twelve "good and true men" to testify as to Lobdell's sanity; this testimony was to be presented to Judge Isaac H. Maynard, Delaware County judge.

Despite one newspaper reporter's declaration that Lobdell was capable and fit to work a farm, twelve men from John Lobdell's community outside Hancock, New York, swore that Lucy Ann Lobdell was insane and incapable of self-government or managing property, mostly because "she frequently dressed in men's attire. Sometimes says she is a hunter. Sometimes claims and acts as if she was in love with another woman and says that [woman] is her ... wife."[100] Harry Walsh had thought she was insane for years. Twenty years before this hearing, he had seen Lobdell at the family saw mill,

> sawing or attempting to saw. She was then dressed in men's clothes and particularly attracted my attention ... from her appearance and conduct at the

time we both came to the conclusion that she was crazy.... She was dressed in men's clothes and had a gun and pretended to be a hunting. After that I saw her in company with another woman traveling the roads. That woman was crazy. They both claimed that they were man and wife and pretended to love each other so that they could not be separated. When they came to my brother's he said they frequently came there together in that way and wanted to be together and sleep together.[101]

John Lobdell testified that his sister had been insane for more than ten years and that he believed the insanity was brought on by "excitement in religious matters." As evidence of insanity he stated:

She has a habit of dressing in men's clothes. At times she has had bad spells where she imagines there are snakes in the room and beasts and at such times she tears her clothes and the bedding in the room. She becomes quarrelsome and unmanageable at times and threatens to burn the building and runs off in the woods alone. She has a woman who she sometimes claims is her wife.[102]

Dr. Ed L. Pettingill, who had never met Lobdell but had heard for years of "a crazy female hunter," declared Lobdell insane and, without ever speaking with Lobdell, Judge Maynard signed the court order to commit. John Lobdell was appointed Committee for the person and property of Lucy Ann Slater, making him responsible for the management of the money he had helped his sibling receive. Lobdell was first removed to the Delaware County poorhouse and from there, on the orders of the superintendent of the poor and certificates signed by two medical doctors, Lobdell was transferred to Willard Insane Asylum in Ovid, New York, in October 1880. The Certificate of Insanity[103] stated Lobdell was insane for the following reasons:

1st: She is uncontrollable, indecent, & immoral and insists on wearing male attire calling herself a huntress.
2nd: She threatens the lives of her companions.
3rd: She does herself violence.

And so the management of Lobdell was transferred from legal containment to incarceration in an insane asylum, where Dr. P.M. Wise studied him, focusing on his gendered appearance and behavior as the manifestations of deviance. Like all other male authorities before him, Wise judged and identified Lobdell on the basis of gender nonconformity, reinforcing the judgment of insanity from the position of psycho-medical authority.[104] "We have no social place for a person who is neither woman nor man" and because such a third sex is not known in Western culture, transgender "violates strong social boundaries."[105] No queer social relationships can form without disturbing the social order because gendering the individual into acknowledged and accepted sexes and behaviors genders society and brings about a sense of order. As a transgendered man, Lobdell threatened the stability of bi-gendered order, especially after gaining a form of legitimacy as a landowner, so he was removed from the third space he created with his body and life and confirmed to a socially sanctioned space of incarceration and restraint within society that rendered him invisible and the public safe. Through the actions and narratives of numerous male authorities creating meaning around Lobdell, definitions of heteronormative normalcy were reinforced by classifying Lobdell as deviant. Traditional, civilized space and gendered spheres were preserved by disallowing Lobdell legitimizing ownership of land or money, and a bi-gender patriarchal balance of power was reestablished by erasing the disruptive energy of the transgendered Other. At age 50, Joseph Israel Lobdell had effectively been eradicated from existence.

• Four •

"A Man in All That the Name Implies"

THE NINETEENTH-CENTURY COMMUNITY surrounding Lobdell viewed his refusal to conform to expected gender presentations and roles as dangerous to the social order built upon traditional understandings of men and women. As a transgendered man, Lobdell disrupted dichotomous categorization of sexed bodies by complicating the traditional assumption that genitals are a clear and truthful indicator of sex. While society viewed him as a person too dangerous for inclusion in society, once incarcerated, sexologists saw him as a specimen to be examined, removing even more subjecthood than did the false obituaries. Rather than expanding concepts, terms, and categories to more accurately reflect a more genderful[1] array of embodiment, sexological authorities developed new terms to explain transgender difference as deviance and frame its meaning from a heteronormative view that positioned Lobdell's gender, sex, and sexuality as mental illness. Lobdell's attempts to name himself and craft an identity from the concepts and terms available at the time were seized first by nineteenth-century psychiatric authorities, and later by twentieth- and twenty-first-century theorists who denied Lobdell's voice and dismissed his words in various exercises of identity piracy grounded in traditional assumptions of sexed bodies. Lobdell's experience reveals the inadequacy and dangers of classifications formed without consideration of the voice of the subject.

Dr. P.M. Wise was the first American sexologist to write about "Lesbian love" in an 1883 article in *Alienist and Neurologist* titled "A Case of Sexual Perversion," which was based on his case study of Lucy Ann Lobdell, who had a "rare form of mental disease."[2] His evaluation was based almost entirely on Lobdell's anatomical sex and gendered behavior, as well as his own ignorance of female desire and sexuality, and selective consideration of Lobdell's own words.

While many writers over the last 50 years have discussed Lobdell as the first lesbian in American medicalized writings, Wise did not label Lobdell *a lesbian*, as a type of person, for concepts about same-sex activities were just starting to be formulated by sexologists, and then focused only on male subjects. Wise's psychological diagnoses of Lobdell, based almost completely on observations of and assumptions about gendered behavior and a skepticism of erotic satisfaction between two female bodies, make for a shaky foundation for a lesbian sexuality, which is understood in the twenty-first century as more complex than unusual gendered behavior and an "odd" attachment between two women. When Lobdell's own words, which repeatedly declare he is a man, are privileged in forming an understanding of his body and sexuality, the label of "lesbian" is completely severed from Lobdell's identity, whether turn-of-the-nineteenth- or twentieth-century understandings of the term are used.

Lobdell was not a lesbian but a transgendered man, and the sexual relationship he had with Marie Perry was not lesbian but a queer form of love and desire that has yet to be named. His physical relationship with his wife, Marie Louise Perry, raises questions about styles of sexuality outside of hetero/homo constructions, which then lead to questions on the nature of female desire for masculinity in intimate partners and how desire is labeled.

The gender violence that began against Lobdell in the nineteenth century carried over into the twentieth century and continues today. An exploration of narratives and scholarly essays about Lobdell in the twentieth and twenty-first centuries shows how writers used nineteenth-century constructions of knowledge based on gender performance and modified them to form new understandings and classifications of sexuality that frame Lobdell as acceptable in an era that views lesbianism more positively. This exploration reveals that while modern writers dismiss sexological definitions of perverse sexuality as ignorant and misguided constructions of knowledge based on heteronormative definitions of normalcy, they likewise rely on traditional, heteronormative concepts and project assumptions about sexed bodies onto Lobdell to shape the meaning they give to their construction of his identity — that of butch lesbian. Those who have written accounts about Lucy Ann Lobdell for familial or historical purposes ignore the issue of sexuality altogether and treat Lobdell as either a passing woman, meaning a woman who passed as a man for the purpose of adventure and economic opportunity, or simply a strong, albeit eccentric, feminist woman ahead of her time.

Such naming and labeling of Lobdell becomes a discursive power play that completely ignores the voice of the subject. The writers of twentieth-century narratives attempt to bring Lobdell out of nineteenth-century condemnation and into identities now recognized as legitimate, but in doing so, they duplicate the same errors that Wise made: they appropriate the authority to identify Lobdell; they privilege the body, specifically the genitals, as the only source of truth; and they privilege the words and concepts of the educated, sexological authority and ignore those of Lobdell himself. While it may have been the intention of these writers to finally grant Lobdell a safe space and legitimate identity, they, too, managed to silence his voice and obscure his transgender. Ironically, their writings reinforce traditional, narrow, binary constructions of sexed bodies and sexuality by insisting that Lobdell is a woman; they allow him either the now-acceptable role of feminist woman or the alternative sexuality of lesbianism, as long as he is imprisoned within dichotomous understandings of the sexed body. The conflation of Lobdell's female anatomy, Wise's classification of him as an invert, and modern misconceptions of him as a lesbian work together to obscure male transgendered history. By rendering his transgenderism invisible, they contain the disruptive power of his body as much as nineteenth-century writers and authorities did.

Privileging Lobdell's voice as an authentic and authoritative source of knowledge and accepting the classification he gave himself as male positions Lobdell as the one who understood the nature of his being, safe within the wilderness, that space that was not controlled by humans or society, that space that granted him the freedom to be who he was. Whenever Lobdell entered civilization, his safety was at risk. While Lobdell was frequently described as wild, it was civilization that was savage, ruled by the laws of the social land that were built around rigid gender and sex constructions that oversimplified and polarized people into two discrete categories of men and women, further restricted by the hetero/homo binary for sexual practices, the understandings of which were based on the genitals of both partners. Civilization was savage in its treatment of Lobdell, who was attacked, mistreated, and stripped of his identity by the law, the general population, his own family, psycho-medical professionals, and writers— both informal and scholarly — of the past 120 years.

This form of transphobic violence also indirectly includes Marie Louise Perry. Historically, the partners of transgendered men have been almost completely dismissed or simply classified as femme lesbians. Marie Louise Perry is one such historic example of invisible trans-queerness. As discussed in the previous chapter, Perry's contemporaries, confused and ignorant of her relationship with Lobdell, dismissed her as odd but harmless, lacking the common sense to return to what they perceived as a better life. Although she repeatedly claimed Joseph as her husband and openly referred to him as a man, her understanding of Lobdell as transgender is not validated any more than Lobdell's claims. Sadly, Perry is often given scant attention in historical writings and only mentioned in modern writings to qualify the label of lesbian layered onto Lobdell, which forces Perry into lesbian classification as well. While Perry's voice was dismissed and ignored in the nineteenth century, it is completely obliterated in the writings of the past 120 years. By keeping Perry's voice inaudible, writers have again rendered Lobdell's transgenderism — and the threat it brings to bigendered social order — nonexistent. This same silencing of Perry's voice also eliminates the disruption that female partners of transgender men create. Not only does their desire for transgendered men challenge the assumed male privilege of sexual access to female bodies, but when that desire is acknowledged as desire for masculinity, it also reinforces the authenticity of transgendered men's embodied masculinity.

The discursive practice of classifying the partners of transgender men as lesbians has worked hand in hand with denying these transgender men a legitimate, visible identity and sexuality that are not based on traditional concepts. An understanding and validation of partners of transgender men needs to be developed, one that recognizes a female desire for masculinity housed in female bodies.

Lobdell is just one example of historic transgendered invisibility. Close study that sifts through sexological writings and case histories for the dismissed and invalidated transgender voice is needed to draw out transgender subjects who have been molded to lesbian and gay classifications. A review of nineteenth- and twentieth-century narratives of people recorded as butch lesbians and women who passed as men would work to further develop the history of transgender men. Because the narratives offered here reveal the erasure of transgenderism, and because study would reveal that the same has been done to transgender women, I argue that there is a need for the historical reclamation of transgender subjects and relationships.

A critique of how writers in the last 120 years have (mis)presented and identified Lobdell and Perry spotlights the problem with labels and identity categories that are formed by those who construct meaning, and therefore truths, from observations and common assumptions while ignoring and disallowing the voices of the experiencing subjects. While Lobdell repeatedly and insistently claimed he was a man, nearly all those writing about him stubbornly categorize him as a woman and, wedding genitals to object of desire, define his relationship with Marie Louise Perry as lesbian. Lobdell is an historic example of trans-invisibility, which can only be remedied by an acknowledgment of transgendered voices, sexualities, and experiences that works to develop a more genderful taxonomy of subjectivity.

During the second half of the nineteenth century, European male doctors developed the field of sexology by combining scientific determinism, social Darwinism, and eugenics. Working from the foundational beliefs that gender was a God-given innate quality in male and female bodies and that the purpose of sexual desire was procreation, sexological pioneers focused their studies on abnormal and perverse sexual practices, those sexual activities outside of and contrary to reproductive sex.[3] In the 1860s, Karl Heinrich Ulrichs presented his theory about same-sex attraction in men, stating he knew first-hand the symptoms and the problems as he himself suffered from the condition. He claimed that one man out of 500 had this condition and he called these men "urnings"—female souls trapped in male bodies, suffering from a hereditary, congenital condition that was not perverse or immoral, but physiological. This condition was presented as distinctly male since Ulrichs, like all sexologists, assumed that women were naturally and passively heterosexual. As an activist for male homosexual civil rights, he argued against Prussian anti-sodomy laws, and in 1864 he published "Vindex," defending urnings as "mental hermaphrodites." The volatile reaction to his philosophies, theories, and publications drove his supporters underground and Ulrichs to exile in Italy.[4]

In 1869 Karl Maria Kerberry campaigned against German anti-sodomy laws and coined the term "homosexual." He agreed with Ulrichs that homosexual desire was innate, but not necessarily effeminate. Also in 1869, Karl Westphal published his theory of sexual inversion, describing effeminate male and masculine female same-sex attraction in *Archiv für Psychiatrie und Nervenkrankheiten*. He agreed that homosexuality was congenital, but pathologized homosexuals as a "defective, degenerate breed" suffering from mental illness, and in need of psychiatric care, not legal persecution.[5]

Assuming that gender expressed a natural inner identity, sexologists established desire and aggression as a natural heterosexual male condition and passivity as a natural attribute and pattern evident in women's gender and sex roles. Because of the Victorian assertion that men were sexually aggressive and women were merely passionless objects of male desire, females who displayed desire for other women were considered to have an unnatural, inverted nature—that of a man. These women were most noticeable when they displayed masculine behaviors and appearances, which were read as an unnatural, and therefore psychologically ill, desire to be *men*, not women who sexually desired other women. This type of sexual inversion was read as a complete reversal of a woman's gender/sex role and defined in terms of gendered—not sexual-behavior.[6] The first psycho-medical analyses of female bodies within same-sex relations examined gendered behavior, as sexual desire in woman was inconceivable.

> Such an assessment of women's sexuality necessarily had fundamental implications for the medical conceptualization of lesbian relations. Indeed, in the context of female passionlessness, there was no place for lesbianism as it is currently understood; if women could not even respond with sexual enthusiasm to the advances of men, how could they possibly stimulate sexual excitement between themselves? In the Victoria system, therefore, a complete inversion or reversal of a woman's sexual character was required for her to act as a lesbian; she had literally to become man-like in her sexual desire.[7]

Although he did not publish his influential book, *Psychopathia Sexualis*, a compendium of sexual perversions intended as a forensic reference for doctors and lawyers, until 1886, Richard von Krafft-Ebbing's influential theories were widely circulated a decade before that date. Most sexological studies had focused on male sexual difference, with scant attention given to women until Krafft-Ebbing's treatment of female sexual difference.

The categories and degrees Krafft-Ebbing developed for female deviance combined sexual, social, and physiological characteristics to form four specific types: women who remained feminine in appearance and behavior but responded to masculine women; women who had a strong desire to wear men's clothes; full inversion, where women assumed a masculine role; and extreme gyandry. This last type of homosexual woman was only recognizable as a woman by her female genitals—all other appearances, actions, and behaviors were those of a man, including a rough, deep voice, masculine features, and a manly walk. Krafft-Ebbing offered preferences for short hair, male attire, and association with men for masculine sports, work, and pastimes as evidence of this type of degeneracy.[8]

According to Carrol Smith-Rosenberg, Krafft-Ebbing focused on behaviors and appearances coded as masculine and enacted by female-bodied persons to link same-sex desire to a rejection of the social expectations of women.

> [He] made gender inversion physiologically manifest. Atavistic throwbacks, the women who "aped" men's roles looked like men. But even more, having rooted social gender in biological sexuality, Krafft-Ebbing proceeded to make dress analogous to gender. Only the abnormal woman would challenge conventional gender distinctions — and by her dress you would know her.... In this way Krafft-Ebbing, through creation of a new medico-sexual subject, the Mannish Lesbian, linked women's rejection of traditional gender roles and their demands for social and economical equality to cross-dressing, sexual perversion, and borderline hermaphroditism.[9]

European doctors developed the field of sexology by using Darwin's method of classification and categorization to chart sexual variations and degrees of perversity. Conventional heteronormative knowledge constructions and binaries of bodies, genders, and desires formed the foundational lens for analysis, positioning masculine men, feminine women, and procreative sex as natural and normal. Through their judgments, writings, and development of taxonomies, sexologists became the storytellers in a new area of knowledge, which fictively contained and controlled sexual threats to social order by naming, defining, and classifying new identities that reinforced traditional categories for legitimate, normal subjects. This process made transgendered bodies virtually invisible, and by the end of the nineteenth century, all difference was construed as sexual and simplified as deviance from conventional forms. Addressing this process of simplification, Lisa Duggan states,

> Multiple variations and meanings were condensed into rigid binary forms of either excess sexuality or inverted gender, "primitive" or overcivilized masculinity and femininity. The production of binaries, and the collapse of sexuality into gender, of difference into deviance, was especially marked in the texts of the new late-nineteenth-century "scientific" sexology.[10]

Through an intersection of physical, psychological, and moral study, these early doctors declared sexual perversions, most especially homosexuality, to be varieties of physiological abnormalities, their congenital degeneracy found in genetic origins, thereby redefining such behaviors and activities as psychological problems. Rather than being immoral acts to be dealt with and punished by clerics or law officials, these issues became conditions that required the knowledge and authority of male sexologists.[11] With the construction of new definitions and classifications, the authority to manage difference moved from law to science.

American doctors, also working from the perspective that established gender categories, traits, and behaviors were natural and normal, built on European theories, but were hampered by distance and translation problems in communication. As a result, the study and development of sexology in America was several years behind that in Europe. By 1880

> [Krafft-Ebbing's] theories concerning the origin and consequences of the sexual perversions were just being picked up and reworked by a handful of medical writers in the United States. Though the concept of "homosexuality" had not yet been clearly developed by these writers (the term itself was first used in an American publication of 1892), a pathological condition (variously named) involving same-sex love and cross-sex behavior was being described in the medical journals for the first time.[12]

Sexology focused on the study and classification of sexual perversions, not cures. According to Carrol Smith-Rosenberg, the goal of sexologists was

> [t]he reassertion of order in a conflicting and changing world. This — not the control of literal sexual behavior — obsessed the sexologists. Within the sexologists' categorical elaborations, perverted behavior did not have to cease. A proxy, it existed to be railed against and thus to give the sexologists a sense of power and reaffirm their faith in their ability to restore order.[13]

Having installed themselves as medical and psychiatric authorities, they were able to reinforce heteronormative categories and definitions of normalcy by reclassifying nonprocreative sexual behaviors and nonconformity to gender classifications as forms of mental illness that must be institutionalized for the sake of both patient and society. All forms of sexual deviance were positioned outside of normalcy; deviant subjects were relegated to the space regulated by state politics, and imagined boundaries and definitions of normalcy were reinforced.

Female inverts — defined by their gendered behavior, not their sexual activities — had been documented in Europe, but not yet in America. Dr. James Kiernan was a disciple of Krafft-Ebbing and America's top sexologist. In 1883 his student, Dr. P.M. Wise, a physician for Willard Insane Asylum, wrote an article for *Alienist and Neurologist* detailing his findings from two years of interviews with, and observations of, his patient, Lucy Ann Lobdell, who suffered from "a rare form of mental disease."[14]

Using Krafft-Ebbing's theories, definitions, and descriptions as guidelines, Wise's analysis focuses on Lobdell's gendered behavior and dismisses his sexual behavior as unsuccessful attempts at being a man, evidence of his inversion. He first notes the nonconformity of Lobdell's gendered appearance as evidence of his illness.

Her voice was coarse and her features were masculine. She was dressed in male attire throughout and declared herself to be a man, giving her name as Joseph Lobdell, a Methodist minister; [she] said she was married and had a wife living. She appeared in good physical health; when admitted, she was in a state of turbulent excitement, but was not confused and gave responsive answers to questions. Her excitement was of an erotic nature and her sexual inclination was perverted. In passing to the ward, she embraced the female attendant in a lewd manner and came near overpowering her before she received assistance. Her conduct on the ward was characterized by the same lascivious conduct, and she made efforts at various times to have sexual intercourse with her associates.[15]

He describes Lobdell's behavior in the ward as lascivious, emphasizing the sexual aggressiveness that belonged to men, declaring it "perverse" in Lobdell, even though such conduct represented mere "efforts," framing such activities as unsuccessful. George Chauncey, Jr., notes that because of the polarization of sexual desire as dominant in men and nonexistent in women, "the perversion described by Wise was not so much in the object of [Lobdell's] sexual desire as in the masculine, aggressive form it took; the woman (Lobdell) had inverted her whole sexual character."[16]

These events became evidence of "paroxysmal attacks of erotomania," the label and diagnosis Wise gave to Lobdell's psychosis. Originally, erotomania referred to love-sickness toward a person of the opposite sex, but the meaning of the term changed. "In the 1892 edition of D. Hack Tuke's authoritative *Dictionary of Psychological Medicine*, 'Erotomania' was defined as a term used for those forms of insanity where there is an intensely morbid desire towards a person of the opposite sex, without sensual passion. Others define it as synonymous with Nymphomania and Satyriasis."[17]

Following patterns of inquiry established by Krafft-Ebbing, Wise notes certain childhood elements as evidence of Lobdell's insanity. Sexologists believed that insanity was often hereditary, and Wise states that Lobdell "inherited an insane history from her mother's antecedents."[18] Lobdell's mother, Sarah, was listed twice in census records as insane.[19] Although details of her insanity are nowhere recorded, no nonconforming gendered behavior was ever noted; however, any form of insanity was believed to have the potential to result in sexual perversion in offspring. Wise also includes an account of Lobdell's youth, offering tomboyism, a characteristic included in virtually all case studies of female inverts, as an early indication of mental instability. "She was peculiar in girlhood, in that she preferred masculine sports and labor; had an aversion to attentions from young men and sought the society of her own sex."[20]

Four • "A Man in All That the Name Implies"

Wise next offers the fact that Lobdell had to be coerced into marrying George Slater as more evidence of illness. "It was after the earnest solicitation of her parents and friends that she consented to marry, in her twentieth year, a man for whom, she has repeatedly stated, she had no affection and from whom she never derived a moment's pleasure, although she endeavored to be a dutiful wife."[21] In addition to his presentation of Lobdell's masculinity as evidence of illness, Wise pathologizes Lobdell's failure to perform expected gender roles and behaviors as mental illness.

Through a confessional style of question-and-answer dialogue, Dr. Wise transforms information on Lobdell's transgender appearance and performance and his sexual peculiarities into diagnoses.

> The confession is a ritual of discourse in which the speaking subject is also the subject of the statement; it is also a ritual that unfolds within a power relationship, for one does not confess without the presence (or virtual presence) of a partner who is not simply the interlocutor but the authority who requires the confession, prescribes and appreciates it, and intervenes in order to judge, punish, forgive, console, and reconcile.[22]

While this obligatory act of speech presents an opportunity for Lobdell to "talk freely about herself and her condition,"[23] Lobdell is not the one to interpret and produce the truth. As the authority at the hospital, Wise listens, interprets, and reports; he thus becomes the storyteller who constructs and presents a narrative of truth about Lobdell. "The one who listened was not simply the forgiving master, the judge who condemned or acquitted; he was the master of truth. His was a hermeneutic function. With regard to the confession, his power was not only to demand it before it was made, or decide what was to follow after it, but also to constitute a discourse of truth on the basis of its decipherment."[24]

Wise understands Lobdell's activities (the ones he selects for inclusion in his study) to be of an erotic nature, though he judges them to be perverse; yet he considers the relationship between Lobdell and Perry beyond understanding. "The attachment [that Lobdell felt for Perry] seemed mutual and, strange as it may seem, led to their leaving their temporary home [in the poorhouse] to commence life in the woods in the relations of husband and wife."[25] Wise notes that when questioning Lobdell, "[she] was quite clear and coherent and she evidently had a vivid recollection of her late 'married life.'"[26] Wise repeatedly states throughout the article that Lobdell is not confused or unintelligible, emphasizing Lobdell's clear-headedness and seeming sanity, yet he clearly doubts the definition of the relationship that Lobdell gives by placing quotation marks around the phrase "married life."

The "vivid recollections" that Lobdell shares with Dr. Wise are of a sexual nature, and although they are clearly stated, Wise expresses disbelief in what he hears. "From this statement it *appears* that she made frequent *attempts* at sexual intercourse with her companion and *believed* them successful; that she *believed* herself to possess virility and the coaptation of a male; that she had not experienced connubial content with her husband, but with her late companion nuptial satisfaction was complete."[27] Wise states that Lobdell believes that sex occurred, but makes his doubt clear by positioning Lobdell's statements as only believable to Lobdell. "Victorian culture believed that sex without men was inconceivable — men were essential to female desire, which was for motherhood."[28]

This article is often cited as the first medical/psychiatric treatment on lesbians in the United States because of the use of the word "Lesbian." But while Wise acknowledges that Lobdell and Perry shared a life together in what he calls "the quiet monotony of this Lesbian love,"[29] he uses the word "Lesbian" as a qualifier of female companionship. His statement that Lobdell suffers from an "abnormal sexual tendency"[30] is attributed to Lobdell's inverted gendered behavior, not homosexual identity. As stated earlier, female inversion was not defined in sexual terms until after the turn of the century, when women's sex roles were somewhat separated from their gender roles, and the bodies of those who were objects of desire were considered in terms of sexual desire.

Wise relied on nineteenth-century dominant discourses on gender, sex, and sexuality to construct Lobdell as a perverse subject. Since Lobdell had a female body with female genitalia, Wise viewed him as a woman whose natural presentation should exhibit femininity, and whose natural inclinations should be a desire for domesticity, family, and a male husband. Wise, and all other sexologists, privileged the genitals as the source of truth in bodies, believing genitals alone determined appropriate gendered behavior, appearances, functions, and desires.

Genitals also determined the function of that body in the sex act. Since procreative sex required penile penetration of the vagina, and women were believed to have no desire, sexologists could not imagine any form of sex between female bodies. "Sex was seen as phallic, by which I mean that, conceptually, sex could only occur in the presence of an imperial and imperious penis."[31] Believing that a penis was essential to sex, they looked for enlarged clitorises on female patients, believing some women, in ignorance and misguided emotion, would attempt to penetrate other women with their oversized clitorises. Wise was unable to conceive of any real act

Four • "A Man in All That the Name Implies"   135

of sex or sexual satisfaction between Lobdell and Perry because there was no phallus involved. Lobdell's assertions and the sexual behaviors at the asylum were aberrations from the procreative norm and, to Wise's thinking, not even possible — therefore, they were insane.

Lisa Duggan explains that deviant sexual practices in women and unnatural emotional attachments "invoked a centuries-old assumption that gender ambiguity in behavior was rooted in ambiguous genitals. Specifically, sexual relations between women were often understood as a cause and/or effect of an enlarged clitoris in at least one of the partners."[32] Wise did declare that Lobdell had "an enlarged clitoris covered by a large relaxed praeputium," about which Lobdell offered more information: "'I may be a woman in one sense, but I have peculiar organs that make me more a man than a woman.' ... She says she has the power to erect this organ in the same way a turtle protrudes its head — her own comparison." Despite two years of observations, Wise was "unable to discover any abnormality of the genitals" other than the enlarged clitoris,[33] and so came no closer to understanding Lobdell's perception of his own sexuality.

Because genitals are also understood to determine sex, even in the twentieth century, Lobdell queered dominant definitions not only of gender but of understandings of the body and sexuality as well. Even though Lobdell was clear and articulate during conversations with Dr. Wise, the doctor could not comprehend what he was hearing because the information did not fit any patterns that he understood as natural and normal, the most basic one being a person with a penis was a man, and a person with a vagina was a woman. Of the two known paradigms available, Lobdell knew he was a man. Using genitals as the sole marker of identity, Wise perceived Lobdell as a woman who suffered from the rejection of womanhood and femininity, even as Lobdell repeatedly told him he was a man.

Wise reports that Lobdell, in his first interview upon entering the asylum, "was not confused and gave responsive answers to questions" and presented himself "dressed in male attire throughout and declared herself to be a man giving her name as Joseph Lobdell."[34] Lobdell explained that even at the time of writing the autobiography he knew he was a man, yet "she did not refer to sexual causes to explain her conduct and mode of life at that time, although she considered herself a man in all that the name implies."[35]

Lobdell was lucid and coherent as he queered dominant understandings of bodies, genders, and desires. His assertions revealed the constructedness of those categories, but because Wise, who adhered to hegemonic truths about those categories, was in a privileged discourse position as a male medical authority, he was the one with power to create the narrative of Lobdell as an insane woman and disseminate it as truth. "The 'truth' that is revealed in [the] process [of confession] is, of course, not found but produced."[36] Considering the repeated report of Lobdell's clear, articulate, lucid conversations with Dr. Wise, I question the diagnosis of insanity and believe Lobdell was framing his relationship with Marie and his understanding of himself in concepts outside Dr. Wise's comprehension.

Wise makes no comments on Lobdell's repeated and reported assertions that he was a man. By deliberately ignoring and dismissing Lobdell's claims of manhood, Wise selectively blends ignorance with information to form his narrative of truth that substantiates his diagnosis of insanity. "Knowledge, after all, is not itself power, although it is the magnetic field of power. Ignorance and opacity collude or compete with knowledge in mobilizing the flows of energy, desire, goods, meanings, persons."[37] Lobdell was a living example that body, gender, and sexuality could not be forced into artificially constructed categories, but Wise used his ignorance, disguised as medical wisdom, to contain the disorder of Lobdell's transgender statement. By countering Lobdell's self-identification as a man with repeated classification as a woman, Wise erased this trans-queer challenge to social order and reinforced the restrictive boundaries of the social body.

While Lobdell received an opportunity to speak freely, his non-normative use of the terms *man*, *husband*, and *wife* granted him no autonomy or success in defining himself as a man. He was in the powerless position of patient and unable to convince authorities to legitimize him as male. "[C]ontests for discursive power can be specified as competitions for the material or rhetorical leverage required to set the terms of, and to profit in some way from, the operations of such an incoherence of definition."[38] The cultural and legal construction of the meaning of Lobdell's transgender as wrong and deviant was passed through a medical lens that reinforced those earlier judgments of Lobdell's difference and simply redefined its context as mental illness, once again reestablishing heteronormative classifications as correct and normal.

By focusing on policing the boundaries of those gendered and sexual behaviors recognized as natural, Wise pathologized the alternatives presented by Lobdell's body and life. By ignoring Lobdell's remarks about being a man, Wise rendered the possibility for a third sex not rooted in genitals invisible and nonexistent. Using his discursive authority as a doctor who published his findings, Wise, as psychiatric storyteller, presented a narrative based "not in [his] command of knowledge, but precisely in [his] ignorance."[39]

Lobdell presented a lived narrative that featured a nontraditional, non-family-based sex, space, body, and sexuality that escaped the conventional binary understandings of body and gender. In his competing narrative that defined Lobdell as insane, Wise reinforced the heteronormative standards that continued to define normalcy, and male privilege, power, and masculinity remained with those bodies with penises.

American sexologists believed that reports on female same-sex desires reflected a condition peculiar to the debauchery in Europe and England, one that did not exist in the United States. In his article, Wise alludes to Westphal's one report of a female case in Germany and Krafft-Ebbing's published analysis of this "anomalous and rare disorder," but declares that Lobdell "possesses little forensic interest, especially in this country, and the case herewith reported is offered as a clinical curiosity in psychiatric medicine."[40] He believes that people like Lobdell are victims of "a pathological condition and a peculiar manifestation of insanity,"[41] one that can't be cured. Dr. Wise's recommendation is "that all such cases be sent to an asylum."[42]

Sexological discussion of female homosexuality did not develop until after Wise's report on Lobdell. In 1895 Havelock Ellis reported in *Alienist and Neurologist* that homosexuality in women was usually an ignorant development of affection between women, encouraged by their close confinement with one another, and difficult to detect because of the common acceptance of female intimacy in friendship.[43] He theorized that such impulses were usually cured when the woman entered into a relationship with a man and subsequent heterosexual education ensued. Those women who accepted the advances of female inverts were usually those women who were "not very attractive to the average man" but "always womanly. One may perhaps say that they are the pick of the women whom the average man would pass by. No doubt this is often the reason why they are open to homosexual advances."[44] Ellis debunks the claims made of the enlarged clitoris, "which has very seldom been found in such cases, and never, so far as I am aware, to an extent that would permit of its use in coitus with another woman."[45]

But his description of the femme presupposes heterosexual rejection and then links her condition to a feminine need for masculinity, which was found in the active invert.

And when they still retain female garments these usually show traits of masculine simplicity, and there is nearly always a disdain for the petty feminine artifices of the toilet. Even when this is not obvious there are all sorts of instinctive gestures and habits which may suggest to female acquaintances the remark that such a person "ought to have been a man." The brusque energetic movements, the attitude of the arms, the direct speech, the inflexions of the voice, the masculine straight forwardness and sense of honor, and especially the attitude towards men, free from any suggestion of either shyness or audacity, will often suggest the underlying psychic abnormality to a keen observer.[46]

Historically, transgenderism has been collapsed into homosexual categories. Because Lobdell is just one such example of hidden transgender subjects, I suggest that this classification of people defined as extreme female inverts needs to be explored for hidden transgendered men.

Through the use of psychoanalysis, which Foucault argues produces a cultural sexuality that maintains a male-dominated power balance, Wise's narrative construction and dissemination of knowledge about Lobdell promotes and validates his authority to render Lobdell invisible, hidden within the walls of the insane asylum. While Foucault focuses on the cultural construction and management of sexuality, his classification of what he called "juridico-discursive" powers parallels the outcome of Wise's analysis of Lobdell, especially when the word *sex* is understood as the physical act and the classification of the body:

> *The cycle of prohibition*: thou shalt not go near, thou shalt not touch, thou shalt not consume, thou shalt not experience pleasure, thou shalt not speak, thou shalt not show thyself; ultimately thou shalt not exist, except in darkness and secrecy. To deal with sex, power employs nothing more than a law of prohibition. Its objective: that sex renounce itself. Its instrument: the threat of punishment that is nothing other than the suppression of sex. Renounce yourself or suffer the penalty of being suppressed; do not appear if you do not want to disappear. Your existence will be maintained only at the cost of your nullification.[47]

Joseph Israel Lobdell was a living example of the dangers of making difference too visible; the price for living openly as a transgendered man was fictive death and secret incarceration away from the world. Lobdell experienced "the violence of the foreclosed life, [as] the one that does not get named as 'living,' the one whose incarceration implies a suspension of life, or a sustained death sentence."[48]

Despite the family's efforts to present Lobdell as dead, in Delaware County, New York, and Honesdale, Pennsylvania, word had spread that the Female Hunter was still alive in a mental hospital, but obituaries constructed from nameless sources reported Lobdell's death again in 1885 in New York and Pennsylvania newspapers.[49] However, Lobdell still lived and was the subject of Dr. James Kiernan's flawed and incorrect — yet influential — reports. Kiernan, Wise's superior, used Wise's case study of Lobdell in lectures and articles he published,[50] but included only part of the information in Wise's writing, along with misquoted information about Lobdell's life, and he also confused Lobdell's youth with one that might be Marie's, resulting in publications rife with inaccurate accounts and pure fiction, yet influential in forming the historical base for lesbian history — these articles are quoted even today.

Perhaps the biggest inaccuracy in Kiernan's report was his declaration that Lobdell had died while in the asylum in 1889.[51] This information appears in histories about Lobdell's life by Woodward, and even in twentieth-century accounts of Lobdell.[52] However, Lobdell had actually been released from Willard that year and two years later in October 1892[53] was admitted into the Binghamton Insane Asylum, where he died in near obscurity May 28, 1912.[54] He was buried in the graveyard at the hospital without a funeral or mourners, and the few family members who knew he was still alive now settled the distribution of his estate.[55] Because of the social stigma of having an insane relative and the embarrassment caused by Lobdell's social disruptions, he was quickly forgotten by his family except as an obscure derogatory term used to label disruptive girls who behaved in unfeminine ways.[56]

Who Is Constructing the Subject?

Judith Butler asks, "If the subject is constructed, then who is constructing the subject?"[57] The meaning given to Lobdell's body, identity, and life changes with various storytellers across the decades. While various people in the nineteenth-century identified Lobdell as a pervert and a deviant — at best, a social disgrace because of his gender presentation — he was identified as a feminist, a passing woman, and a lesbian in the twentieth century.

By the 1990s, some family members openly embraced Lobdell as a strong, feisty woman, presenting narratives of actions and behaviors positioned as revered acts of nonconformity that challenged patriarchal social structures that subordinated women. Others were appalled that such a scandalous ancestor would be discussed at all. Those family members who wrote about Lucy Ann Lobdell treated her as an early feminist hero. In 1996 Ernest James published a short compilation of Lucy's autobiography, several folkloric articles, and a Lobdell family genealogy. His only commentary on Lobdell is this: "Today, Lucy Ann would have been the CEO of a corporation, a well known educator or a politician. Discrimination of the type experienced by Lucy Ann and others like her has been a loss to this great country."[58] While James clearly means to defend and support Lobdell, the phrase "others like her" is vague; it could simply mean feminist women. Any consideration of sexuality or transgenderism is completely obscured.

In *The Echo*, a small newsletter published in Delaware County, New York, by the Basket Historical Society, the area where Lobdell first left home as a man, Susan Crawson Shields, Lucy Ann Lobdell's great-great-granddaughter, shares the story of Lucy Ann as compiled from family lore, legal documents, meticulous genealogical research, a couple of folk histories, and several nineteenth-century newspaper articles. She highlights Lobdell's feminist demands, sensational life "dressed as a man," and wanderings with Marie Perry. While Shields does state that after Lobdell's incarceration at Willard, "a brokenhearted Marie left the area never to be heard of again," there is no clear discussion of Marie as Lobdell's wife or the exact nature of their relationship. "The most interesting fact of Lucy Ann's life, is when one considers where she would stand in todays world. Her view on 'women's lib,' wearing pants, equal wages, etc. would fit right in. Her exploits with Maria Perry would not even make news items in our era. If anything, the fact that she was 'The Female Hunter' would be the most newsworthy item about her. Lucy Ann was merely born 'ahead of her time,' 130 years too soon. A voice crying in the wilderness of things to come?"[59]

In both instances of family writing, all sexuality has been removed from the story and Lobdell is positioned simply as a feminist hero, born before her time, and projected forward to a utopian future when people "like" Lobdell would not simply be accepted, but actually be successful and revered. However, it is unclear what people "like" Lobdell are like; sexuality and transgenderism have been made nonexistent. Yet Shields's words make an intuitive prediction about the boundaries Lobdell did illuminate and shatter.

Fascinated with nineteenth-century historical accounts of Lobdell in Minnesota, Mindy Desens wrote an article for the local Litchfield newsletter.[60] Referring to Lobdell throughout the article as Lucy, Desens explains how, "in disguise," Lobdell, an abandoned, single mother "determined to earn her independence through hard work," ventured to Minnesota to find "well-paying employment." In this romanticized narrative, Desens frames Lobdell as a hard-working, well-liked woman who suffers from being arrested for impersonating a man and is subsequently mistreated by the citizens of Manannah, and then returns home to the heartbreak of finding her daughter adopted out. Unaware of Lobdell's life in Pennsylvania as a wandering hunter or his relationship with Marie, Desens offers up the Minnesota experience as the cause of psychological damage that led to Lobdell's commitment. Presenting Lobdell as "the victim of 19th century society's unwillingness to accept her as she was," she positions Lobdell as a brave and rebellious early feminist, stating that it was "tragic that she lost her own identity in the struggle." Ironically, Desens reads Lobdell's masculinity as unreal and frames his ostracized expulsion from Manannah as defeat and loss in his struggle to form a personal identity.

Because of the efforts of Ellen Dwyer, who "rescued the nineteenth-century casebooks from the basement of the abandoned Chapin building" at the Willard Insane Asylum,[61] Lobdell's story became fodder for academic analysis and inquiry. Theorists, historians, and essayists became the next group of storytellers to grant meaning to Lobdell and his life as they resurrected Lucy Ann Lobdell as the first lesbian in American psycho-medical writing. In their efforts to build a legitimate lesbian history, they sought for what they knew rather than objectively examining difference. By assuming the man/woman binary as a starting point for analysis, these new authorities blinded themselves to Lobdell's transgender and categorized his difference as sexual. Using a twentieth-century hetero-/homosexual binary and its attending concepts and vocabulary (which did not exist in the nineteenth-century), they defined Lobdell's nonconforming behavior as lesbianism and obscured Lobdell's transgenderism. The social construction of sexed bodies as an absolute man/woman dichotomy is compounded by its connection to the construction of sexuality as an absolute dichotomy of hetero-/homosexuality.

Because categories of sexuality are constructed in historically and culturally specific ways, epistemological elements complicate the analysis of past sexualities and embodiments. Judith Halberstam states that

> lesbian scholarship ... has generally understood same-sex nineteenth-century and early-twentieth-century desire as either in the model of romantic friendship or along the lines of mannish identification. It now seems highly likely, however, that many other models existed beyond the either-or proposition of

an asexual friendship or a butch-femme sexual dynamic. Indeed, before the emergence of what we now understand as "lesbian" identities, same-sex desire worked through any number of different channels, including the Tribade and The Female Husband.[62]

Problematically, twentieth-century writers used the term *lesbian* in its modern context, a meaning distilled from decades of various female gender and sexual experiences, expressions, and lifestyles that resist heteronormative constructs. They also assumed that both female bodies in a relationship identified as women, and thereby automatically classified both Lobdell and Perry as lesbian. But Lobdell did not identify as a woman and repeatedly declared he was a man to family, community members, legal officials, and his doctor, despite the trouble it brought to his life.

Claiming the position of authority, twentieth-century writers moved subjects out of psycho-medical jurisdiction, and used new concepts and classifications that validated homosexual identity, but they tended to read all difference simplistically within these new terms, concepts, and binaries. Crafting narratives about historical lesbians, writers used these new vocabularies and concepts, dismissed Lobdell's words, and focused on an interpretation of the relationship between his body and Marie's meant to be liberating, but which once again erased his transgenderism. Lobdell's words were no defense against his automatic classification as a woman by those who, basing their conclusions in traditional assumptions that genitals determine sexed identity, became the new gatekeepers of truth and meaning.

Jonathan Katz uses the files from Willard to discuss, at some length, Lucy Ann Lobdell as a nineteenth-century passing woman. He advises that

> since the old ways of viewing such [passing] women are confused and clouded by outmoded, limiting preconceptions, labels, and stereotypes, the reports of these lives should be read carefully and closely, with an open mind and a fresh eye for meaningful detail.... Examination of these passing women's lives exposes the historically relative character of "masculinity" and "femininity," helping to reveal the person behind the stereotype, the human actor behind the role, as well as the socially conditioned character of role and stereotype.... Despite their masculine masquerade, the females considered here [in this chapter on passing women] can be understood not as imitation men, but as real women, women who refused to accept the traditional, socially assigned fate of their sex, women whose particular revolt took the form of passing as men.[63]

Ironically, even within his deliberate attempt to understand and present Lobdell outside of traditional, gendered concepts, and despite the fact that he includes the entirety of Wise's article, Katz falls victim to his own "limiting preconceptions" and is the first twentieth-century writer to ignore

Lobdell's insistence that he was a man, and classify Lobdell merely as a feminist lesbian within the category of passing women.

> The key to understanding Lobdell's difficulties and later decline into madness seems to lie in the conflict of this assertive, intelligent, proud female with that behavior her society declared proper and improper for women. As a feminist, Lobdell early pushed against these social restraints and limiting definitions, a woman finally trapped and doomed by her inability to work her way free of them.[64]

Katz also validates Wise's diagnosis of Lobdell as insane and in his *Almanac* states that "in an earlier age, the mental disturbance and threatening behavior of an individual like Lucy Ann Lobdell might have been ignored, or managed by local religious or legal authorities."[65] Lobdell was, indeed, a feminist, but I believe he did work his way free of social restraints and limiting definitions, which made him extremely dangerous to society. Lobdell's gender behavior was viewed as "threatening" and he was managed by legal and psycho-medical authorities; his consequent incarceration was more evidence of society's fearful move to restore order than true diagnosis of mental illness.

Lobdell's conflict with the society around him was obvious, but his conflict with twentieth-century academics and theorists is not. Katz presents Lobdell as a tragic subject, "doomed" by "her" own inability to either reconcile gender identity and expression with normalizing presentations and enactments or successfully rise above them, a disability that led directly to madness. I suggest that the diagnosis of insanity is based more on an acute and severe case of transphobic anxiety suffered by the civilization around him than Lobdell's actual frame of mind. To preserve order and patriarchal power structures, society needed to eliminate Lobdell's challenge to bi-gendered, bi-sexed social constructions of identity. No doubt years of incarceration in a madhouse had the potential to drive Lobdell past sanity.

In "Making Sexual History: Obsessions of a Quarter Century," an article written for the Winter 2003 edition of *CLAGSnews*, a publication for the Center of Lesbian and Gay Studies at the City University of New York, Katz shares his own experience of finding nineteenth- and twentieth-century case histories and creating a compilation from these hidden stories that would help recover a gay and lesbian past. While his classification of Lobdell as a lesbian was merely inferred within the contexts of his previous discussions, he clearly identifies him as such in this article:

> Documented tales of women who dressed and passed as men, and had sexual affairs with women, showed how women's history and feminism were illuminated by the documents of "lesbian" history. (One of those "Passing Women," Lucy Ann Lobdell, the first to be labeled a "lesbian" in an 1883 American medical journal, was also called "The Female Hunter of Long Eddy," after a small town in Sullivan County, New York, a county ... to which I'll return.)[66]

Katz projects the modern concept of lesbianism onto Wise's archaic use of the phrase "Lesbian love" and obscures the ignorance and misconceptions that attended its use with Lobdell. In trying to help people find a voice and a legitimate past as lesbian, he continues to deny Lobdell's transgenderism, obscuring it as he cites the very source that makes it clearly visible.

Scholarly writers discussing nineteenth-century passing women make it clear that passing did not automatically mean these women were lesbian, but it did mean they were women disguising themselves as men for the purpose of gaining male advantage to mobility, male spaces, employment, and financial opportunities. Several include Lobdell as a passing woman and focus solely on Lobdell's wandering adventures and desire to do men's work for men's wages, rendering his transgender and its threat to social order completely invisible.[67] "The idea of counterfeiting [passing], then both reduces male impersonation to an economic opportunity and collapses it into the phenomenon of social climbing. In other words, if male impersonation can be safely explained in terms of economic advantage, then the gender crisis it also names can be avoided."[68] And if passing is seen as merely masquerading as men, it also denies authenticity to female masculinity.

In *Odd Girls and Twilight Lovers: A History of Lesbian Life in Twentieth-Century America* and *Surpassing the Love of Men*, Lillian Faderman discusses Lucy Ann Lobdell merely as an example of an early transvestite feminist and offers no discussion of Lobdell's sexuality despite the context of her books. In the *Encyclopedia of Lesbian, Gay, Bisexual and Transgender History in America*, Faderman's entry on Lobdell states that

> Lucy Ann Lobdell has the distinction of being one of the first subjects of an American medical article on female-female sexual relations, Dr. P.M. Wise's "Case of Sexual Perversion" (1883). Lobdell, a nineteenth-century crossdresser, would perhaps have dubbed herself "transgender" had she lived in the modern era.[69]

Despite the nod to transgender identity, she insists on referring to Lobdell as *she*, *her*, and *Lucy*, identifying him as a woman, disregarding

Four • "A Man in All That the Name Implies" 145

the label she herself offers, and rendering his transgenderism invisible, or, at the very least, unimportant and somehow not real enough to acknowledge him as a man.[70] Faderman acknowledges that people who see themselves "trapped in the bodies" of the opposite sex "usually consider themselves 'transsexual' rather than lesbian, and modern medical technology has even permitted them to choose to alter their sex to be consonant with their self image."[71] Yet she consistently does not acknowledge Lobdell's transgender.

When sexuality is a component of the discussion around Lobdell, he is framed as a lesbian. Carrol Smith-Rosenberg offers Lucy Ann Lobdell as a nineteenth-century example of a transvestite lesbian who called "herself" Reverend Joseph Israel Lobdell. As proof of Lobdell's lesbianism, she cites Wise's article as "the first American article on lesbianism."[72] In her book *Sapphic Slashers*, Lisa Duggan analyzes how nineteenth-century newspaper articles on same-sex female love and relationships presented difference in the form of the dangerous female. The inclusion of Lobdell as one such woman sensationalized by the press implies a lesbian identity for Lobdell, obscuring his transgender.

Electronic storytellers of numerous websites offer Lucy Ann Lobdell as a nineteenth-century example of a passing woman, cross-dressing to find greater earning potential and opportunity disguised as a man, an act that also allowed "her" to live as female husband to "her" wife. These sites list Lucy Ann Lobdell as an historical lesbian, often claiming her as the first woman recognized as such by medical authorities.[73] Some even offer Lobdell as the etymological source for the word "lesbian" as it is used today. One site, GLBT Terminology, states, "It is unclear just how long the term 'lesbian' has actually been in use in reference to homosexual women, but it appeared in this context for the first time in 1883, in an article about the crossdressing Lucy Ann Lobdell in the *Alienist and Neurologist* medical journal."[74] These websites show a lack of thorough research into or informed understanding of the birth and development of modern lesbian identity. The same information is obviously borrowed and passed from site to site, often word for word, and the forced classification of Lobdell as a lesbian woman works to keep his transgender hidden and nonexistent.

For these writers, traditional understandings of the sexed body "are reinforced by the Western sex-gender code that links anatomical sex to gender identity and gender role to erotic object of desire ... and in dominant U.S. culture, gender identity and sexual preference remain fused to biological sex."[75] In all these presentations and interpretations of Lobdell's life, not once is his conscious understanding and presentation of himself as a man validated. Writers presume the authority to define and classify him based on his genitals alone, obscuring his masculinity and the full potential of the disruptive power of his transgender body and life. Many also pick and choose which of Lobdell's words to use in their classification of Lobdell as a lesbian woman, granting validity to Lobdell's feminist arguments and open relationship with Marie Perry, but ignoring completely his words pertaining to himself as "a man in all that the name implies."[76] Acknowledging Lobdell's self-defining words as legitimate markers of his identity places him accurately in transgender — not lesbian — history and casts completely different meanings on his life, his incarcerations, and his relationship with Marie. "Transgender history should allow the gender ambiguous to speak; too often ... the histories of women who pass as men or the narratives of transgender men attempt to rationalize rather than represent transgender lives in the glory of all their contradictions."[77]

All discussion of Lobdell as a cross-dressing passing woman is invalid. Early (twentieth-century) definitions of nineteenth-century passing women describe them as women who dressed as men for the purpose of seeking greater advantages in mobility and economic opportunities as well as social freedoms reserved for men, often including intimate relationships with women. Their male appearances were merely a disguise that enabled them to gain unrestricted access to the public male world of opportunity. Lobdell offers this very reason in the autobiography and, however logical it may have sounded in the feminist argument of the narrative, it was still a dangerous statement in 1855, but not nearly as dangerous as the truth he confessed to Dr. Wise, that he considered himself a man at that time. Despite the argument that male attire would make life for an ambitious woman easier, his experiences in Bethany and Minnesota brought only moderate financial success and a great deal of trouble and loss. After meeting Marie, Lobdell only rarely found employment as a menial laborer on rural farms and he avoided seeking employment in towns. The majority of the time, he and Marie voluntarily lived as vagrants, outside of society, surviving poverty by building shelters in the woods and living off the land.

Dressing in male clothes to create a safe opportunity to be with women certainly was not effective for Lobdell, considering the violent responses from citizens of Bethany and Manannah when he was exposed. After meeting Marie, he did not enjoy anonymity for very long. Once his female body was discovered in the jail in Stroudsburg, Lobdell became the

Four • "A Man in All That the Name Implies" 147

subject of scandal and rumor. Word spread quickly from town to town, and law officials kept each other posted about Lobdell. The exploits and lifestyle of the Female Hunter were well known and written about widely; the *New York Times* alone published three stories about Lobdell, and he was a frequent subject in local newspaper narratives, which continually revealed the connection between Lucy and Joe Lobdell. Often Lobdell and Perry were scorned for their relationship, their marriage mocked by the use of derisive words. Lobdell was regularly arrested for vagrancy upon entering Honesdale, although Marie was not, and many attempts were made to force him into female clothing, suggesting that Lobdell's transgender was being punished — not his homelessness. Wearing men's clothes did not give Lobdell any amount of advantage, privacy, or secrecy, only hardship, whereas adopting female clothes would have eliminated public curiosity and fear and legal harassment.

As much attention as Lobdell's hunting and other masculine activities drew, women who hunted and did farm work were not rare in poor, rural areas, especially if they were widows.[78] As long as they dressed in somewhat feminine clothes and maintained that they were women, they drew only passing notice. If Lobdell's only motivation had been a relationship with a woman, he could have avoided a great deal of the conflict he experienced after being exposed by changing back into women's clothes and not identifying as a man. As stated earlier, society experienced a general ignorance about female sexuality and had no understanding of relationships that today would be referred to as lesbian. Female romantic friendships were encouraged and viewed as appropriate, even laudable. Lobdell could have lived as Lucy Ann in relative safety and obscurity with Marie as a couple of widows — perhaps eccentric, but not insane.

Lobdell's stubborn insistence on presenting himself as a man despite the trouble and mistreatment he received in doing so proves he was not merely an opportunistic passing woman. Lobdell insisted on wearing men's clothes and living as a man not because he was a butch lesbian, but because he identified as male. The only descriptive imagery given in his autobiography is a male one. The inclusion of Talmage's detailed description of Lobdell can be read as an artistic rendering of his self-image — that of a man. Lobdell's naked rage in the Honesdale jail cell was uncharacteristic and occurred when yet another attempt was made to force him into women's clothes. Wearing female clothing was unbearable for Lobdell, even just long enough to escape legal trouble. Lobdell did not use male attire as a method of creating and sustaining a disguise that would allow him to have an intimate life with Marie; he presented as a man because he identified as a man. Transgendered people "are motivated by the desire to be themselves."[79] Lobdell wore men's clothes because he identified as male and did so years before any of his known relationships with women.

> [Transgendered people] consistently and publicly express an ongoing commitment to their claimed gender identities through the same visual representational strategies used by others to signify that gender. [Transgenderists express their identities] through a non-corporeal change in public gender expression that is nevertheless more complex than a simple change of clothes.[80]

Those who persist in naming Lobdell a lesbian reveal either incomplete researching efforts or their own inability to understand people outside the man/woman, male/female binaries, even when they warn others not to allow their thinking to get caught in restrictive, artificial, dichotomous constructions. While it is true that Lobdell openly acknowledged Marie as his wife while they were together and even afterward, and boldly stated the sexual satisfaction he found in his relationship with her to Dr. Wise, he also repeatedly stated to everyone that he was a man "in all that the name implies."[81]

In contrast, Lobdell claimed male identity openly throughout his adult life and attempted to reconcile the absence of a penis by explaining to Dr. Wise that while "I may be a woman in one sense, I have peculiar organs that make me more a man than a woman" because his clitoris could grow "the same way a turtle protrudes its head."[82] Transgender identity is based on how one relates to one's self, and for decades Lobdell adamantly rejected female identification and repeatedly insisted that he was a man, lived a male identity, and assumed the role of male husband in his relationship with Marie, despite the trouble it brought to his life.

While the complete absence of Marie Louise Perry, or else her presentation as merely Lobdell's faithful friend, in writings that position Lobdell simply as a folkloric hero denies Lobdell's sexuality altogether, the forced placement of Perry into a lesbian category compounds the erasure of Lobdell's transgender by making trans-queer sexuality invisible. Often, Perry is used merely as a qualifier for Lobdell's assigned lesbianism; little is mentioned of her and she is tacitly presented also as a lesbian because of her female body. In the writings of Katz and Duggan there is no discussion of Marie other than what can be found within quoted material, such as newspaper articles and sexologists' reports. Faderman does not

Four • "A Man in All That the Name Implies"   149

mention Marie at all and Smith-Rosenberg gives only a short discussion of Marie as Lobdell's faithful wife.

Marie's acceptance of Lobdell as a man queers contemporary understandings of lesbian relationships. Discussions of homosexuality rely on the assumption that there are only two sexes. "One of the dangers involved in an exclusive consideration of heterosexuality and homosexuality is that of neglecting the diversity of sexual and gender positions available."[83] The acknowledgment of transgender complicates the meaning of the emotional and sexual interaction of two biological female bodies. Discussion and analysis of the Lobdell/Perry relationship through the use of limited and limiting vocabularies, definitions, and concepts eliminates the possible categories that queer same-sex classifications. Rendering trans-queerness invisible also denies an understanding of sexuality outside of contemporary binaries of sex and gender, and, of course, the threat such knowledge constructions would have on established classifications of lesbianism. Acknowledging Marie Perry's trans-queerness challenges classification of her as the femme partner in a lesbian relationship. "Through the transgression of loving someone who is differently gendered ... it is possible for someone who does not appear to be a gender outlaw to become one."[84] Acknowledging Perry's trans-queerness, along with Lobdell's, opens a path of exploration into new concepts and possibilities as it helps to legitimize transgender identity and sexuality.

In contrast to the theorists who have persistently classified Lobdell as a passing woman and lesbian, John M. Sloop of Vanderbilt University has argued that Lobdell belongs as a historical subject in the transgender canon.

> Of attempts to hoist identities onto others, or to deny identities to others that they adapted or may have chosen for themselves, Eve Sedgwick warns that, "To alienate conclusively, definitionally, from anyone on any theoretical ground the authority to describe and name their own sexual desire is a terribly consequential seizure." When we are dealing with a corpse, especially one with so little discursive record from which to speak, the ability to arrange such a seizure is perhaps easier while the consequences, especially for those still "in the flesh," is no less severe. Indeed, whether it be an historical case such as [Lobdell's], or a more contemporary one, we are well advised to be wary of the ways in which critics and historians remember the corpse, using concepts such as denial, repression, fear, or internalized shame, in ways that, as C. Jacob Hale argues, "tend to dismiss the agency of the subject once animated in that dead flesh." Moreover, and perhaps more importantly, such dismissals of identificatory categories often marginalize or culturally devalue positions claimed by the animated subject for all others who would wish to identify with it.[85]

Sloop examines the ways Lobdell and his relationship with Marie have been disciplined into contemporary definitions, categories, and classifications, and also analyzes the effects of the filtering and altering of Lobdell's identity by twentieth-century writers. He likewise explores the possible motives for identity piracy and the consequent results of a wrongful addition to lesbian history and the occlusion of transgendered history.

The collective appropriation of Lobdell's identity as a lunatic, an invert, a passing woman, an early feminist woman, and a lesbian has occluded his transgender, his own claims to manhood, and a trans-queer sexuality outside the hetero-/homosexuality binary, for it creates inauthentic definitions and classifications for him. The accretion of pirated identities forms various artificial, fictive figures that are held up in place of the authentic person. The nineteenth-century constructions of identities for Lobdell show him to be a less-than-human Other, outside of natural constructs, mentally diseased and unfit to live in society, a form of monster with the subversive potential to destabilize social order.

Twentieth-century authorities fashioned identities for Lobdell that more closely resemble a golem, an animated monster created entirely from lifeless material. Through narrative creation, writers have layered their own meanings onto Lobdell's body and fashioned him as a feminist hero or lesbian model while denying the life and identity that Lobdell persistently lived. Medieval legends tell about ancient holy men who created golems who would work for them, "motivated by a charm, a Shem, or paper inscribed with one of the names of God. This charm was placed in the mouth or inserted into the head of the inert mass, which thereafter could move about and obey commands until the Shem was removed."[86] Once the paper was removed from the golem's mouth, it would crumble back to dust.

Many twentieth-century writers have used Lobdell like a golem, faultily crafting an empty persona and imprinting meaning on a passive, lifeless surface that would help them create narratives about passing women and lesbians. When Lobdell's voice is reestablished, these fictive identity constructions fall away, creating a path to explore transgender identity, sexuality, and history. As transgender embodiment queers contemporary sex, sexuality, and gender binaries, Lobdell's transgender still carries the power of the original definition of monster:

> "Monster" is derived from the Latin noun *monstrum*, "a divine portent," itself formed on the root of the verb *monere*, "to warn." It came to refer to living things of anomalous shape or structure, or to fabulous creatures like the

Four • "A Man in All That the Name Implies"   151

sphinx who were composed of strikingly incongruous parts, because the ancients considered the appearance of such beings to be a sign of some impending supernatural event. Monsters, like angels, functioned as messengers and heralds of the extraordinary. They served to announce impending revelation, saying, in effect, "Pay attention; something of profound importance is happening."[87]

This view positions the disruption transgendered bodies and sexualities bring to traditional binaries as emancipatory, dislodging genitals as the sole criteria for determining gender, sex, and sexuality.

> Lately, however, a more radical change has occurred. Some transgender theorists and activists have begun to insist that the binary model is hopelessly flawed and needs to be abandoned. They argue not only for an increased fluidity, but want to have gender unhooked from genitals and speak of a "rainbow" of gender. There is no good reason, they say, why the accident of being born with a penis or a vagina should prevent one from fully experiencing what life is like as a woman or a man.[88]

Transgenderists queer the established binary categories of man/woman, highlight the gap between heterosexuality and homosexuality, and point out the need to examine what and who have been excluded from that binary. As Foucault has stated, social identities are effects of ways knowledge is constructed and organized, so the acknowledgment of transgendered sexes and sexualities that already exist will form new legitimate classifications that challenge heterosexual norms without being homosexual. "In this process, bisexual and transgender identities can become viable cultural possibilities, and a broad-based political coalition established."[89]

Traditional binaries, all based in traditional gender dynamics, keep power relations in place by offering only two positions within classifications, and no matter what the specific binary is, the positions are dominant/subordinate, more value/less value. Transgender has the potential to rupture the social constructions of gender and sex and open a path to that third space of subjectivity. Such freedom and enlightenment granted by new concepts requires development of new definitions and vocabularies that acknowledge the third space between the polar opposites of man/woman and masculine/feminine. "In order to think in new ways about gender issues like transsexualism and transgenderism we need a new language reflective of that thinking."[90]

Judith Butler states that identity categories are oppressive structures that artificially lock people into restrictive spaces, yet are liberatory when new ones contest the restrictions of that very oppression. So they are troublesome but still necessary. "Sex radicals and social constructionists such as Gayle Rubin, Jeffrey Escoffier and Pat Califia argue that conceptually separating gender from sex is crucial for understanding the sociopolitical meanings of sex and gender. By fusing sex, gender identity and sexual preference, Western gender ideology denies human variability and choice and advances biological determinism."[91] Acknowledging transgenderism as legitimate opens the possibility of making forms of difference that already exist outside traditional binaries visible. Foucault states that "particular forms of knowledge, and the ways of being that they engender, become 'naturalized,' in culturally and historically specific ways."[92] But first those forms of knowledge must be established by making difference visible through new ways of categorizing.

While Judith Halberstam recognizes that "no system of classification can successfully catalogue or explain the infinite vagaries of human diversity," she argues for the production of new taxonomies,[93] what Eve K. Sedgwick calls "nonce taxonomies."[94] For this new development to reflect a third space authentically, subjects within it need to name themselves. Bornstein learned "from working in the Women's Movement that one of the first steps in claiming power is to speak one's own voice: to name oneself."[95] And when transgenderists name themselves, they seize the power to claim legitimate, natural, healthy identities as they break open stagnant, restrictive, artificial binaries. Mackenzie argues that "by rejecting medical definitions and categorizations that stigmatize [transgenderists] as having a 'psychological disorder,' transsexuals and transgenderists can shift the emphasis from a personal 'disorder' to a cultural 'disorder.' This shift forms the nucleus of the Gender Movement."[96]

Bornstein imagines a gender revolution set in motion by third-space subjects who make visible a plethora of variable genders, thereby forcing social recognition and acceptance of gender variance as they free everyone from gender oppression. She believes "it's up to each transgressively gendered person to create a space for this life as Third."[97] Of course, certain dangers come with living openly as transgendered due to inevitable social prejudices and biases, and so not everyone is willing to make their life a political statement. But for those who are, like Joseph Israel Lobdell, their voices need to be heard and their transgender needs to be acknowledged as legitimate.

"The current gender system relies heavily on everyone's agreement that it's inflexible."[98] Opening up the gender binary to register all gender expressions and identities requires the visibility of third-space subjects.

> Indeed, it may be precisely through practices which underscore disidentification with those regulatory norms by which sexual difference is materialized

Four • *"A Man in All That the Name Implies"*   153

that both feminist and queer politics are mobilized. Such collective disidentifications can facilitate a reconceptualization of which bodies matter, and which bodies are yet to emerge as critical matters of concern.[99]

Acknowledging Joseph Israel Lobdell as an historic transgender man would work to bolster and legitimize the development of such third-space subjects.

In light of the monumental effort it took to contain Lobdell's disruptive energy and threat to heteronormative social constructs, the dominant power structures and institutions do not appear to have been victorious. Incarcerated but never corrected or cured, Lobdell lived his life stubbornly insisting he was a man and persistently declaring Marie was his wife, resistant to all social, legal, and medical authorities that held control over him. Consciously defying established power, uncontrollably subversive, Lobdell's body became "something that smacks of revolt, or promised freedom, of the coming age of a different law"; not ruled by fear of ridicule or legal restraints, he embodied "revolution and happiness; or revolution and a different body, one that is newer and more beautiful; or indeed, revolution and pleasure."[100] Placing Lobdell within transgender history heals the disjuncture between Lobdell's self-knowledge and twentieth-century writers' interpretations of him and his life and sexuality as it adds to a transgender foundation.

Appendix A:
Narrative of Lucy Ann Lobdell, the Female Hunter of Delaware and Sullivan Counties, N.Y.

NEW YORK:
PUBLISHED FOR THE AUTHORESS
1855

NARRATIVE

PART ONE

Many of my readers will no doubt recollect some of the persons and places referred to in this little book, and as they pass over the record of my strange destiny, many of the incidents will seem almost impossible; yet in this, as in most other cases, truth is stranger than fiction.

My father and mother, James and Sarah Lobdell, were born in the town of Westerlo, Albany county, New-York. They had been married but about two years, when a little daughter blessed their union. This little innocent was born but to bloom for a few short months upon earth, before her Heavenly Father called her to himself. It may be the earthly parents loved the child too fondly, with too exclusive devotion, and God took away their idol. She had just begun to lisp the endearing words — Father!

Mother! — just budded in infantile beauty and sportiveness, when the stern mandate was issued; and disease attacked the delicate frame; the bright eyes grew dim; the prattling tongue was stilled; the merry laugh was changed to that of silence which the last trumpet only shall break.

She was two years, one month, and ten days old when she died. The only child — it was a bitter bereavement, and the parents sorrowed as those without hope. Not for a long period could they be resigned to this terrible affliction, and with humble faith say, They will, O Lord, not mine be done! Yet time brought it accustomed consolations, and they learned to think more that the loved one was present in heaven, and less that it was lost to earth.

I was the second child of my parents, and was born December 2, 1829. I was named Lucy Ann. As I was the only living child, it is not strange that I became their pet — almost spoiled child. Well, years passed over my infant head, and at length memory began to show signs of an existence. And now for an incident, here and there, as that fateful friend may bring before me those happy days of youth. When care was a stranger, I was ofttimes strolling the little wood that was but a short distance from my home, and oft did I get lost chasing and searching for the little Robin red-breast as she warbled her lays at morn and eve; and, now and then, stopping to cull the wild flowers that thronged my pleasant pathway, till tired and weary, I sank upon some mossy spot, and cried myself to sleep. But, by and by, I would be awakened by the call of my distressed mother; and away I would hurry to answer the summons, and gladden the heart of that fond one. But at length mother bethought herself of tying a bell on the little truant, and then her ear was gladdened by that tell-tale of my retreat. Time passes, and I hurry to my fourteenth year, and again find an observation. I was then at school, and possessed a temperament which made me foremost in mischief as well as in study. My delight in each was about equal. I was ever and anon trying to get my lesson, and at the same time, thinking and acting mischief together. I would frequently contrive, during the hours of study, to read from another book, which I would conceal from the teacher's eye, and still have my lesson more perfect than half the scholars who were more studious, but less vivacious.

It happened one night I was at a spelling class that my train of thought was to take a different direction, for after school was dismissed, a Mr. William Smith asked to see me safe home. I at once took his offered arm, and away we tripped homeward, chatting and laughing at some foolish remark we might mistake for wit and sentiment. We at length were getting to be the objects of remark, as day after day passed in its turn; and we arranged the business of almost every day so as to have an interview, which we would ofttimes while away in telling and laughing over the news of the day. But at length, father began to look after and into my love affairs, as he termed them; at the same time, he said I must discard Mr. Smith at once. To this, I answered nothing, but resolved to tell Mr. Smith father's commands, as soon as I should have an opportunity, which, by and by, soon came around. When I had told the story to him, he said father had no right to control or do as he had said. I, of course, was of the same opinion; and we soon found that we were in love, and vowed that nothing should or could be done to separate us. We, however, concluded to see each other no more for the present, for we had agreed to open a correspondence. As Mr. Smith's father lived in a tenant house of my father's, which was about a quarter of a mile from that in which we lived, it need surprise none that I received letters from Mr. Smith frequently, for Mr. Smith passed our door every morning, and our chosen post-office was under a large stone which was concealed beneath a large clump of May rose-bushes; so we corresponded in that way for a long time. But those things were destined to take a turn — the long concealed plans and letters were tale-bearers to a third and fourth persons. One day, I was going to make an afternoon's call, and as I was busy getting off, I accidentally left my key in the trunk which held those letters from the sight of any and all except the author and myself. After I had gone, my key was discovered by my sisters Mary and Sarah, who were just wise enough to take a survey of my trunk and its contents. The result, of course, was the discovery of a dozen or more love-letters; and all our sorrows and complaints became known. My sisters deeply sympathized with and pitied me, which roused my pride; and the result was, I got sick of the idea of loving Mr. Smith.

I will leave Mr. Smith for a while, and introduce a Mr. St. John to the reader. He was one of my old school-mates. And one day, in the fall of the year, after school was closed, Mr. Smith and myself had accidentally met at a Mr. Stone's, at whose house I had called for the purpose of buying and carrying some very choice plums home to mother. As I knew that I should be reported to my parents if I should say a word or act in any way as if on friendly terms with Mr. Smith, I took it into my head to appear as cool as possible toward him that afternoon, hoping he would leave before I did, or not go home when I did at all events; but I was disappointed, for as soon as I started for home, he walked along with me, and wished to carry my plums for me. I refused, and we walked on a little way and met Mr. St. John. He was riding for his health; and as he saw me carrying my plums, he offered to go back and carry them home. I told him it was but a little way, and I had already refused Mr. Smith's politeness, and turned to proceed on my homeward course, when he called to me, and said he had heard some news, and would, in a few days, call at my home and tell me the same. I bid him do so, and then walked on. Mr. Smith, in the meantime, had waited and heard all. I reached home in a few minutes, and then told mother all the news, and she finally said I was a good girl.

In a few days, I received a letter from Mr. Smith offering me his heart and hand in marriage, and requesting a positive and final answer. I accordingly penned a word in reply; told him I was not my own mistress yet, and as I was too young, I must be silent as to a part I felt I was not yet fitted to act. In a few days, Mr. St. John called, and said he had heard I was going to be married to Mr. Smith, and this is what he had heard and wished to tell me. I told him I thought there was a mistake somewhere, as I was ignorant as yet of any such thing. His keen eye was bent toward me as I made this reply; and I saw in that gaze a look that still seems to be written on the pages of the heart, and never can be forgotten. I can scarce analyze, now, the impression that look made upon me. Hope, fear, love, death — all seem to be blended in wild confusion as I recall that interview. I seemed to see a strange and gloomy future. I felt, when in the presence of Mr. St. John, an unusually gloomy and restless spirit, for upon that fair, young brow and cheek were written, as with a pen of fire, the marks of Consumption! Days and months passed, and, by and by, came that messenger, Death, and tore from my young heart my loved, beautiful one, and they laid him away beneath the cold ground! My heart had found its kindred spirit, but that spirit had soared away and found its mansion on high. I could not yet follow; I must wait till I, too, am called, and then I may find that loved one, and be at rest for ever!

About two years passed away, and I found I must apply my mind to exercises that would banish care and grief from its presence. I struggled with life's uneven way, and in a few years, I became acquainted with a George Washington Slater. He appeared an innocent sort of a boy; and as he was quite agreeable, I kept his company for some five or six months; and as I one night came home and found him there, I began talking and telling him that I should be obliged to discard him, as father was not willing that I should have any thing more to say to him whatever. As I turned away, I saw that all was not well with Mr. Slater, for, as pale as death, he stood partly leaning against the wall, watching me as I was talking with my cousin, A. Lobdell. I at length found myself alone with Mr. Slater, and I almost trembled to meet his pale countenance, for I felt such a pity for the poor fellow that I arose from my seat, and walked to where he was standing, and asked him what made him look so very pale. He made no reply, and I then took hold of his arm, and asked again what made him look so dejected and cold towards me. I met those sorrowful eyes bent upon mine with a pity which I mistook for love; he pressed me to his beating heart, and a sigh escaped from his lips which marked and told that story that the tongue refused to utter. He again pressed me to his heaving bosom, and imprinted a wild kiss upon my brow, and told me a tale of how he loved; how he loved without one hope; how he had struggled to be free; and how vain was it for him to endeavor to forget me. I told him I would see him once more, and he tore himself away with a half hope; for it seemed to me as if a strange power, a wild and dizzy dram, bade me tell him I might and would allow him to visit me once more. He came again, and I saw a fever racking and torturing his frame. My father said he was love-sick, and tauntingly told me I had better have him, as he might die, or I might be disappointed, if, indeed, I was not despairing already. I left his presence, and walked into the other room where Mr. Slater was, and told him he had better try and get down to Mr. Hallock's, where he had spoken of going, for I well knew my father would rejoice if he died. He then arose, and went reeling away; and as I saw his retreating figure slowly lost to view, I wondered if he could bear the pain and anxious pity I then felt for him. Night came, and at nine o'clock, I retired to my bed-room, but not to sleep, for the God that made me gave me a tender heart, and nerved me with a daring spirit; I therefore waited until all was quiet, and then arose and dressed myself in my brother's clothes, stole out of my bedroom window, and went to the stable, and took one of father's horses, and away I rode to learn what had become of Mr. Slater. I at length learned his whereabouts, without being discovered, for I saw some one was up in a room about five miles from my home. I at once alighted, and looked in at a window, and saw Mr. Slater and some one standing beside his bed that appeared to be a doctor. I then left and ran to where I had tied my horse, and jumped upon his back with a lighter heart than I had when I dismounted, for I felt that some kind hand would aid and take care of him. When I got within a half a mile of home, it commenced raining very hard, and I got as wet as I could. I was in a pickle as to what I should do to dry brother's clothes; I therefore built a fire in the parlor, ad told mother when she asked me what I was doing, that I felt sick, and was going to take a dose of hemlock tea to get in a sweat; so when the tea was boiling, and I had got warmed, and enjoying a perspiration, I felt quite well, and brother's clothes were quite dry. I then retired, and soon forgot all my anxieties and trouble. I awoke the next morning, and the sun's beautiful rays spoke in warm whispers, not to be misinterpreted, of its Maker, God! When I appeared before my mirror, I learned how much an adventure added health and beauty to the cheek. But in about a week, I think, Mr. Slater came to father's again, and he looked so pale and weak that I asked him to stop over night, for if, indeed, father meant and was determined to cross my way, he should have a privilege. Mr. Slater informed me he had been under the doctor's care since he left me last; how he had broke his fever, and how very sick he had been. I went out into the kitchen, and put over the tea kettle to get him some tea, for he said he had hardly eaten anything since he had been ill. I, after a long time, coaxed him to eat some of my cookies, and at last I prevailed. We were in the sitting-room alone, and brother came in and saw me combing Mr. Slater's hair, and arranging it in its most usual way; for, reader, I pitied him because he had no home — no kind mother to comfort, or sister to care for him; they all were scattered over the cold-hearted world; his father was a drunkard, and long ago had left him; and thus poor George had no home. I, under these circumstances, resolved to be his friend, if I was driven from my father's house the next moment.

I will now attempt to give the reader a description of his person and report among the sons of men. He was rather tall, and of a slender form; his hair of a jet black, and eyes of deep blue, and of an ordinary size; and as I looked upon him, I saw his eyes were clouded with sadness, and his pale, white forehead looked beautiful, but care-worn. I gazed in wonder upon one so beautiful, so innocent, and yet an outcast. He had heretofore had the name of being very industrious and cunning, which I knew was true to the letter. I felt I knew not how; but, in other words, that I was forming an acquaintance with Mr. Slater that I might repent if not carefully looked after. I therefore made up my mind to leave home, and go to a school then in Coxsackie, Green county, N.Y. I think it was in the month of June that I left off going to our District school, and prepared to go to Coxsackie, but before I left, I was expecting to see Mr. Slater again; I accordingly waited until after he came before I should settle the question. Well, at length the day came, and with it, true to his courage, came Mr. Slater. When father saw him coming in, I hurried him into the parlor, for fear he would say something to wound the feelings of George; but it seemed I was not destined to get off in this way, for in about an hour, father walked into the room with a paper in his hand, and sat down and commenced reading. I saw a sneering glance was, now and then, sent toward me and Mr. Slater. I arose in a few minutes and left the room, and very soon after, Mr. Slater followed suit; and as the moon, that bright sister of the night, was looking down upon the earth in all her splendor, I put on my shawl and bonnet, and asked Mr. Slater to take a walk with me just out in the door-yard. He accompanied me, and I then told him I was going to Coxsackie to school, and thought it would be best to break off all our keeping company together, for I felt that father was each day growing more bitter against him. I told him to try to see if he could not love some other more than me, for I knew that I was the first lady that had kept his company. One thing I should have stated in its proper place, that is, when Mr. Slater first came to our house to pay me a visit, I asked father if I had better receive his addresses; he said, yes; for, he said, if you treat him well, he will feel himself somebody, and, perhaps, grow to fill a respectable station; for, he said, he behaves well for one so young. The consequence of my obedience the reader has half read. Mr. Slater said he would abide by what I thought was best. I then prepared to go to school at Coxsackie; and, in a few days, things had taken a change, and I was at school.

Well, time passed slowly away, and I had not heard one syllable from my George since I left home. I passed through many little adventures while stopping there, and became acquainted with but few, as I had but little relish for society, except some particular friends that I there became acquainted with, by the introduction of my aunt, with whom I was stopping. I received a letter one day from home, wishing me to come and make them a visit. I accordingly penned a reply, and told them when I could come. I at length went home, as I had appointed, and staid a week or two. I did not inquire for one whom I expected to hear from, nor did I hear a word about him. I could not bear to look around, for the old familiar scenes revived recollections of pleasant walks, merry tales, and innocent sports, in the company of one whom I could no longer see. The charm was gone while the charmer was absent. Memory of the old times made the present distasteful. I could not bear to stay there, and so I went back again sooner than I had expected when I started to go home. Father wrote and said if I wanted to live at Coxsackie he would sell out and buy there, if I wanted him to. I wrote him a letter and told him I was not going to stay there, and I at the same time told him of lands that were selling very cheap in Delaware and Sullivan Counties, and concluded by telling him a dream I had about the Delaware. I received a letter a short time after, stating father had offered his place for sale and was going a viewing in Delaware and Sullivan Counties with the intent of purchasing a place, if he found any to suit him. I was pleased to hear this, and wrote to father I would go with him if he purchased. In a few days brother came after me and told me father had gone a viewing; and so I went home again, and in three weeks I was living in Delaware County, with father, mother, sisters, and brother.

I had been there but about a month or so when Mr. Slater came there, and all our former acquaintance was renewed. I then knew it was my time to talk to father in regard to Mr. Slater. I told him my design for coming into the woods was to avoid him. I told my father he first told me to stay with George, and then, when I had won his heart, bade me break it. I told him my heart had no joy in him, for my early love was no more, and his dear remains were mouldering back to their mother earth; and as George was a good workman, and an innocent boy, I had told him I would have him if I could get your consent. This news seemed to sink deep in his heart, and he said he was afraid Mr. Slater would not use me well if I should have him. And he said he wanted me to wait till the next fall, and then if I wished to marry Mr. Slater he would consent. I told him I would wait and was in no hurry to get married, if Mr. Slater was willing. He then said he would hire him to work for him and then I would have a chance to learn more of his true character. I told George what father had said, and asked him if he would not wait. He said he had come to marry me, as I had promised, and did not wish to wait. And to cut the story short, we were married, and father and mother had given their consent. It was too late now to repent or retrace my steps, nor did I wish to; for a while things went on very well, it seemed to all appearance, and I too late learned Mr. Slater's disposition.

It at length happened that a Methodist meeting was going to be held about two miles from our house, and as I wished to attend that I might learn the quality of preaching in the woods, Mr. Slater went with me, and after the preacher had finished his sermon, he said he was willing to preach again if any one sinner wished or would rise to have the brethren pray for him. At the end of this remark Mr. Slater rose, to intimate his desire to be remembered. I also rose on seeing his wish to become a Christian. They then appointed a meeting the next evening, and we went again the next night, and they had an anxious seat, so called, for the inquirers to occupy that evening. I believe four others came forward and expressed a desire to get religion; and it seemed as if a revival had commenced at once. Those meetings continued for some two or three weeks, and at the end of that time Mr. Slater, myself, and twenty or more others, experienced and professed religion.

As the ministers had visited our house very frequently I had become quite a curious person for them to talk with, as my sentiments varied from theirs with regard to their belief very much. But they finally prevailed on us to have our names set on their class book; and as it happened one day, the preachers were both at our house, and I was telling and expressing my ideas as nearly as I possibly could, when Mr. Slater said he felt very much indisposed, and withdrew, and walked up to the chamber bed-room and laid down. I soon followed him and inquired if he did not feel any better. He said he did not, but affirmed his belief that he was going to die. I asked him what in the world had made him think so? He could give no reasons, I saw, but seemed and appeared as very strange. He then wished me to promise, if he died, that I would not marry again. I would not make a promise of so unusual and selfish a bearing. I laughed at him a little, and told him to go to sleep, and I thought he would feel better. I told him he was a strange boy, and coaxed him to try to sleep. He at length said he would, and I went down stairs again. It happened that when he came down he was quite well, but appeared very cold towards me, and behaved very differently from his usual manner. Well, it happened the next Sunday that we went up to meeting, and after meeting we went over with Doctor Hale and his lady (a cousin of mine). As we went to go home, we promised to visit them some appointed evening that I do not now recollect, but we fulfilled our appointment, at least; and as the subject of religion arose for our discourse, Dr. Hale remarked that I was going ahead of the preacher in speaking at meetings; and he said he thought I did wrong in speaking after nine o'clock in meetings. At this Mr. Slater began, and said I was going to leave him, and going off with the Dominie to help him preach. I made no reply to this false assertion, but took up the Bible, then on the stand before me, and opened and read aloud the sixth verse of the eighteenth chapter of St. Matthew, for it was the first sentence that met my eye as I opened the Bible, which read thus: "But whoso shall offend one of these little ones which believe in me, it were better for him that a millstone were hanged about his neck, and that he were drowned in the depths of the sea." I read no further, but commenced weeping, for I felt that that woe might be dealt on the heads of my cousin and companion, for a great deal that they had said I have not given place here — it is not my nature to afflict the afflicted. But truth must come if indeed I say anything; and now we will look and see where Mr. Hale is, and how he felt after talking to me as he did. It happened that we staid (George and myself,) all night with them, and as I got up in the morning I saw that Mr. Hale was worried about something, and at last he came to me and asked me to forgive him, "for," said he, "I have slept but little all night fearing I had wounded your feelings." I told him I could forgive him if my Heavenly Father could. But whether God has forgiven him or not is not in my power to say. But in a short time the news came to me that Doctor Hale was crazy, and soon after he was sent to the asylum at Utica. He appears to be quite rational at times, but he is there now at the asylum, a poor crazy being.

I will attempt to follow Mr. Slater's proceedings. After my school had closed, (for I was teaching a district school at that time,) Mr. Slater and myself moved from our folks about two miles, I think in the month of March, for he had hired to work for a Mr. LaValley, and so we lived in a tenant house of his. As Mr. LaValley had a saw-mill opposite our house, Mr. Slater told me that Mr. Edwin Allen, the sawyer, wanted to board with us, and as he said he should have to be gone all day while he worked for Mr. LaValley, I would not be so lonesome if Mr. Allen was there at his meals three times a day. I told him it put me to a great deal of inconvenience to board but one hand, as I should be at as much confinement in getting regular meals as though I had a dozen boarders; but however, if he wished me to do so, I would board him. So, in April, I think, Mr. Allen came to board, as Mr. Slater said we had ought to accommodate him. As I had a violin, and played it quite often, Mr. Allen, after a little acquaintance, would occasionally ask me to play a tune for him. I would sometimes play, as I did not wish to show any respect to persons, for when night came round Mr. Slater would come home with some half a dozen hands from Mr. LaValley's, and then he would get the violin and wish me to play. I would play, of course, but after a while I put my violin into the wood stove, for I had no relish for the society it was bringing. This did not suit Mr. Slater at all, and he said he would get another. I told him I would not play any more for a gang of card-players and swearers. He ripped out an oath, and said I could as I pleased. In the meantime Mr. Allen was there, and as George came from his work he would begin some of his vulgar talk, and because I did not notice him or his speaking, he would appear sulky, and say but little, perhaps, the whole evening. Mr. Allen was a professor of religion, and we would converse together on some topic of a different character from the low one Mr. Slater had announced.

Things were permitted to go on in this style but a little while before I understood Mr. Slater's proceedings quite well; for he came home one day and said he was going to the depot store to get some tobacco, and should probably be back in a few hours, unless he went to our folks' house, and then he would stay all night. Night came, but no Mr. Slater, so I went to bed at about ten o'clock, for Mr. Allen had set up and been down to Mr. LaValley's to see if Mr. Slater had not got back as far as there, for it was in the time of a freshet, and the creek was very high, and he did not know but Mr. Slater might have found the bridge gone away, and in attempting to get round to the other road have been lost in the woods, as it was a dark, foggy afternoon and night. I felt worried, and after I had gone to bed I kept awake and could not sleep. It was about two o'clock, I should suppose, when Mr. Slater came in, with a lantern in his hand, and he came directly to my bed and asked me where Mr. Allen was. I told him that Mr. Allen and a cousin, Mr. Smith, were upstairs in bed. I made no inquiries as to the reason of his first question, singular as it was, only asked if anything had happened, or if he wanted Mr. Allen. He said no; and I dropped the subject as if nothing unusual was contained in the question. He soon came to bed, and I pretended to be very sleepy, for I saw and felt by his actions something was brewing. He at length began and said I had got so I would not speak to him now-a-days, if Mr. Allen was present. He said he had to work like a d — d slave now-a-days, and that I had got tired of him. I told him Mr. Allen must be dismissed in the morning, as I would board him no longer. He hardly knew what to say to this reply, and he said as Mr. Allen's time was almost out I should say nothing to him, as people would think it strange if he went away. I said it was strange, and as I had wronged him so much by not talking with him, and entering upon a subject I knew nothing about, as I had not been in the habit of talking on so unlearned a subject, I should not practice the art before Mr. Allen, and I accordingly heard no more about it that night, and when I awoke in the morning Mr. Slater had gone to his work. I know not what he thought, but I concluded he thought I would say nothing to Mr. Allen of his talk; but he was disappointed if he did, for I had told Mr. Allen previous to that night that I believed Mr. Slater was jealous of his being there, as I had learned by a great many unguarded remarks Mr. Slater had made; and now the actions of the preceding night spoke louder than words. Mr. Allen accordingly left boarding at our house right away. And now I will pass over a few months and give place to the last story while I lived with Mr. Slater.

In the month of September, 1852, I was over to my father's one Sunday, and a cousin of mine, a Miss Helen LaValley, from Delhi, Delaware County, N.Y., was at Mr. Roderik LaValley's, where Mr. Slater worked, on a visit, and she came with me the night before to our folks', and while we were there a Mr. Chandaler came to our house with a Mr. Thomas Smith, a cousin of mine, and a half brother to the Mr. Wm. F. Smith, my first gallant, as the reader will recollect in the first part of my history. Mr. Chandaler, it appeared, came to our folks' for the purpose of inviting them, brother and sisters, to a quilting at Mr. Taylor's, some three or four miles from our folks'. He also gave Miss LaValley and myself an invitation, and told me to invite Mr. Slater to a bee on the same afternoon, at Mr. Taylor's, as the gentlemen had a bee as well as the ladies, and then in the evening they were going to have a dance. I told him if Mr. Slater would come I did not know but I would, as Miss LaValley was a stranger in the place, and said she would not go without [me], and [as] the quilting was to be that week, Friday, I had time to arrange matters in that respect. Thursday at length came round, and in the morning I asked Mr. Slater if he was going to the bee the next day. He said he was, and said he was going to wait on a Miss Yandes, and that I would have to get some one to wait me if I went, for he had told me a few days before that I must go with Miss LaValley, as she wished, as she was a stranger in the place, and a cousin. So, about noon Miss LaValley came up from Mr. R. LaValley's and said Mr. Slater was going the next day to the afternoon party, and as she had some errand over to Mr. John Spirbeck's, she wanted to go with her and stay all night, as Mr. Slater had given his consent; and as it was but a little way from father's I could go there in the afternoon, and then ride with brother and sisters, as they were going as far as Mr. Chandaler's with their team. I told Miss LaValley I had no objections, and could go as well as not, as I was alone and had nothing to see to but Mr. Slater. She accordingly went back to Mr. LaValley's and fixed and came along for me about five o'clock. I went with her to Mr. Spirbeck's and stopped over night, and in the morning I went down to father's and waited till it was time to start for the quilting. Brother got up his ponies after dinner and drove up to Mr. Spirbeck's after Miss LaValley. They came back in a few minutes, and sisters and myself were waiting and ready to go.

Now we will take one look at the party. Some forty or fifty ladies, both young and old, had about finished the quilting operations when we arrived, and we therefore got there just in time for tea. We had an elegant supper — as good as the county was able to scare up. As I did not see Mr.

Slater appear, I began to conclude something was wrong and out of tune somewhere. But I was not long to be kept in conjectures, for a Mr. Buell Smith, a half brother to Mr. William F. Smith, who was working at Mr. R. LaValley's, came to me and asked how I enjoyed myself. I told him as well as I had anticipated. I then asked him if Mr. Slater had come; he said no. I asked him if he was coming; he replied in the negative, and said Mr. Slater told him he had not at any time intended to go; and that he said he did not intend to go when he told me he was going; "for," said he, "Mr. Slater said he wanted to make a fool of you just for the fun of it." I then felt he had some design in getting me to come, so I felt a little annoyed for a few moments, and then dismissed the matter and joined in the dance.

Well, in the course of the evening a gentleman asked me if I would play then a tune on a violin. I told him I would try; so the violin was brought, and all appeared to be [at] attention, and I played some two or three tunes for the party. I received their acknowledgements, and then excused myself from playing more that evening, and the party broke up at a dark hour, which was just before day; and as it was about a mile or over to Mr. Chandaler's, he walked with me, and brother and Miss LaValley was with us in going to Mr. Chandaler's, across lots about a quarter of a mile to the railroad. We at length reached Mr. Chandaler's, and by the time brother's ponies were ready, it began to be daylight. Miss LaValley and myself were to stop at Mr. Yandes' and wait till Mr. B. Smith came along with Mr. LaValley's team, as he passed there drawing lumber, and then, when he came back, we rode up as far as Mr. LaValley's. I them went home, as it was but a little way from Mr. LaValley's. I had been home but a few minutes before Mr. Slater came in. He began to tell me he had heard I had a beau last night, and that I had played the violin for the company. I told him that as he did not come, I had a right to engage an escort; and as I had been his tool for a fool, he could hardly make it appear I had done anything but what he had intended me to do. At this he began to curse and rave like a demon; he at length stopped a minute, as I had remained silent, and asked when I was going to have another spree. I answered, I thought I should go to father's that afternoon, as it was a pleasant day, and Saturday too. He replied, he did not care where I went, if I went to hell; and after he had got through he went back to work again, and I went down to Mr. LaValley's, and told Cousin Almira and Helen how Mr. Slater had acted, in part, and she cried, and told me she would not live and bear so much of him. She, Helen, then told me what he had said at the dinner table. He said he had given five dollars to be married, and that he would give five or ten more to be unmarried, which was a mistake; for he told me before I was married that he had some considerable money coming to him out at Westerlo, and that he could not get it when he left, as it was not then due; so finding he had no money to pay the marriage fee, I told him brother would arrange and attend to those matters. I told brother, as I handed him some cash, to settle the marriage fee when we were married, which he did; and that was the way Mr. Slater paid the five dollars to be married. And, again, that amount he spoke of at Westerlo, I never heard or saw any thing of it whatever afterward. But again to my story.

Miss Helen said I must stop with her till morning, and then she would go over to father's with me; and so I staid at Mr. LaValley's till after tea, and then George came in, and I told him what I had heard. He made no reply to it, but said I had better come along home with him, and stop my noise. I told him I had promised to stay at Mr. LaValley's that night with Helen, which I did, for I was afraid to go back with him. That night I dreamed Mr. Slater stuck a knife into my side, which caused a great deal of blood to run from the wound. I dreamed I saw the blood roll down, drop by drop, which I have since found interpreted to the letter.

I went with cousin the next day to Mr. Smith's, the father of Mr. William F. Smith. As he is a second husband to mother's sister, I told her what had happened, and she said Peter (for that was her husband's given name) told her, when he came last night, he knew I would get a blast from Slater, for he had been to work that afternoon with him threshing buckwheat. I asked no questions as to what had been said, for I well knew Peter was an enemy of mine since I had refused to marry his son, William. While I was there, brother came in, and wanted to know where we were going. I told him I had started to go to father's, so he went back with us, for he had started to go to my house. When I got home, I told our folks how Mr. Slater had conducted himself in part; that I was afraid to live with him any longer. Brother said I should not go back any more, but might live with him the next summer, as he was going to build a house on his land, and then I should keep house for him; but father said I had better try and live with Mr. Slater since I was married to him. I told him I would try and do as he said, if he would let me move my things over and live at his house; for I told him that the house where we lived would not be fit to live in the coming winter, as it was so open and cold. He said I could move over if Mr. Slater would agree to it. So, in a few days, I rode over home to see how things got along. I found my house in confusion and shame. It appeared that Mr. Slater had been there, as I afterward learned, and got some of the neighbors to see what a wasteful and mean housekeeper I was; and to make this a point of shame, he had, that Saturday night I stayed at Mr. LaValley's, went and made a fire and cooked some rice which he burned on the kettle; and as the next day was Sunday, he cooked some more in another kettle or spider, and then [ate] from all the dishes he could find, and left them all dirty, and looking anything but decent for the neighbors to see and charge me. He had also milked the cow, and got the milk arranged in a manner to suit his time of inspection. He had not had the cow but a few days, but it afterwards, as you shall hear, helped him to make out his stories to my friends in Westerlo.

Well, when I saw Mr. Slater at Mr. LaValley's that day, I found that he was willing to move me over home; so he went back with me, and drove the cow to father's, and stayed all night, and the next day he took father's oxen, and moved one load of things home. He then said he should be coming over there on Saturday, and he could move the rest by hand. It happened to be rainy after that for a few days, and George came over to our house, and he and brother went up to a Mr. John Gearse's to get some beef he ordered. When they came back it was in the night, and as it was very dark, they had got lost in the woods, and it was after nine o'clock before they found their way home. After they got home, mother cooked some beef for their supper; and as it rained now and then the next day, Mr. Slater stayed there, and was tormenting and laughing to see me cry, and mother was watching to see what he would do and say till, at length, she could bear no more, and she told him to leave her house instantly, and not to darken her door again till he could make up his mind to treat me a little better than a brute. He obeyed, and took some of his clothes with him, and went to Mr. LaValley's, and told a few stories of how he had been misused by the whole family, which was false as it was told fair. He came over again on Sunday, and Mr. Thomas Smith and Mr. John Chandaler with him. He asked me for his clothes, and I got them for him; and when he got out of the door, he spoke and said he would give me his cow. I said, "Why George, are you going off?" He said he did not know but that he should. I then said, "Well, if you go, be a good boy;" and that was the last I saw of him till the next spring. After I heard that Mr. Slater had gone, I wrote a letter to my uncle, Truman Ingalls, who was living in Westerlo, as I supposed he would be likely to go there as any where. I will here give the reader a copy of the same:

Hancock, Monday, Oct. 24th, 1852

Respected Uncle:

You will no doubt hear the story of Mr. Slater if he comes to Westerlo, as he has left this place in rather queer circumstances. Last Saturday, I have been informed, he left Mr. LaValley's for Westerlo, or California, or parts unknown, without saying a word to me as to where he was going. I wish you to ascertain, if he comes to Westerlo, why he left, and, if possible, ascertain his complaints, as his actions go to show that there must be some cause for his leaving. Mr. Woolcoot came here, and told father that he had bought a cow which Mr. Slater gave me a few days before he left, and that he had paid Mr. Slater for the same. He drove her away a little while ago. George has moved me over to father's, and so I did not know what was going on; and he has left me without any thing to live on, except one bushel and a half of potatoes; and now as the cow has gone, I hardly know what to do; and as I expect ere long to become a mother, it seems to me that the Lord will prepare a place of rest in heaven for me — a poor, forsaken child; and I almost feel the assurance that He will take me to a place of rest ere long; and were I deprived of this hope, I, of all creatures, should be most miserable!

Please answer this as soon as you can, and let me know whether you have heard anything in regard to Mr. Slater's departure or complaints.

P.S. — Be sure to have his statements entire, that justice and truth may yet triumph, and the guilty learn that there is a God that protects the widow.

Yours, respectfully,

L.A. Slater

In a short time, I received the following answer, which I copy here also:

Westerlo, Oct. 30th, 1852

Mrs. Slater:

We received your letter day before yesterday, and in answer to your inquiry, George W. Slater arrived in this vicinity last Sabbath, and staid at Gardener Udell's that night. Mrs. Udell was here on Thursday, and told us the reasons he had assigned for his leaving you. The first and most serious charge was, that you went to sprees, and had other men to wait upon you at home. Another was, that you would not do anything; that he had got a cow, and you would not milk it, or take care of anything; and also another, that your whole family misused him [in] the worst way. These are the most prominent reasons that he assigned. He said that he had done all that he could do to live; that you had seventy dollars of his wages and a cow. Another reason of his leaving you I should have stated in its proper place — that your family had driven him off; and he also stated that he thought if you was entirely away from your folks, he might possibly live with you. Buel has written a letter to Mr. Martin, stating that your family has misused Mr. Slater very much, the truth of which is best known to yourselves; and if you have taken any unjustifiable course with Mr. Slater, you alone will have to suffer the consequences. But I think you may congratulate yourself very much in that you have lived as long with him. You have exceeded my most sanguine expectations; and you may well feel consoled that you are no worse off, for it is easier to take care of one than a half dozen children. Bought wit is the best when not bought too dear; and now I know of no better way than to make the best of it, and to profit in the future, from the past lest a worse thing befall you.

Yours, with due respect,
T. Ingalls.

P. S.—Mr. Slater was at Smith Lamb's on Thursday. He bought a jewharp and some hair-oil; he had candles with him. So it goes, and so on, and so on.

This, reader, was the answer I received from my uncle. It so happens that I have a book-account of all the money Mr. Slater let me have, which was just ten cents, and that I took to pay the postage of his sister's letter. He commenced work at Mr. LaValley's on Tuesday, February 14th, 1852, and was to have fourteen dollars per month and left the place the 23d of October, 1852. But [he] lost over a month's work while at Mr. LaValley's, and I wonder where the seventy dollars of his wages came from, that he said I had. I will tell you what became of his money—it went in a like manner, or similar one, that the cow did, and some of my things that he was going to move over to father's by hand—some were sold, and some given to Peter Smith, Esq., by George W. Slater; and as I have a book-account of all the articles bought by Mr. Slater for me, it amounts to something less than five dollars, and turns out to be less that the marriage fees he paid for; and as father has a book-account of the provisions he let us have when Mr. Allen was boarding with us, I imagine Mr. Allen paid the wrong man for his board when he paid Mr. Slater, as he told me he had paid him for his board; and this, gentlemen and ladies, is a sketch, here and there, of the treatment I received at the hands of a jealous husband. And has anyone been guilty of setting Mr. Slater up? If so, they will be cursed for it. We read in the Holy Book, "Cursed is he that parteth man and wife." Has Mr. Smith had a word of news to tell Mr. Slater? If so, when Mr. Slater left, why did Mr. William F. Smith come and see me right away, almost, and say he knew I could not live with Mr. Slater, and tell mother if I ever went to live with Mr. Slater again to horse-whip me; and why did he send a letter to me, which I shall copy here for the reader to judge:

Coxsackie, May 24th, 1858

Mrs. Lucy A. Slater:

I must style you so, if I once thought otherwise. I often think of the pleasure that I have taken when I had the happiness of your sweet company.

Although it has been a long time since you and I took comfort together, and those days have passed and gone, still my mind often wanders back to by-gone days. I have often thought of a union between you and I; but the Lord has so seen fit that we shall never enjoy each other's troubles. You must write as soon as you receive this. Direct to William F. Smith, Coxsackie.

From one that will ever stand your friend as long as there is a drop of warm blood running in his veins.

My love, to you, from your most affectionate friend,

William F. Smith.
Lucy A. Slater.

P.S.— Remember, love, remember!

William F. Smith.
Lucy A. Slater.

And, now, where do we hear Mr. William Smith is? We hear that he is sick and in a distant land, and among strangers; and as he has no money, he writes for his father to send him some; and we hear again that his father wrote to his dying boy that he could not help him; and we hear that Mr. P. Smith has yet another son who joined the United States Dragoon Company, and went to California. That son has deserted, as he is not yet of age. We hear that Mr. P. Smith has a cancer that is speaking in tones not to be misunderstood, "Prepare to meet thy God!" Does it appear that any one has been "accursed" for sin? If so, these words are being fulfilled— "Vengeance is mine, saith the Lord, and I will repay." And, now, reader, how think you I struggle with so much sorrow and disappointment. I lean upon the promises of the Great Jehovah; I can say, "Thy will, not mine, O Lord, be done." I have a clear conscience, and feel that if this earthly tabernacle of mine should be dissolved, I have "a building of God, a house not made with hands, eternal in the heavens!"

PART II

I am now going to relate some hunting stories; how I first was induced to learn to shoot.

I was in my tenth or twelfth year when I had the charge of some hundred chickens, turkeys, and geese, that I used to raise and sell, and then I had half the money I made in that business and in tending the dairy; and so when I went to Coxsackie, I had money I had made in raising calves and poultry to pay for my schooling, and all the expenses I incurred in going to school. In consequence of my keeping poultry, I learned to shoot the hawk, the weasel, the mink, and even down to the rat; so after I had moved to father's, and Mr. Slater had gone away, I used often to go hunting to drive care and sorrow away; for when I was upon the mountain's brow, chasing the wild deer, it was exciting for me; and as times were hard, and provisions high, I was often asked by father, who had become decrepi[t], if I could not go and shoot him some venison, as he was obliged to stop hunting. I used to feel sorry to see my poor father so lame, and hear him ask me to shoot him some deer. I at length put on a hunting suit in pursuit of some meat.

Our little store of meat was almost exhausted, and I had hunted some length of time with but little success, till one morning I heard mother say we were quite out of meat; and when I had got ready to go hunting, I felt rather discouraged. So I wandered up the mountain that morning, without expecting to see any thing, as usual, but as I got upon the top, I heard a stick crack, and I stopped and looked this way and then that, but could see nothing; so I started to go in the direction I had heard the noise. As I started, I saw a deer running as fast as it could jump; so I ran, too, for some twenty rods or more, after it, and then stopped to see if I could see anything of the deer. I looked about a hundred yards, and I saw a fawn coming towards me; so I got behind a log, and took aim at it, but the rifle did not go off; so I looked and saw that there was no powder in the tube. I primed her, and by that time the deer had got nearer to me; so I crept up to a log that was between myself and the deer, and took aim, and the rifle went off, and so did the deer. I began to think that I should have to coax the deer to me next time, and hold the rifle against him in order to kill him. But I was not permitted to laugh at my stupid and wild shot long before I saw the deer drop down. I loaded my rifle again, and walked up to him. I saw he was dead; and close beside him, I knelt down, and offered up a prayer of thankfulness to my Heavenly Father that he had not forgot my toil from day to day, but had provided as we had luck. This was the first deer that I had the fortune to kill, and thus I had not got into the spirit of hunting much.

I recollect one night I was going to watch my deer-lick, and as it was a beautiful night for watching, a bright moonlight, I went up the mountain just before dark, and as I had a place of concealment, I sat there waiting for the deer. I had been there but a little while before I heard the bushes crack somewhat to the left of where I sat; so I kept as still as possible, and waited for the deer to come nearer. I at length heard one stamp, and then blow; I knew at once that they had smelled my track when I came up the mountain, and so I kept as still as possible and waited a little while. I had heard it thunder some length of time, but did not think that I was going to get caught out upon the mountain at night, and get lost. As I sat there listening to the concert of the deer, it, on a sudden, began to grow dark; I turned to look at the moon, and saw it was just going under some dark clouds then over my head. I jumped up to see if a shower was at hand, and saw a sharp flash of lightning that showed too plainly that I was swamped. I therefore started in the direction of the house, and as it began to sprinkle, I hurried along as fast as possible. In my hurry, I mistook my course, and instead of going east went north. It was very dark; I kept one hand before my eyes to ward off the bushes, and my rifle served as a cane to measure my steps down the mountain. I at length thought I was using rather a dangerous staff, as the lock might catch in a bush and go off; so I fired the contents I had destined for a deer into the forest. The report reached the ears of mother, and she told our folks I was lost, for I appeared to be north of the house almost. In the meantime, I was slowly feeling my way down, as I supposed, to the creek that passes our door; but I found myself mistake, for I came into a chopping, and, now and then, I found myself entangled in a brush-heap. I finally concluded I had got out on a creek that came from a pine swamp a little north of our house — some two miles. So I followed the stream down, and I could see, now and then, by the flashes of lightning, that I was going to have a time of it; so I hurried as fast as the darkness would permit, and at length I conceived I was within call of the house, so I gave a wild whoop some half a dozen times, and then listened for an answer from the house. In a few minutes, I heard the voice of my dear sister Mary. She and my mother had been listening and calling me for a long time, as I afterwards learned, before I hallooed. And, now, as I am penning this, it seems as if the wind's low sigh bears that welcome voice again to my ear; but, no, it is not so, for I know that I am far from my loved ones at home, struggling with my might to earn and give them a better station than is now their lot. But again to my story.

I answered the call again and again, till at last I saw a light coming toward me, I then, in a few moments, saw the forms of my brother and sister appearing. I stood still a few moments, and allowed them to near me; they came through the bushes pretty fast, and [every so often], sister Mary would call to get the direction of my whereabouts. We soon met, and I discovered I had come off minus shoes and stocking-feet, as I had left them in the bushes some where. I was obliged to stop hunting a few days on account of sore feet. But I soon prepared to go again; and as there were moonlight nights, I went up on a clearing of brother's, some two miles from home, and watched for deer. I had been there but a short time, when I heard something coming which I knew to be a deer, for in a few moments, he made his appearance in the open field; and as I allowed him to walk round and round the field for the purpose of learning their manner of acting, I saw he was very careful; for he would just take a bit of grass in his mouth, and while chewing it, look around every way. He at last got within two rods of the rock on which I lay concealed, and then as I raised my rifle, the fellow jumped so rapidly, that I did not fire, for I thought he would stop in a minute; but, no, he was on the safe side of the hedge ere he paused. I felt provoked at myself a hundred times for allowing the deer to escape in so foolish a manner, but it was a lesson for me afterwards.

I will now take the reader to an excursion on a cold winter's morn. The sun had not yet risen to warm and illuminate the cold earth, but I could just see sufficiently to climb up the mountain quite well. I crawled along very slowly, and was just raising the last hedge, so as to look over its summit, when I discovered, about twelve rods from me, an animal that I at once supposed to be a panther. As I looked at the fellow, he stopped behind a large tree, and appeared to be looking in the direction that I stood. In a moment, he started around the tree to come toward me. As soon as I got a fair sight at his heart, I fired, and, O horror! such a noise as I heard in an instant caused my hair to stand erect, I believe, for I felt a cold sensation crawl over me that seemed to freeze the blood in my veins. The moment I fired, the animal turned and jumped, and ran out of sight; I reloaded my rifle, and ran after him. I was bothered so much at intervals to find his tracks, that I thought I would go back after chasing him a few miles. I supposed, from the appearance of things, that the ball must have hit him some where near the back-bone, as some places I saw where he had fallen down, and rubbed his hair off against the rocks and trees. It was snowing so very fast, that I relinquished the chase for that day, and went home. The next day, I started again. After I had been out about two hours, it again commenced snowing; but I thought I would not go back this time without taking a pretty good search; so I looked among the rocks and hills till about noon, as I supposed, and then thought I must go back so as to reach home by night. I was walking along very fast, when the idea occurred to me that I was lost, for I had long since ceased to find my track, and now it appeared that I was on a strange ridge of mountains. So I began to look around to find some familiar spot, or marked tree, but it was of no use; not a single thing could I find or recognize. I therefore fired off my pistols as signals of distress. I loaded and fired every little while and listened to hear my folks fire in some answer somewhere; but not a sound could be heard save the whistling of the wind, as it drove the flakes of snow against my chilled frame. I then commenced running round and round, supposing, in the meantime, I was taking a different course, till I came round to the place from whence I started. At length I sat down in the snow to rest, and was startled to hear a distant sound somewhat similar to the noise I had heard the panther make the day before. I jumped up, and looked at my pistols and rifle to see if they were in order, and then started in the direction of the noise; I thought I might as well meet the panther as stop and freeze, for I had not a match with me to build a fire, and if night came on, I knew that I should perish with the cold; so I determined or rather courted to meet the panther again.

When I arrived at the spot where I had calculated the noise came from, I discovered the tracks of a man, and so I followed them, and, in a few minutes, came out right above the house on a hill. I at once walked into the house, and mother said that father had just gone out with his rifle, supposing I had killed all the deer in the woods, having heard me fire so frequently near the ridge back of the house, not even dreaming that I was lost; so I stepped out doors and fired off my rifle and pistols to let him know that I had returned. I had never before been so lost in the woods in daylight, and so I was the more confused.

As I have greatly enlarged on the first part of this work, I shall be obliged to pass over some hundred little hunting adventures, and give them a place in my next book. But those days have passed, and I have left those happy scenes; for after the work of Mr. Talmage, the ped[d]ler, came before the public, in 1854, my hunting grounds were infested with hunters, and thus I was obliged last winter to hunt but little. I will copy his work here, as I may make truth appear convincing as it regards my present occupation:

Bridgeport, Conn., Jan. 2, 1853

Mr. Pomeroy — Sir: I received a letter a few days ago from a friend of mine, from this State, traveling as a [peddler] in the wild portions of Delaware and Sullivan counties, N.Y., in which he related an account of an adventure he had, which, if you think worth the trouble, you will please correct mistakes and improper language, and give it a place in your paper. The story is as follows; I give it in his own words:

"I must relate an adventure that I met with a few days since. As I was trudging along one afternoon, in the town of Freemont, one of the border towns of Sullivan county, I was overtaken by what I, at first, supposed was a young man, with a rifle on his shoulder. Being well pleased with the idea of having company through the woods, I turned round and said, 'Good afternoon, sir.' 'Good afternoon,' replied my new acquaintance, but in a tone of voice that sounded rather peculiar. My suspicions were at once aroused, and to satisfy myself, I made some inquiries in regard to hunting, which were readily answered by the young lady whom I had thus encountered. She said that she had been out ever since daylight; had followed a buck nearly all day, and had got but one shot and wounded him; but as there was little snow, she could not get him, and was going to try him the next day, hoping that she could get another shot, and was quite certain that she could kill him. Although I can not give a very clear idea of her appearance, I will try to describe her dress. The only article of female apparel visible was a close-fitting hood upon her head, such as is often worn by deer hunters; next, an India-rubber over-coat. Her nether limbs were encased in a pair of snug-fitting corduroy pants, and a pair of Indian moccasins were upon her feet. She had a good looking rifle upon her shoulder, and a brace of double-barreled pistols in the side-pockets of her coat, while a most formidable hunting-knife hung suspended by her side. Wishing to witness her skill with her hunting instruments, I commenced bantering her in regard to shooting. She smiled, and said that she was as good a shot as was in the woods, and to convince me, took out her hunting-knife, and cut a ring, about four inches in diameter, on a tree, with a small spot in the center; then stepping back thirty yards, and drawing up one of her pistols, put both balls inside the ring. She then, at eighteen rods from the tree, fired a ball from her rifle into the very center. We shortly came to her father's house, and I gladly accepted of an invitation to stop there overnight.

"The maiden-hunter instead of setting down to rest as most hunters do when they get home, remarked that she had the chores to do. So, out she went, and fed, watered, and stabled a pair of young horses, a yoke of oxen, and three cows. She then went to the saw-mill, and brought back a slab on her shoulder, that I should not liked to have carried, and with an axe and saw, she soon worked it up into stove-wood. Her next business was to change her dress, and get tea, which she did in a manner which would have been creditable to a more scientific cook. After tea, she finished up the usual house-work, and then sat down and commenced plying her needle in the most lady-like manner. I ascertained that her mother was quite feeble, and her father confined to the house with the rheumatism. The whole family were intelligent, well-educated, and communicative. They had moved from Scholharie county into the woods about three years before; and the father was taken lame the first winter after their arrival, and has not been able to do anything since, and Lucy Ann, as her mother called her, has taken charge of, ploughed, planted, and harvested the farm; learned to chop wood, drive the team, and do all the necessary work.

"Game being plenty, she had learned how to use her father's rifle and spent some of her leisure time in hunting. She had not killed a deer yet, but expressed her determination to kill one, at least, before New-Year's. She boasted of having shot any quantity of squirrels, partridges, and other small game. After chatting some time, she brought a violin from a closet, and played fifteen or twenty tunes, and also sang a few songs, accompanying herself on the violin, in a style that showed she was from being destitute of musical skill. After spending a pleasant evening, we retired. The next morning she was up at four o'clock, and before sunrise, had the breakfast out of the way, and her work out of doors and in the house done; and when I left, a few minutes after sunrise, she had got on her hunting-suit, and was loading her rifle for another chase after the deer."

After the above piece was published, in many different papers, some people were curious to see and hear me play the violin. I, of course, would not refuse so trifling a request. But when the story began to be noised around, that Mr. Slater had reported, I found that I was subjected to the insults of wicked persons when I was traveling or away from home. And as Mr. Slater's story was false about my going to sprees, and having other men wait on me at home, and as the only "spree" I went to was at a Mr. Taylor's, I hardly admit that Mr. Chandaler waited on me home, for I think I rather waited on him home, as he was pilot no farther than his house, where my brother's wagon was in waiting. And that was the only time men waited on me home which gave Mr. Slater such a story to report about me. He well knew that nothing else would touch my feelings like a report of that nature, so he hesitated not to sink me, if possible, in the eyes of the public and my friends. But I had a clear conscience, and I waited to proclaim the truth. After some lapse of time, and after my child was born, Mr. Slater came back, and proposed living together again, as he said that at the time he went off, he was almost crazy and confused. I told him that I could take care of one child, and that I feared he might get crazy again. So I thought it proper for him to wait a while till he had become rich, as he said before he went away, he should always be a poor man while he had me to take care of; and as I thought that I could get along without his care, he had better try and see what he could do. So he stayed at Mr. LaValley's some months, and worked very steady. But as I was not to be shaken in my resolution, he finally went off to Westerlo again to live. After living there some length, he got someone to write a letter for him to me, which I will copy here:

Westerlo, Oct. 5th, 1854

Miss Lucy A. Lobdell,

    (As you call yourself, but which is Slater truly, but I address you as you call yourself to please you,) in truth, I wish it were as it was once — peace and harmony. Then I took comfort in my home, and in your presence; but now you, perhaps, will not agree with me. Let that be as it may, I will say that I am well, and hope these few lines will find you enjoying the same blessing. If you could but know the lonely hours that I spend in Westerlo, you would have some words of comfort to send me. Aunt Becky is in this place, and said that you was sick. Sorry was I to hear that; but I hope that you will gain your health soon. This news I have just heard, but how long you had been ill, I did not hear. I wish you to write as soon as you get this, and let me know how you and that dear little child are. I long to see it once more, and if I hear favorable news from you, I will be in your place soon. But if you talk as if you would like to see the best friend you have in the world, you must say something favorable to me; for I do not wish to come and go to any place unless I am wanted. You must give my best wishes to your parents, and brothers and sisters, and all inquiring friends. Tell them I wish to see them all. Now I will close, and say, I bid you do as you see best for yourself. You are capable of doing your own business; and I hope that you will not forget your best friend,

G.W. Slater

Well, reader, I somehow could not swallow down the words, "best friend." I too well understood the meaning. I had once before listened to his winning words; and when he had once got me within his bounds, you see a sketch here and there of his treatment toward me — the slave of my choice. My "wit was bought too dear" to be caught with smooth words which I did not believe; for I too well knew the plans of the destroyer. I too well have learned the form of the serpent when he would charm the innocent little bird till, step by step, it hops into the jaws of the reptile, and is no more. Well, after I received Mr. Slater's letter, I wrote a reply, stating to him that he might come and see his child; but, at the conclusion, said that I did not believe he would see me again; for I had made up my mind to leave after reading his letter; and as I had several reasons for leaving home, of which I will treat on, I at once will state them. First, my father was lame, and in consequence, I had worked in-doors and out; and as hard times were crowding upon us, I made up my mind to dress in men's attire to seek labor, as I was used to men's work. And as I might work harder at house-work, and get only a dollar per week, and I was capable of doing men's work, and getting men's wages, I resolved to try, after hearing that Mr. Slater was coming, to get work away among strangers.

I accordingly got up one morning, and it seemed as if I must go that day. I did not dare to tell our folks my calculations, for I knew that they would say I was crazy, and tie me up, perhaps. So I went upstairs, saying I was going to dress, and go a hunting as I was accustomed to. I hurried and put on a suit of clothes, and then my hunting suit outside. When I came downstairs; mother came toward me, and was going to take hold of me to see what made me look so thickly dressed. I saw her move, and stepped out doors saying that I must hurry, as it was getting late. I drove the cow up before I left, and then hurried up the mountain. I could not even kiss my little Helen, nor tell her how her mother was going to seek employment to get a little spot to live, and earn something for her as she grew up. So, I stole away with a heavy heart, for I knew I was going among strangers, who did not know my circumstances, or see my heart, so broken, and know its struggles. As I was walking down to the Hankins Depot, I met one of our nearest neighbors. He called to me, and asked me where I was going. I made no reply, but walked on; but I had got but a few yards, when I heard [him] say, "There goes the female hunter." I kept on walking in the meantime a pretty good pace, and then I stepped a little one side in the bushes to change my hunting attire. I in a few minutes saw someone pass the road who appeared to be in search of me. After the lapse of a short time, I walked out of the woods in a different direction, and went to Miss Hankins's, and she kept me over night. I arose in the morning at four o'clock, and walked to the Calicoon Depot, and bought a ticket for Narrowsburg.

I must now leave the reader for a short time, and then I intend to write another book, in which I shall give a full account of my adventures whilst I adopted male attire; and as I am about to leave the reader for a short time, allow me to state the reasons for my adoption of man's apparel. The first reason, then, is this: I have no home of my own; but it is true that I have a father's house, and could be permitted to stay there, and, at the same time, I should be obliged to toil from morning till night, and then I could demand but a dollar per week; and how much, I ask, would this do to support a child and myself[?] I tell you, ladies and gentlemen, woman has taken upon herself the curse that was laid on father Adam and [m]other Eve; for by the sweat of her brow does she eat her bread, and in sorrow does she bring forth children. Again, woman is the weaker vessel, and she toils from morning till night, and then the way her sorrows cease is this—her children are to be attended to; she must dress and undress them for bed; after their little voices are hushed, she must sit up and look after the preparations for breakfast, and, probably, nine, ten, eleven, or twelve o'clock comes round before she can go to rest. Again, she must be up at early dawn to get breakfast, and whilst the breakfast is cooking, she must wash and dress some half a dozen children. After finishing up the usual morning's house-work, such as washing dishes, making beds, and filing the kitchen-floor, then comes the dinner as usual. Then comes the husband—the puddings have been burned a trifle when mother was busy at something else; then come complaints in regard to the pudding. Well, mother was busy with Bridget or Patrick, settling some quarrel or blows, and now mother has made father a little out of taste with the dinner. And this is the way the world is jogging along.

And, now, I ask, if a man can do a woman's work any quicker or better than a woman herself; or could he collect his thoughts sufficiently to say his prayers with a clear idea? No; if he was confused and housed up with the children all day, he would not hesitate to take the burden off his children's shoulders, and allow woman's wages to be on an equality with those of the man. Is there one, indeed, who can look upon that little daughter, and feel that she soon will grow up to toil for the unequal sum allotted to compensate her toil[?] I feel that I can not submit to see all the bondage with which woman is oppressed, and listen to the voice of fashion, and repose upon the bosom of death. I can not be reconciled to die, and feel my poor babe will be obliged to toil and feel the wrongs that are unjustly heaped upon her. I am a mother; I love my offspring even better than words can tell. I can not bear to die and leave that little one to struggle in every way to live as I have had to do.

Again, we see the girl that is obliged to work day by day, and has no home; we see that one toil on- on- on; and the scene becomes changed. We behold her married for the sake of getting a home. Well, suppose we look into that home for a short period — what do we perceive? For a short period, we discover that all is very well. At length, the man becomes tired of being at home, for some reason or another. Perhaps he does not find it quite so pleasing to sit at home in the evening and hear the baby cry. It is less tedious to walk over to the hotel and learn the news, while mother loves her darling, and will try to soothe his sufferings into slumber; for, indeed, he is crying with pain, and can not tell why he suffers. Thus we see the home our child has found. Ah! she indeed has found a home — a habitation of care and sorrow! She indeed hugs the cords that bind her there. Again, the husband comes home a little the worse for wine or rum. The mother marks that staggering form as he wends his way to the bed whereon he goes to sleep and forget the care he now throws away in a whirl of drunkenness. Mother clings tighter to that babe, and cries to that Being of Wisdom to enable her to bear the ills that thus betide her. Well. We will follow her yet a little further. We behold that the father has squandered all his living in drunkenness. He has become a drunkard; his home is now a hovel of wretchedness and misery. The mother is obliged to toil, day by day, for her little ones, and she can scarcely get a morsel of food for herself, as she will toil and feed on the crumbs. And, now, we see again that mother has fallen. Her babes are left to the charity of the world. They have no kind parent to kiss away the tear that co[u]rses down their pale cheeks; no mother to pillow their heads upon her heaving bosom. And when thus deprived of a tender mother, we need not wonder that our jails are filled with criminals. The warmth of a mother's love has long ago been extinguished; and thus the heart has had a sad blight thrown upon its life to make its darkness more terrible.

And now, reader, you have read, in part, a history of your unfortunate writer; but may God grant that you may never experience the sorrow I now feel. I am among strangers penning this little book. I am not permitted to lay the pen aside and kiss the child of my bosom. No; I am far away, struggling with my pen to lift the veil that has so long shrouded the hearts of fathers and mothers as regards the future of their offspring.

And now you, perhaps, are rich and have plenty. Could you bear to suppose that the little child you so fondly love should, after your body is crumbling back to earth again, be obliged to toil with the common class, and drudge, day by day, for a scanty livelihood, when, if you had been a prudent man, you might have foreseen and provided for the evil. Help, one and all, to aid woman, the weaker vessel. If she is willing to toil, give her wages equal with that of man. And as in sorrow she bears her own curse, (nay, indeed, she helps to bear a man's burden also,) secure to her the rights, or permit her to wear the pants, and breathe the pure air of heaven, and you stay and be convinced at home with the children how pleasant a task it is to act the part that woman must act. I suppose that you will laugh at the idea of such a manner of convincing; but I suppose it will not do to convince the man of feeling, who can see and pity, and lend a helping hand to release the afflicted, the child of your bosom, the choice of your heart, young man.

And, now, as I have done speaking of these bodies, these tenements of clay, let me speak of the spirit that dwells therein; let me tell you of a promised rest to the faithful; to those that serve God and love to serve him. Had I been deprived of a hope in this life, I could not have borne the keen arrows that have been hurled, and wound[ed] me continually. But my Heavenly Father has protected and supported me in all my trials; and if I but meet the approbation of my Heavenly Friend, I shall not fall by the hand of my enemies. And now I must close with remarks; and as I am about to say farewell, permit me to invite you to choose my Friend to go with, and support you through the short journey of life; for as the

Scriptures saith, "Man that is born of a woman hath but a few days, and they are full of trouble." It is a true saying, that every heart feels its own sorrows. Let me point you to one who will be a friend that sticketh closer than a brother; and for wisdom, search the Scriptures, for in them you have eternal life; and although I may never behold your face in the flesh, I feel that I shall meet you at the great Judgment Day. And then how happy I should feel, if I, in writing this little scrawl, had persuaded a brother or sister, in the flesh, to love God, and keep his commandments, that they may have a right to the tree of life, and enter in through the gates to that great city. And though some do call me a strange sort of being, I thank God, in whom I believe, and in whom I trust, and who is my defense, and I can praise Him, that He has given me a heart, that He will mould and fashion after His holy will; and as nothing is more calculated to make a heaven on earth than the love of God, I can say, that my affliction has taught me a thousand truths of His loving kindness; for whomsoever the Lord loveth, He chasteneth, and scourgeth every son and daughter of Adam. And though the hand that has written this may crumble and mingle with dust again, yet this work may remain as our works will follow us. And as the present day and age of the world appears to be black with iniquity, I would say take the Word of God for your counsel and guide. If you love God, and keep his commandments, you will get to heaven in spite of professed preachers, or churches, or the devil and all his dominies; and though your name may be cast out as evil, you can rejoice, knowing that if you but endure to the end you will be saved. Amen!

         Your humble servant,
         L.A. Lobdell

Appendix B:
Lunacy Testimonials

In the County Court, Delaware County
In the Matter of Lucy Ann Slater, a Supposed Lunatic

On reading and filing the petition of John F. Lobdell of the Town of Hancock in the County of Delaware dated the 31st day of May 1880, and the affidavits of John F. Lobdell, Sidney K. Lobdell, and Walter Peak of the same place annexed to the said petition and on motion of W.J. Welsh of counsel for the petitioner, it is ordered that a commission in the nature of a writ de lunatico inqui[rendo], be issued out of and under the seal of this court in the usual form, directed to Arthur More counselor at law and of the county of Delaware to inquire by a jury of the said county and of the neighborhood where the said Lucy Ann Slater resides of the lunacy of the said Lucy Ann Slater, and that the Sheriff of said county be instructed in said commission to summon such jury.

And it is further ordered, that the said commission be executed at or at some convenient place near to the residence of the said Lucy Ann Lobdell and that previous notice of the time and place of such execution be given to the said Lucy Ann Slater and to the person having the care of him.

And it is further ordered, that upon the execution of the said commission the person or persons having the care or custody of the said Lucy Ann Lobdell do produce him before the said commissioner and jury to be inspected and examined by them whenever requested to do so by such commissioners.

Dated June 7th, 1880.

(Signature): Isaac H. Maynard, Delaware County Judge

In the County Court in and for the County of Delaware; In the Matter of Lucy Ann Slater, a Supposed Lunatic. State of New York, County of Delaware.

John F. Lobdell being duly sworn says that he is the brother of the above named Lucy Ann Slater also the said Lucy Ann Slater before the War of the Southern Rebeleon married a man by the name of George Slater: that said Slater inlisted, was taken prisoner and died in the army[,] leaving his said wife a widow with one child for whom he never provided. That the said Lucy Ann Slater has no property (of any worth) but deponant believes that she is now intitled to a pension, deponant therefore asks to be appointed a committee of the person and estate of the said Lucy Ann Slater, to [illegible] him to proceed in the matter of her pension and for other purposes and that the proper proceedings be had for that purpose.

Sworn before me this 2nd day of June, 1880—

(Signatures) John F. Lobdell, John W. Gould, Notary Public

In the County Court in and for the County of Delaware; In the Matter of Lucy Ann Slater, a Supposed Lunatic. State of New York, County of Delaware

Sidney K. Lobdell being duly sworn says that he resides in the town of Hancock in the said county of Delaware that he now is[,] and has been for over six years last past wile [sic] acquainted with the above Lucy Ann Slater of the same town of Hancock. That the said Lucy Ann Slater [illegible] the whole of the time for at least six years last past has been of unsound mind and understanding, rendering her unfit to have the government of herself or the management of her affairs.

But deponant further says that he has very frequently seen the said Lucy Ann Slater within the last two years, and that according to the best of his judgment and belief, the said Lucy Ann Slater has been during the whole of that time of unsound mind and understanding. That the habits, doings, language and actions of the said Lucy Ann Slater during the past two years have been those of an insane person. She frequently claims that she is a man and has a wife, sometimes dresses in men's clothes and uses such other language as to convince the deponent that she is a conferred lunatic and has been so called by those who knew her for many years last past.

Deponant further says that the said Lucy Ann Slater now resides and has for the last 15 months resided with her brother John F. Lobdell at the town of Hancock aforesaid and that her brother provides for her. That sometimes the said Lucy will take her clothes off of her person[,] being then difficult to control or manage.

Sworn to before me this 2nd day of June 1880.

(Signatures): Sidney K. Lobdell, John W. Gould, Notary Public

In the County Court in and for the County of Delaware in the State of New York; In the Matter of Lucy Ann Slater, a Supposed Lunatic. State of New York, County of Delaware

Walter Peak being duly sworn says that he resides in the town of Fairmont in said county. That he now is and has been for over twenty years acquainted with Lucy Ann Slater of the town of Hancock in the County of Delaware, that the said Lucy Ann Slater for the last six years or more has been more or less affected by an alienation of mind rendering her unfit for the time being to have the government of her affairs. And deponent further says that he has seen the said Lucy Ann Slater frequently within the past two years: and according to the best of his judgment and belief, the said Lucy Ann Slater has been during the whole of that time of unsound mind and understanding.

And deponent further says that the language and actions of the said Lucy Ann Slater during the last two years have been those of an insane person. That she very frequently dressed in men's attire. Sometimes says she is a hunter. Sometimes claims and acts as if she was in love with another woman and says that that husband is her husband or wife, is vulgar and incoherent in her conversations. Said deponent believes that she is still of unsound mind and understanding and unfit for the government of herself or management of her affairs.

Sworn to before me this 31st day of May, 1880.

Signatures: Walter Peak, John Newton, Notary Public

In the County Court in and for the County of Delaware in the State of New York; In the Matter of Lucy Ann Slater, a Supposed Lunatic

To the County Court in and for the County of Delaware in the State of New York:

The petition of John F. Lobdell of the town of Hancock in said County of Delaware respectfully shows that Lucy Ann Slater[,] who resides in said town of Hancock and who is the sister of your petitioner, now is, and, for a space of over twenty years last past has been so far deprived of her reason and understanding as to be all together unfit and unable to govern herself or manage her affairs[,] as well more fully appear by the affidavits here to annexed.

Your petitioner therefore prays that a commission in the nature of a writ [de] lunatico inqui[rendo], may issue out of and render the seal of the court to refuse [illegible] into the lunacy of the said Lucy Ann Slater and to be directed to such persons as to the court may seem proper.

(Illegible Signature — Attorney) John F. Lobdell (signature)

State of New York, County of Delaware: On this 31st day of May 1880 before me personally appeared the above named John F. Lobdell and [illegible] that he has read the above petition subscribed by him and knows the contents thereof and that some is true of his own knowledge except as to the matters herein stated to be alleged on information and belief and as to those matters he believes it to be true.

(Signature) John Newton, Notary Public

Delaware County Court; In the Matter of Lucy Ann Slater, a Supposed Lunatic

On reading and filing the inquisition in the above matter, taken under a commission issued out of the Delaware County Court from which it appears that the jury have found the said Lucy Ann Slater is a lunatic and of unsound mind, so that she is incapable of the government of herself, or of the management of her lands, tenements, goods, and chattels, and from which it appears that the said Lucy Ann Slater is possessed of certain real estate and [illegible] right to a pension in said inquisition described, and on filing other papers and testimony herein used on the motion.

Now on motion of [illegible signature of lawyer] attorneys for the petitioner John F. Lobdell, it is ordered that the findings of the jury upon the execution of the said commission, as set forth in inquisition be, and the same is hereby confirmed. And on reading and filing the petition of John F. Lobdell, a brother of said lunatic dated the day of June 1, 1880, praying for the appointment of a committee of the person and estate of the said Lucy Ann Slater and the consent of Helen Crawson[,] the only child of said lunatic, it is on like motion, ordered that the said John F. Lobdell be, and he is hereby appointed the committee of the person and estate of the said Lucy Ann Slater upon his filing with the clerk of this court a bond with two sufficient sureties to be approved by the judge of this court in the penalty of one thousand dollars and conditioned for the faithful performance of his trusts as such committee according to the statute and the rules and practice of the court, and to account, whenever required, in conformity with such rules and practice.

(Signature) [illegible first name] Maynard, Delaware County Judge

Delaware County Court; In the Matter of Lucy Ann Slater, a Supposed Lunatic

The petition of John F. Lobdell in the town of Hancock in the County of Delaware respectfully shows: that the commission heretofore issued out of this court in pursuance of an order made of the eighth day of June 1880, directed to Arthur More to inquire into the lunacy of Lucy Ann Slater of the town of Hancock aforesaid, who is the sister of your petitioner[,] has been duly executed and returned by the commissioner and filed in the office of the clerk of this court. That from the inquisitions annexed to the said commission and returned therewith, it appears that the jury have found the said Lucy Ann Slater is a lunatic and of unsound mind so that she is incapable of the government of herself or the management of her lands, goods, and chattels, as by reference to said inquisition will more fully appear.

Your petitioner therefore prays: that he may be appointed the committee of the person and estate of the said Lucy Ann Slater upon his giving security for the faithful performance as trust as such committee according to the statute and in accordance with the rules and practice of the court. And for such other or further order as the court may think proper to order.

[Illegible signature of lawyer] Signature of John F. Lobdell

On this 19th day of June 1880 before me the undersigned[,] a notary public[,] personally appeared the above named John F. Lobdell and made oath that he has [illegible] the above petition subscribed by him and knows the contents thereof and that the same is true of his own knowledge except as to the matters which are herein stated to be on his information or belief, and as to those matters he believes it to be true.

(Signature) John W. Gould, Notary Public

Delaware County Court; In the Matter of Lucy Ann Slater, a Supposed Lunatic

I, Helen Crawson, daughter and only child of the said Lucy Ann Slater above named[,] do hereby consent that John F. Lobdell of the town of Hancock in said County of Delaware be appointed committee of the person and estate of the said Lucy Ann Slater and I do hereby request the said court to appoint the said John F. Lobdell as such committee.

Dated this 19th day of June 1880

(Signature) Helen A. Crawson

On this 19th day of June 1880 before me the subscriber personally came Helen Crawson to me known to be the same person described in and who executed the foregoing consent and acknowledged that she executed the same.

(Signature) John W. Gould, Notary Public

Delaware Co. Court; In the Matter of Lucy Ann Slater, a Supposed Lunatic; Petition: read on Motion, June 28, 1880. Filed June 29, 1880

Know all men by these presents. That we, John F. Lobdell of the town of Hancock in the County of Delaware and State of New York and Sidney K. Lobdell and John F. Cagwin of the same place[,] are held and firmly bound unto Rauson A. Grant [,] Clerk of the County of Delaware[,] and to his succession or successions in office in the jurial sum of one thousand dollars to be paid to the same clerk or to his successors as aforesaid, for which payment well and truly to be made we bind ourselves, our heirs, executors, and administrators jointly and severely firmly by these presents, sealed with our seals and dated the 19th day of June 1880.

Whereas the said John F. Lobdell has made application by petition to be appointed committee of the estate and person of Lucy Ann Slater of the town of Hancock in said county of Delaware, who by an inquisition taken under a commission issued out of said court previous thereto been found a lunatic.

Now therefore, the condition of this obligation is such that if the above bounden John F. Lobdell shall faithfully perform the trust reposed in him as such committee according to the Statute, and shall render an account whenever required, in conformity to the rules and practices of the said court and shall observe the orders and directions of said court in relation to such trust, then this obligation to be void otherwise to remain in full force and virtue.

Sealed and delivered in the presence of H.W.M. Koon

(Signatures) John F. Lobdell, Sidney K. Lobdell, John F. Cagwin

County of Delaware: On this 19th day of June 1880 before me personally appeared the above named John F. Lobdell, Sidney K. Lobdell, and John F. Cagwin known to me to be the individuals described in and who executed the above undertaking and severally acknowledged that they executed the same.

(Signature) John W. Gould, Notary Public, County of Delaware

(Signatures) Sidney K. Lobdell and John F. Cagwin above named being severally sworn each for himself says that that he is a resident of the State of New York and a freeholder therein and worth double the sum specified in said undertaking over all his debts and liabilities and [illegible] of property exempt by law from execution.

Sworn to before me on this 19th day of June 1880.

(Signatures) Sidney K. Lobdell, John f. Cagwin, John W. Gould

The People of the State of New York to Arthur More of the County of Delaware;

Greeting:

Know ye, that we have assigned to you, to inquire, by the oaths of good and lawful men of the County of Delaware by whom the truth of the matter may be better known whether Lucy Ann Slater of the town of Hancock in said county, is a lunatic or enjoys lucid intervals so that she is not sufficient for the government of herself, or the management of her lands, tenements, goods and chattels, and if so from what time, after what manner and how, and what lands and tenements[,] goods and chattels she owns or is entitled to, and of what value the lands and tenements[,] goods and chattels owned by her or to which she may be entitled are and how much the issues and profits thereof are worth by the year and what is the value of her goods and chattels and personal estate; and who are the nearest heirs of the said Lucy Ann Lobdell who will be entitled to her estate in case of her death and of what age. And therefore we command you, that at a certain day and place or at certain days and places which you for that purpose shall appoint you diligently make inquisition in the premises, and that you cause reasonable notice of the time and place by you appointed for that purpose to be given to the said Lucy Ann Slater; and that you send the inquisition which you shall therefore make, under your seal and the seals of those persons by whom it shall be made, distinctly and plainly and without delay to our County Court together with this writ.

And by the tenor of these presents we command the Sheriff of the County of Delaware that at a certain day and place or at certain days and places which you shall make known to him, he cause to come before you so many and such good and lawful men of his bailiwick as you shall direct by whom the trust of the matter aforesaid may be better inquired into.

Witness (Signature) Hon. Isaac H. Maynard, County Judge of Delaware County at Delhi the 8th day of June 1880.

(Signatures) H.W.J. Walsh, Attorney, R.A. Grant, Clerk

[lines of crossed out writing]

Delaware County Court; In the Matter of Lucy Ann Slater, a Supposed Lunatic. State of New York, County of Delaware, Writ de Lunatico Inqui[rendo]
(The execution of its commission appears in the schedule and ___ hereto annexed on June 17, 1880. Signatures Arthur More, Commissioner, R.A. Grant, County Clerk)

Arthur More[,] having been duly appointed by order of this Court a Commissioner in the above entitled proceedings being duly sworn, deposed and says that he will faithfully and fairly execute said commission and perform the duties as such commissioner and make a true return and report therein according to the best of his ability.

Sworn to before me this 15th day of June 1880.

(Signatures) Arthur More, S.S. Doolittle = Notary Public, Deposit, N.Y.

Delaware County Court; In the Matter of Lucy Ann Slater, a Supposed Lunatic

To Lucy Ann Slater
Take notice that a commission to inquire as to your lunacy, a lunatic, issued out of and under the seal of the County Court of Delaware County

and directed to the undersigned as commissioner[,] will be executed at the house of John F. Lobdell in the town of Hancock, Delaware County on the 16th day of June, instant at 10:00 A.M.

Dated June 9th, 1880. (Signature) Arthur More, Commissioner

Delaware County SS

John F. Lobdell of the town of Hancock in said County being duly sworn says: at the said town of Hancock on the 11th day of June 1880, he served on Lucy Ann Slater of said town of Hancock the above notice by then and there delivery to and leaving with her the said Lucy Ann Slater a true copy of said notice and he further says that he knows the person so served to be the person mentioned and disclosed in said notice.

Sworn to me before me [illegible] June 1880.

(Signature) John F. Lobdell

To the Sheriff of the County of Delaware, by virtue of a commission in the nature of a writ de lunatico inqui[r]endo issued out of and under the seal of the County Court of Delaware County bearing date the eighth day of June 1880, to me whose name is subscribed hereto directed, to inquire if Lucy Ann Slater of the town of Hancock in the County of Delaware be a lunatic or not.

There are therefore to require you to cause to come and appear before us twelve honest and lawful men of the County aforesaid and of the neighborhood where the said Lucy Ann Slater resides on the 16th day of June 1880 by 10:00 in the forenoon of the same day at the house of John F. Lobdell, in said town of Hancock, then and there upon their oaths to inquir[e] of the lunacy of the said Lucy Ann Slater; and of all such matters and things as shall be given them in charge by virtue of said commission. Hereof fail not at your peril.

Given under my hand and seal this 9th day of June 1880.

(Signature) Arthur More, Commissioner

The execution of this precept appears with the panel hereto annexed.

(Signatures)

John Crawford — Sheriff

F.O. Wheeler — Deputy

Names of jurors summoned to inquire according to the tenor of the precept hereto annexed: John Lobdell — Sidney K. Lobdell — Ebenezer Sperbeak —

Oscar Haight — Henry Shifer — Amasa Clark — David Milk — George [illegible] — Stephen Ryden — Elson Stephens — William W. Maines — John Truman

I hereby certify that on the 11th day of June 1880 at the town of Hancock in the County of Delaware, N.Y., I summoned the above named persons as jurors by then and these [illegible] to and [illegible] to each of said persons. This annexed precept also so stating to each, time and place when and where they [illegible] to appear and the purpose for which they were summoned.

Dated June 14th, 1880.

John Crawford — Sheriff

F.O. Wheeler — Deputy

An inquisition which at the residence of John F. Lobdell in the town of Hancock in the County of Delaware on the 16th day of June in the year one thousand eight hundred and eighty before Arthur More a commissioner appointed by virtue of a commission in the nature of a writ de lunatico inqui[r]endo out of and under the seal of the County Court of the County of Delaware N.Y. dated on the 8th day of June 1880 directed to the said commissioner to inquire [illegible] of the lunacy of Lucy Ann Slater upon the oaths of Sidney K. Lobdell, Ebenezer Spearback, Oscar Haight, Henry Phifer, George H. Milk, Stephen Ryder, Edson Stephens, William W. Main, John Turman, John Birdirupp, David Milk, and Amassa Clark, good and lawful men of the said county who[,] being summoned[,] sworn and charged upon their oaths[,] say that the said Lucy Ann Slater at the time of taking this inquisition is a lunatic and of unsound mind and does not enjoy lucid intervals so that she is incapable of the government of herself or of the management of her lands, goods, and chattels, and that she has been in the same state of lunacy for the space of ten years lastpast.

That the said Lucy Ann Slater has occasionally [?] for many years past been afflicted with mental alienation, but what [illegible] mental alienation or her present lunacy the jurors aforesaid have no information and know not. And the jurors aforesaid upon their oaths aforesaid further say that whether the said Lucy Ann Slater being in that state has alienated any lands and tenements or not the jurors aforesaid know not. And the jurors aforesaid upon their oaths aforesaid do further say that the following lands and tenements situated in the County of Wayne in the state of Pennsylvania to wit, about four or five acres situated about one mile from Narrowsburgh, yet remain to her the said Lucy Ann Slater. That the said lands and tenements above described are worth about $10. And the jurors aforesaid upon their oaths aforesaid do further say that the said Lucy Ann Slater has no other property of any kinds either real or personal, but they say that it is understood that the husband of said Lucy Ann Slater died in the service of the United States as a soldier during the last war and that the said Lucy Ann Slater is probably entitled to a pension from the United States government.

And the jurors aforesaid upon their oaths aforesaid do further say that Helen Crawson[,] the daughter and heir at law and only next of kin[,] resides with said Lucy Ann Slater in the town of Hancock[,] Delaware County. That the said Helen Crawson is twenty seven years of age, and that the said Lucy Ann Slater is about fifty one years of age. And that the said Helen Crawson will be entitled to the estate of the said Lucy Ann Slater on her decease.

In witness whereof as well the said commission as the jurors aforesaid have to this inquisition set their hands and [illegible] above written.

(Signatures)

Arthur More   Stephen Ryder   W.W. Main   John R. Inman
John Biedekapp   Edson Stephens   Oscar Haight   Henry Pheifer
Amassa Clark   George H. Milk   David Milk
Ebenezer Spearback   Sidney K. Lobdell

Delaware County Court; In the Matter of the Lunacy of Lucy Ann Slater
Inquisition Ken J. Marble, Attorney

June 16th, 1880

Memorandum of testimony where in the above matter at the house of John F. Lobdell in the town of Hancock in said County. The following named jurors having been called and sworn, to wit, Sidney K. Lobdell, Ebenezer Pheifer, George H. Milk, Stephen Ryder, Edson Stephens, William W. Main, John Inman, John Biedekapp, David Milk, Amassa Clark.

John F. Lobdell being sworn says:

I reside in the town of Hancock[,] Delaware County[,] N.Y. I am forty seven years old. I am acquainted with Lucy Ann Slater and have known her 35 or 40 years. She is a sister of mine. She is about 51 years old. She resides here in the town of Hancock in a house here on my premises. I provide for her and her daughter and her daughter's two children who live with her. Have provided for her going on two years. I should call her insane. She has been insane for more than ten years. Her mother was insane before her.

She has a habit of dressing in men's clothes. At times she has had spells where she imagines there are snakes in the room and beasts and at such times she tears her clothes and the bedding in the room. She becomes quarrelsome and unmanageable at times and threatens to burn the building and runs off in the woods alone. She has a woman who she sometimes claims is her wife — this woman is also insane. [F]rom what I see and know of her she [Lucy] is of unsound mind at all times but she is at some times worse than at others. She at times uses very bad language. She has but one child[,] a daughter whose name is now Helen Crawson.

The bad spells as I call them come at about once in two weeks when she has her raving(?) spells. I know she has not sufficient understanding or ability for the government of herself or the management of her property. Nor does she have lucid intervals where she is capable of governing herself or managing her property. She has been in her present condition of mind for more than twenty years.

She has a small piece of land of four or five acres situated near Narrowsburgh in Wayne County[,] Pennsylvania. I don't think it is worth more than $10. Is a very rocky poor place. She has never sold any lands and has no other lands or tenements. She has no personal property of any kind nor has she any interest in any real estate or personal property except the single piece of land I have mentioned. I think her insanity was to some extent caused by excitement in religious matters.

She has never lost any children who died having children. She came here where she now lives about March 1879.

(Signature) John F. Lobdell

Subscribed and sworn to before me June 16th, 1880.

(Signature) Arthur More, Commissioner

Ed L. Pettingill sworn says:

I reside in Hancock[,] N.Y. I am a practicing physician. I have seen Lucy Ann Slater today, never was acquainted with her before. I have frequently heard of her as a crazy female hunter. I have examined her today. I consider her insane to the best of my judgment. I should consider her incapable of governing herself or managing her property. I think her incompetent for any kind of businys.

(Signature) Ed. L. Pettingill M.D.

Subscribed and sworn to before me June 16th, 1880.

Arthur More, Commissioner

William W. Main sworn says:

    I reside in the town of Hancock[,] Del. Co. I am about fifty years old. I am acquainted with Lucy Ann Slater and have known her for about twenty years. On one subject her mind is not sound but on other matters have heard her talk quite sensibly. I have never had an intimate acquaintance with her and am not familiar with her habits and customs. *I know that she sometimes dresses in men's clothes and it is on that subject that I think her of unsound mind.* I have lived in this vicinity about twelve years and during that time she has been away most of that time except about one or two years.

(Signature) William Main

Subscribed and sworn to before me June 16, 1880.

Arthur More, Commissioner

Edwin Stephens sworn says:

    I reside in the town of Hancock Delaware County. I am acquainted with Lucy Ann Slater and have seen her more or less for the past nine years. I consider her from what I have seen of her insane. I do not think she is capable of governing herself or of taking care of herself or of doing any kind of businys. I don't know whether she has any property or not. It has been the general talk ever since I knew her that she was a crazy person.

Edwin Stevens

Subscribed and sworn to before me June 16, 1880.

Arthur More, Commissioner

Inid Ryder sworn says:

    I reside in the town of Hancock and have about thirty years. I am nearly seventy four years old. I am acquainted with Lucy Ann Slater. I have known her more or less ever since I have lived in the town. She used to come to our house quite often and does job[s], was there about a week ago. I should call her insane. I think she has been so as much as 15 or 16 years. I do not consider her capable of taking care of herself or of managing her property. I don't know of her having any property. The general speech of the people in the neighborhood and vicinity is that she is a crazy person.

I know that she is at times very wild and violent.

Inid [his X mark] Ryder

Subscribed and sworn to before me June 16, 1880, Arthur More

John F. Lobdell recalled:

Her maiden name was Lucy Ann Lobdell. Her husband was George Slater. He was in the Union Army during the Revolution, at least he enlisted and went in the army. The general understanding is that he died in the service and I suppose Lucy Ann is entitled to a pension. She received from the government about two years ago about $300 for Bounty and Commissary [illegible]. She paid $60 of it for the small piece of land mentioned in my former testimony, and bought a horse for about $60. She said she let one George Walsh have her horse. She also bought an old wagon, a [illegible], a fiddle, and an old watch. I don't know what has become of this property. She hasn't got it now.

(Signature) John F. Lobdell

Subscribed and sworn to before me June 16, 1880

Arthur More, Commissioner

Harry Walsh sworn says:

I reside in Hancock[,] N.Y. and have for about 22 years last-past and have been more or less acquainted with Lucy Ann Slater for the past 20 or 25 years. Have met her a good many times and have seen her traveling along the roads. The first that I discovered anything about Lucy which led me to believe she was insane was about 20 or 25 years ago when she was in her father's saw mill sawing or attempting to saw. She was then dressed in men's clothes and particularly attracted my attention. Someone was with me. We stopped some [illegible] and from her appearance and conduct at the time we both came to the conclusion that she was crazy.

Some years ago I met her at [the home of] Mr. David Hallock in Wayne County, Pennsylvania. I was satisfied then that she was crazy. She was dressed in men's clothes and had a gun and pretended to be a hunting.

After that I saw her in company with another woman traveling along the roads. That woman was crazy. They both claimed that they were man and wife and pretended to love each other so that they could not be separated. When they came to my brother's he said they frequently came there together in that way and wanted to be together and sleep together. I saw her once at Hancock with her husband at the time he existed? She was in the bar room[,] according to men[,] singing to her husband. There was no mistake but that she was then insane. I cannot swear positively that it was her husband, but she claimed it was her husband with her. Have seen her at other times and think she is insane without doubt and incapable governing herself or of managing her property.

Harry Walsh

Subscribed and sworn to before me June 16, 1880.

Arthur More, Commissioner

June 29, 1880
Delaware County Court; In the matter of Lucy Ann Slater, supposed lunatic

[Illegible name], Attorney

In Media Res:

Place of such execution be given to the said Lucy Ann Slater and to the person having the care of him.

And it is further ordered, that upon that upon the execution of the said commission the person or persons having the care or custody of the said Lucy Ann Lobdell do produce him before the said commission and jury to be inspected and examined by them whenever required to do so by such commissioners.

Dated June 7th, 1880.

Isaac H. Maynard, Delaware County Judge

Appendix C: Wise's "Case of Sexual Perversion"

From *Alienist and Neurologist: A Quarterly Journal of Scientific, Clinical and Forensic Psychiatry and Neurology*, volume 4 (January 1883): 87–91.

Case of Sexual Perversion

P. M. Wise, M.D., Willard, N.Y.
Assistant Physician of the Willard Asylum for the Insane

The case of sexual perversion herewith reported, has been under the writer's observation for the past two years and since the development of positive insanity. The early history of her abnormal sexual tendency is incomplete, but from a variety of sources, enough information has been gleaned to afford a brief history of a remarkable life and of a rare form of mental disease.

Case — Lucy Ann Slater, *alias*, the Rev. Joseph Lobdell, was admitted to the Willard Asylum, October 12th, 1880; aged 56, widow, without occupation and a declared vagrant. Her voice was course and her features were masculine. She was dressed in male attire throughout and declared herself to be a man, giving her name as Joseph Lobdell, a Methodist minister; said she was married and had a wife living. She appeared in good physical health; when admitted, she was in a state of turbulent excitement, but was not confused and gave responsive answers to questions. Her excitement was of an erotic nature and her sexual inclination was perverted. In passing to the ward, she embraced the female attendant in a lewd manner and came near overpowering her before she received assistance. Her conduct on the ward was characterized by the same lascivious conduct, and she made efforts at various times to have sexual intercourse with her associates. Several weeks after her admission she became quiet and depressed, but would talk freely about herself and her condition. She gave her correct name at this time and her own history, which was sufficiently corroborated by other evidence to prove that her recollection of early life was not distorted by her late psychosis.

It appears she was the daughter of a lumberman living in the mountainous region of Delaware Co., N.Y.[,] that she inherited an insane history from her mother's antecedents. She was peculiar in girlhood, in that she preferred masculine sports and labor; had an aversion to attentions from young men and sought the society of her own sex. It was after the earnest solicitation of her parents and friends that she consented to marry, in her twentieth year, a man for whom, she has repeatedly stated, she had no affection and from whom she never derived a moment's pleasure, although she endeavored to be a dutiful wife. Within two years she was deserted by her husband and shortly after gave birth to a female child, now living. Thenceforward, she followed her inclination to indulge in masculine vocations most freely; donned male attire, spending much of the time in the woods with a rifle, and became so expert in its use that she was renowned throughout the county as the "Female Hunter of Long Eddy." She continued to follow the life of trapper and hunter and spent several years in Northern Minnesota among the Indians. Upon her return to her native county she published a book giving an account of her life and a narrative of her woods experience that is said to have been well written, although in quaint style. Unfortunately the reporter has been unable to procure a copy of this book as it is now very scarce. She states, however, that she did not refer to sexual causes to explain her conduct and mode of life at that time, although she considered herself a man in all that the name implies. During the few years following her return from the West, she met with many reverses, and in ill health she received shelter and care in the alms-house. There she became attached to a young woman of good education, who had been left by her husband in a destitute condition and was receiving charitable aid. The attachment seemed mutual and, strange as it may seem, led to their leaving their temporary home to commence life in the woods in the relations of husband and wife. The unsexed woman assumed the name of Joseph Lobdell and the pair lived in this relation for the subsequent decade; "Joe," as she was familiarly known, following her masculine vocation of hunting and trapping and thus supplying themselves with the necessaries of life.

An incident occurred in 1876 to interrupt the quiet monotony of this Lesbian love. "Joe" and her assumed wife made a visit to a neighboring village, ten miles distant, where "he" was recognized, was arrested as a vagrant and lodged in jail.

On the authority of a local correspondent, I learn that there is now among the records of the Wayne Co. (Pa.) Court, a document that was drawn up by the "wife" after she found "Joe" was in jail. "It is a petition for the release of her 'husband, Joseph Israel Lobdell' from prison, because of 'his' failing health. The pen used by the writer was a stick whittled to a point and split; the ink was pokeberry juice. The chirography is faultless and the language used is a model of clear, correct English." The petition had the desired effect and "Joe" was released from jail. For the following three years they lived together quietly and without noticeable incident, when "Joe" had a maniacal attack that resulted in her committal to the asylum before-mentioned.

The statement of the patient in the interval of quiet that followed soon after her admission to the asylum was quite clear and coherent and she evidently had a vivid recollection of her late "married life." From this statement it appears that she made frequent attempts at sexual intercourse with her companion and believed them successful; that she believed herself to possess virility and the coaptation of a male; that she had not experienced connubial content with her husband, but with her late companion nuptial satisfaction was complete. In nearly her own words; "I may be a woman in one sense, but I have peculiar organs that make me more a man than a woman." I have been unable to discover any abnormality of the genitals, except an enlarged clitoris covered by a large relaxed praeputium. She says she has the power to erect this organ in the same way a turtle protrudes its head — her own comparison. She disclaims onanistic practices.[1] Cessation of menstrual function occurred early in womanhood, the date having passed from her recollection. During the two years she has been under observation in the Willard Asylum she has had repeated paroxysmal attacks of erotomania and exhilaration, without periodicity, followed by corresponding periods of mental and physical depression. Dementia has been progressive and she is fast losing her memory and capacity for coherent discourse.

Westphal[2] reports the case of a female,* that resembles in its salient features the foregoing; who, at the age of twenty, acquired regular desire

---

*Archiv für Psych., Band II, Heft I.

towards her own sex. The sexual organs were normal and she practiced onanism. Having attempted to violate a female relative for the purpose of gratifying her desires and being repulsed, she became depressed with paroxysms of mania. He also reports the case of a male, and contributes an article with Dr. Servaes* upon the same subject several years later. In a contribution† and later, an exhaustive essay,‡ Krafft-Ebbing gives an analysis of the published observations of this anomalous and rare disorder to the present time. With his own additions they number seventeen of both sexes and represent various degrees of perversion. In all but one of these cases there was a neurotic diathesis with positive symptoms of insanity. He discusses fully the relation of society to these sufferers and suggests they should be excepted from legal enactments for the punishment of unnatural lewdness; thus allowing them to follow their inclinations, so far as they are harmless, to an extent not reaching public and flagrant offense.

It would be more charitable and just if society would protect them from the ridicule and aspersion they must always suffer, if their responsibility is legally admitted, by recognizing them as the victims of a distressing monodelusional form of insanity. It is reasonable to consider true sexual perversion as always a pathological condition and a peculiar manifestation of insanity.

The subject possesses little forensic interest, especially in this country, and the case herewith reported is offered as a clinical curiosity in psychiatric medicine.

Archiv für Psych., Band VI, Heft II.
†*Zeitschrift fuer Psych.*, Band XXXIII, Heft 2.
‡*Zeitschrift fuer Psych.*, Band XXXVIII, Heft 2 and 3.

Appendix D:
Excerpt from The History of Meeker County

From A. C. Smith's *Meeker County History: A Historical Sketch of Meeker County, Minnesota from It's First Settlement to July 4th, 1876.* A.C. Smith; President of the Bar and Old Settler's Associations For Said County, Litchfield, Minn. Belfoy & Joubert Publishers, 1877.

CHAPTER X: A Wild Woman's History — The Slayer of Hundreds of Bears and Wild-Cats.

Honesdale, Pa. July 20th, 1876. — "There" said Sheriff Spencer, as he pushed open the ponderous door of one of the cells of the county jail in this place, "There is a woman with a history."

On a low chair in a cell in the jail at Honesdale, Pa., July 20th, 1876, sat a most singular looking person. A round, wrinkled, sun-burned face, small head crowned with thick, shaggy gray hair, that fell down over and almost concealed the blackest and sharpest of eyes; a slender body clothed in scant and shabby female garb, and lower limbs encased in tattered trousers. There was the occupant of the cell — Lucy Ann Lobdee NEE Slater, better known thereabouts as "the female hunter of Long Eddy."

About 45 years ago a family named Lobdell lived in Delaware County, N.Y., at what is now the village of Long Eddy on the Delaware river and Erie railway, then sparsely settled. Lumbering was the main business of the settlers of the vicinity. The Lobdells dwelt in a cabin in the woods where a daughter, the subject of our sketch[,] was born. From the time this child was old enough to walk she was a great favorite among the hardy woodchoppers and raftsmen. They often took her off to the logging camp and kept her there for days at a time, and she early became inured to the hardships of their life. The lumbermen in those days were all good hunters, and always carried their rifles with them. Before Lucy Ann was eight years old they had taught her the use of the rifle, and she soon became as good a shot as there was in the settlement. At the age of twelve she could outshoot any of the men, and handled the ax with the ease of an old chopper. Before she had reached the age of sixteen she had killed numerous deer, and an absence of two or three days alone in the woods was for her not an uncommon thing. She once killed a full sized panther, and the hide of the animal is now in the possession of an ex-sheriff of Wayne Co. Pa. Notwithstanding her masculine tastes Lucy Ann's name, as a girl and woman, was free from reproach. The breath of slander never reached her, and she could have had her choice of a husband from the most exemplary young men in the vicinity. But she had no inclination to marry and she rejected all offers.

A raftsman named Henry Slater came into the settlement about 1850. He formed the acquaintance of Lucy Ann and to the surprise of everybody, they were married. Slater proposed to Lucy Ann, and she told him that they would shoot at a mark with a rifle. If he beat her shots she would marry him, if not she would stay with her parents. The trial of skill took place and Slater was victorious.

Slater proved a worthless scape-grace and neglected and abused his wife. A year after they were married Mrs. Slater gave birth to a daughter. Before the child was two weeks old Slater deserted both child and wife, leaving them in destitute circumstances. Slater never returned, but was occasionally heard of in New York, and on the Hudson river, a worthless, drunken, vagabond.

The sorrowing wife went back to her parents, and after two years spent in trying to get along and maintain herself respectably by doing woman's work, but with poor success, she laid aside the apparel of her sex, donned men's clothing, and taking her rifle went into the woods to earn a living for herself and child.

For eight or ten long years she roamed the forests of Sullivan and Delaware counties, in New York, and Wayne and Pike in Pennsylvania, and spent two years in Meeker county, Minnesota.

She had cabins in various place[s], and would visit the old home about once a year, and only appeared in settlements and villages to sell her game and furs and to procure ammunition.

Excerpt from The History of Meeker County

On one of her visits to her child when it was about four years old, her parents complained of having its care on their hands. She therefore took it away and placed it in the Delhi poor-house, and left her old stamping ground for New York and thence up the Hudson river — still in men's apparel — and, strange to say passed and repassed her husband on the Hudson River railroad without being recognized by him, her disguise was so complete.

From Albany she passed west over the Central New York, and finally turned up in Minnesota, and says she taught three singing schools on the way, to provide means of transportation.

She spent a short time in St. Paul where she made but few acquaintances and among them was an Edwin Gribble, who had some dealings with her, but Edwin hadn't the remotest suspicion that she was a female, or he would perhaps have been less free with her. Gribble had reason to know that Lucy Ann was somewhat eccentric, not only on account of the wildness of her tastes, but in the way she dressed, her costume in the summer of 1856 having consisted of a pair of calico pants, a calico coat and a calico vest and hat. In this cool but rather odd suit of clothes, Lucy Ann hung around for some time waiting for a chance to make a strike. At this time Gribble occupied a claim on the upper shore of Lake Minnetonka, near Cook's and adjoining him was a claim which had been jumped by a man, who employed Lobdell to occupy it in his absence, and [both of them] spent some time together upon that claim. The claim-jumper, however, finally disappeared, leaving Lobdell alone to watch his land. This was about the time that Gribble and Lucy got pretty thick, tramping together through the woods in pursuit of game, and sleeping together under the same blanket when they wooed the gentle goddess of slumber under the umbrageous forest trees around Minnetonka. But Gribble didn't dream that Lucy was a lone female, and hence he felt that his familiarity with her entitles him to a suspension of public opinion until he can prove his innocence of any evil intention. Well, after hunting with Lucy for a while, and pleasing her with the eloquence of his tales of love, and his experiences as a jurist and politician, Lucy got tired of waiting for the return of the claim-jumper and also of Gribble's pretty talk, and expressed an inclination to strike out further into the wilderness. And right here, Gribble did a handsome stroke of business. The claimant of the land failing to appear, it naturally became the property of the occupant, and Gribble thereupon purchased Lucy's right to the soil, and gave her that seventy-five dollar rifle which she carried for so many years afterwards in consideration of a quit-claim to the land, which she made out and transferred to Gribble. Then Lucy with Gribble's gun on her shoulder, set out for Meeker County.

She had the $75 rifle, and spent her first winter (1856–7) with another person[,] both in male attire, on the old Kandiyohi town-site on the north of Kandiyohi lakes.

The two were employed to reside on and thus hold possession of the new town-site, by the Minneapolis proprietors. Her companion spent the winter with her, but never for a moment suspected that he was wintering with a woman. At times when provisions fell short, they were compelled to live on squirrels for their meat.

And on one occasion, her companion was compelled to visit the Mississippi river settlements for supplies, and before his return, she, failing to find the necessary squirrel[s], relied upon those brought in by the cat, her only companion, for supplies — the cat furnished squirrels when the rifle could not reach them.

The last we heard of "puss" he was in the care of Noah White, of Kandiyohi county; he was a favorite in that settlement for a number of years and died of old age.

The Summer of '57 Lucy Ann appeared in Manannah, boarding a short time in a place, doing chores, chopping wood, hunting, washing dishes, etc., for her board. She was handy at anything; those with whom she was acquainted seemed to enjoy her company — her male apparel often requiring her to sleep in close proximity with others of the male gender — but with no indiscretion and with no suspicion that she was other than what appeared on the surface.

For the purpose of completing her disguise she had assumed the name of La-Roi Lobdell.

She ever seemed well pleased with her disguise, and the difficulty that would naturally interpose in resuming, without loss of character, her natural and appropriate raiment probably induced her to continue the deception. She claimed to have assumed this disguise, originally in order to better get away from home, without detection by a drunken husband.

She had but little money and was a splendid hunter and was offensive to none, and, as before remarked, was good company and a "hale fellow well met" with all the young people in the neighborhood, committing no sins or indiscretions.

In the summer of 1858, by accident, "Satan, with the aid of original sin," discovered and exposed her sex. The blue code of Connecticut was

Excerpt from **The History of Meeker County**

consulted, and the law was invoked to purge the community of the scandal.

The county attorney, Wm. Richards, now of the city of New York, filed an information against Mrs. Slater before John Robson, Esq. J. P., then contesting the jurisdiction of this count with J. B. Atkinson, Esq., as judge of the only court we had, alleging "that, whereas, one Lobdell, being a woman, falsely impersonates a man, to the great scandal of the community, and against the peace and dignity of the State of Minnesota," and asked that she be dealt with according to the law, that so pernicious an example might not be repeated in this land of steady habits. U. S. Willie, Esq., a young lawyer from Virginia, then residing at Forest City, appealed for the prisoner, and A. C. Smith as counsel.

The plea of NOT GUILTY was interposed, and the legal evidence to prove the necessary fact could not easily be obtained, and was left in doubt, and the court, after taking the case under advisement, finally ruled that the right of females to "wear the pants" had been recognized from the time of Justinian, and that the doctrine was too well settled to be upset in the case at bar, and Mrs. Slater was therefore discharged.

This denouement had the effect to discredit her in the settlement, subjecting her to insult from the vicious on every hand. She became deranged pending the proceedings, and, as it were, an outcast in society — an object of commiseration and sympathy, and soon thereafter a public charge.

On recovering from the mental shock, she expressed a willingness to return to her family and friends, but had no means save her rifle, and nobody in the settlement able to purchase that.

Mrs. Slater was finally sent home at the expense of Meeker county, under the direction of Capt. A. D. Pierce, then of Manannah.

Soon thereafter Capt. Pierce received a letter from Mrs. Slater's parents, thanking him and the county most heartily for their kindness in returning her to her friends.

In 1859 she again appeared on her old stamping ground, "the basket," and still in male attire. We conclude this novel romance in the langue of the *New York Times*:

> She at time would recount her experiences in the forest, and asserted that in the eight years she had killed 150 deer, eleven bears, numerous wild-cats and foxes, besides trapping hundreds of mink and other fur bearing animals. She had hand-to-hand contests with both wounded deer and bear, as ugly seams and scars upon her body amply testified. For two or three years after

her return she led a mendicant sort of life through the valley, and finally entered the poor-house at Delhi, to which she had sent her child several years previously. This child, however, had some time before been taken out of the institution by a farmer of Damascus township, Wayne county, Pennsylvania, named David Fortman, and given a home at his house.

In the spring of 1865 a young woman was let off an Erie railway passenger train at Basket station, or Long Eddy. She could not pay her fare any further, and said she had no particular point to which she was going. She gave her name as Mrs. Wilson, and said she had been deserted by her husband at Jersey City, where she had been living for some months. He was an employee of the Erie railway company, and had eloped with the daughter of the lady with which they boarded. Mrs. Wilson said that she was the daughter of highly respectable parents, name Perry of Lynn, Mass., and that she had run away from home with, and married James Wilson, her parents having opposed the match. The station agent and others at Basket station kindly offered to make up a purse for the unfortunate woman, and send her back to her parents, but she declined the offer, saying she was ashamed to meet them, and did not wish them to know of her whereabouts. She was in feeble health, and fearing that she might become a burden on strangers, she went to Delhi, and entered the poor-house.

Lucy Ann Slater was still an inmate of the almshouse, and a singular attachment had sprung up between her and the new comer, Mrs. Wilson, probably owing to the similarity of cause of which had forced them to become paupers. The following year both of them left the county house and nothing was heard of either of them for two years.

In the summer of 1868 a party of fishermen discovered two strange persons living in a cave in Barrett township, Monroe county, Pa. They were a man and woman. Soon thereafter there appeared in one of the villages a tall, gaunt man, carrying a rifle and leading a half-grown bear cub by a string tied about his neck. The man was bare-headed and his clothing was torn and dirty. Accompanying him was a woman about twenty-five years old, shabbily dressed, but giving evidence of more intelligence than the man, who called himself the Rev. Joseph Lobdell, and said that the woman was his wife. As they walked about, the man delivered noisy and meaningless "sermons," declaring that he was a prophet of the new dispensation, and that the bear had been sent to him by the Lord to guard him in the wilderness. For two years these vagrants wandered about that portion of the country, living in caves, and subsisting on roots, berries, and game killed by the man. At last they were arrested and lodged in jail at Stroudsb[u]rg, where they were kept several weeks. While in jail the discovery was made they were both women.

Subsequently the authorities learned that they belonged to Delaware county, N.Y., and thither they were sent. This pretended man and wife were Lucy Ann Slater and Mrs. Wilson, who had been leading this vagabond life for four years.

In the meantime Mary Ann Slater, the daughter of Lucy Ann, who had been taken from the Delhi almshouse in 1859 or 1860, had found an excellent home, and had grown up to be an intelligent and attractive young woman. A young man named Stone lived near by with his widowed mother,

Excerpt from The History of Meeker County

who he supported. He loved Mary Ann, and being a worthy and promising youth, the foster father of the girl saw no reason to oppose a match between her and the widow's son. The widow, however, was so strongly set against her son marrying the young lady that the whole neighborhood wondered. A number of young men in the neighborhood were jealous of Stone, and one dark night they waylaid Mary Ann. The outrage drove her almost insane, but Stone's affection was undiminished. He still pressed his claim for her hand. At length when their marriage seemed certain, Mrs. Stone revealed a state of affairs which fully accounted for her opposition. She told her son that she was not a widow, and that Henry Slater was his father as well as the father of Mary Ann.

Lucy Ann Slater and Mrs. Wilson again left the Delhi poor-house and have ever since been living in caves and cabins in the woods. The former is at times entirely deranged. All last winter they lived in a cave ten miles from Honesdale, but they divided their time between Monroe county and this. Lucy Ann wandered into this village the other day, and out of common decency she was arrested, and placed in jail where we found her at the commencement of this chapter.

Chapter Notes

Introduction

1. See Ellen Dwyer, *Homes for the Mad: Life Inside Two Nineteenth-Century Asylums* (New Brunswick, NJ: Rutgers University Press, 1987).
2. P. M. Wise, "A Case of Sexual Perversion," *Alienist and Neurologist: A Quarterly Journal of Scientific, Clinical and Forensic Psychiatry and Neurology* 4 (January 1883): 89.
3. Ibid., p. 87.
4. Ibid., 90.
5. Ibid., 88.
6. Ibid., 89.
7. "Ze" or "sie" can be used in place of "he" or "she," and "hir" can be used to replace "his" or "her." In writing, sometimes people use "s/he."
8. See Judith Halberstam, *In a Queer Time and Place: Transgender Bodies, Subcultural Lives* (New York and London: New York University Press, 2005).
9. Wise, "A Case of Sexual Perversion," 88.
10. Leslie Feinberg, *Transgender Liberation: Making History from Joan of Arc to Dennis Rodman* (Boston: Beacon Press, 1996), 1.

Chapter One

1. George L. Mosse, "Nationalism and Respectability: Normal and Abnormal Sexuality in the Nineteenth Century," *Journal of Contemporary History* 17, no. 2, *Sexuality in History* (April 1982): 230.
2. For a full discussion of experimental religions in nineteenth-century America, see Gayle V. Fischer, *Pantaloons and Power: A Nineteenth Century Dress Reform in the United States* (Kent, Ohio: Kent State University Press, 2001).
3. See G. J. Barker-Benfield, *The Horrors of the Half-Known Life: Male Attitudes Toward Women and Sexuality in Nineteenth-Century America* (New York: Harper & Row, 1976), for a full discussion of the causes and effects of adventurous bachelors in nineteenth-century America.
4. Barker-Benfield, *The Horrors of the Half-Known Life*, 45.
5. Ibid., 200.
6. See Judith Butler's "Introduction to Bodies That Matter," in *Women, Autobiography, Theory*, ed. Sidonie Smith and Julia Watson (Madison: University of Wisconsin Press, 1998), for a full discussion on the performativity of gender.
7. Jonathan Ned Katz, *Gay/Lesbian Almanac: A New Documentary* (New York: Carroll & Graf, 1983), 139.

Notes — Chapter One

8. Mosse, "Nationalism and Respectability," 229.
9. See Barbara Welter, "The Cult of True Womanhood: 1820–1860," *American Quarterly* 18, no. 2, part 1 (Summer 1966): 151–74.
10. See Sheryl Hurner, "Discursive Identity Formation of Suffrage Women: Reframing the 'Cult of True Womanhood' Through Song," *Western Journal of Communication* 70, no. 3 (July 2006): 235.
11. Miriam Forman-Brunell, *Girlhood in America, an Encyclopedia*, volume 1 (Santa Barbara, CA: ABC-CLIO, 2001), 250.
12. Ibid., 248.
13. Ibid., 250–52.
14. For a fuller discussion of nineteenth-century scientific notions on women's bodies, see Barker-Benfield, *The Horrors of the Half-Known Life*, chapter 22, "The Physical Decline of American Women."
15. Forman-Brunell, *Girlhood in America*, volume 1, 253.
16. Lucy Ann Lobdell, *Narrative of the Female Hunter of Delaware and Sullivan Counties, N.Y.* (New York: Published for author, 1855), 4.
17. Lucy Ann was born in 1829 and states that she started school when she was either ten or twelve, so this date is calculated to be her earliest potential date of attending school.
18. Lucy Ann Lobdell, *Narrative of the Female Hunter*, 30.
19. Ibid.
20. Ibid., 16.
21. Barker-Benfield, *The Horrors of the Half-Known Life*, 21.
22. Ibid.
23. Lucy Ann Lobdell, *Narrative of the Female Hunter*, 4.
24. Interview with Susan Crawson Shields, Lucy Ann's great-great-granddaughter, May 2000.
25. Lucy Ann Lobdell, *Narrative of the Female Hunter*, 6.
26. Ibid., 8.
27. Ibid.
28. Ibid., 8–9.
29. Ibid., 9.
30. Ibid., 10.
31. Ibid.
32. Ibid., 11.
33. Ibid., 12.
34. Native Americans were living there at the time, although the government referred to the area as a wilderness.
35. Leslie D. LaValley, *Basket Letters: A History of That Mountainous Region of the Upper Delaware That Was Once Known as the South Woods and the Wilds of the Basket* (Walton, NY: Reporter Co., Inc., in cooperation with the Basket Historical Society of the Upper Delaware Valley, 1990), 138.
36. Lucy Ann Lobdell, *Narrative of the Female Hunter*, 13.
37. Ibid., 14.
38. Wise, "A Case of Sexual Perversion," 88.
39. Welter, "The Cult of True Womanhood," 170.
40. Lucy Ann Lobdell, *Narrative of the Female Hunter*, 16.
41. Ibid., 17.
42. Ibid.
43. Ibid., 19.
44. Ibid., 18.
45. Ibid., 19.
46. Ibid., 15.
47. Ibid.
48. Ibid., 16.

49. Ibid., 22.

50. "The Female Hunter," *Wayne Citizen*, August 24, 1871. This statement comes from one of the men who escorted Lobdell back to New York State after a short time in jail in Stroudsburg, Pennsylvania. He learned this information from neighbors near the Lobdell family home.

51. Lucy Ann Lobdell, *Narrative of the Female Hunter*, 22.

52. Brian Gabrial, "A Woman's Place: Defiance and Obedience—Newspaper Stories About Women During the Trial of John Brown," *Journalism* 25, no. 1 (Winter 2008): 7.

53. Carrol Smith-Rosenberg, *Disorderly Conduct: Visions of Gender in Victorian America* (New York: Oxford University Press, 1985), 25.

54. Marie later stated that she and Joe were followers of Swedenborg, the founder of a controversial religion based on visions that he claimed he received directly from God. See Guinnip's letter to Friend Woodward in the Lobdell file at the Wayne County Historical Society in Honesdale, Pennsylvania.

55. Lucy Ann Lobdell, *Narrative of the Female Hunter*, 28.

56. Ibid., 46.

57. Hurner, "Discursive Identity Formation of Suffrage Women," 236.

58. Welter, "The Cult of True Womanhood," 161.

59. Lucy Ann Lobdell, *Narrative of the Female Hunter*, 30.

60. Ibid., 34.

61. Ibid., 32.

62. Ibid., 36. Note: A second book has never been discovered by either Lucy or Joseph Lobdell.

63. Ibid.

64. Lucy records the newspaper article in her narrative, but does not give the name of either the author or the publication, only that it comes from Bridgeport, Connecticut, and is dated January 2, 1853.

65. According to *Merriam Webster's Collegiate Dictionary*, 10th edition (1993), a rod is equal to 16.5 feet. Lucy hit her mark with a black-powder pistol at a distance of 297 feet.

66. Lucy Ann Lobdell, *Narrative of the Female Hunter*, 37.

67. Ibid.

68. Ibid., 38.

69. Ibid., 39.

70. Rose Weitz, "A History of Women's Bodies," in *The Politics of Women's Bodies: Sexuality, Appearance, and Behavior*, ed. Rose Weitz (New York: Oxford University Press, 2003), 4.

71. Lucy Ann Lobdell, *Narrative of the Female Hunter*, 42–43.

72. Ibid., 43.

73. Ibid.

74. Ibid.

75. Ibid., 43–44.

76. Ibid., 45.

77. Ibid.

78. Helene E. Roberts, "The Exquisite Slave: The Role of Clothes in the Making of the Victorian Woman," *Signs: Journal of Women in Culture and Society* 2, no. 3 (1977): 554–69.

79. Fischer, *Pantaloons and Power*, 77.

80. Carrol Smith-Rosenberg, "The Female Animal Medical and Biological Views of Woman and Her Role in Nineteenth-Century America," *Journal of American History* 60, no. 2 (September 1973): 338.

81. According to Sidonie Smith's "The Autobiographical Manifesto: Identities, Temporalities, Politics," in *Autobiography and Questions of Gender*, ed. Shirley Neuman (London: Frank Cass & Co., 1991), a manifesto explains the reasons for the actions taken for it announces publicly the individual's experience and brings to light issues and experiences hidden in the shadows of the margins (191), confronts cultural constructions of identities and their sanctioned, legitimized performances while intervening culturally in the authorizing fictions sustained by repetition, and speaks to the future (194).

82. Welter, "The Cult of True Womanhood," 152.
83. Barker-Benfield, *The Horrors of the Half-Known Life*, 45.
84. Fischer, *Pantaloons and Power*, 84.
85. Lucy Ann Lobdell, *Narrative of the Female Hunter*, 41.
86. LaValley, *Basket Letters*, 139.
87. Ibid.
88. Interview with Doug Lobdell, Sr., June 14, 1999.
89. LaValley, *Basket Letters*, 138.
90. Ibid., 139.
91. Guinnip, personal letter to Friend Woodward.
92. Lunacy testimonials on Lucy Ann Lobdell Slater (Delhi, New York, Delaware County seat).
93. Lucy Ann Lobdell, *Narrative of the Female Hunter*, 41.
94. Wise, "A Case of Sexual Perversion," 88.
95. Ibid.
96. Lucy Ann Lobdell, *Narrative of the Female Hunter*, 46.
97. Leslie Feinberg, *Transgender Warrior: Making History from Joan of Arc to Dennis Rodman* (Boston: Beacon Press, 1996), x.

Chapter Two

1. The oldest sources for this story, which are contemporary with Joseph's lifetime, list the town as Bethany, while later sources that rely on legend and gossip list the town as Dyberry, Pennsylvania, a small town along the Lackawaxen River and outside of Honesdale in Wayne County, Pennsylvania.
2. See Sally Soden, "Oral History of Irma Kimble Simons," August 15, 2005, in the Wayne County Historical Society in Honesdale, Pennsylvania
3. See Frank P. Woodward, "Lucy Ann Lobdell — Female Hunter of Long Eddy," from "Spooking Around Memory's Garret" (Wayne County Historical Society in Honesdale, Pennsylvania)
4. "The Man-Woman: Lucy Ann Lobdell in Town," *Port Jervis Evening Gazette*, August 10, 1876.
5. Compiled from "The Man-Woman: Lucy Ann Lobdell in Town," *Port Jervis Evening Gazette*, . For the original sources of the story of the Bethany incident, see "Lucy Ann Lobdell Dead," *Stamford Mirror*, June 23, 1885; "A Queer Married Couple," *Warren Ledger*, November 9, 1883; Woodward, "Lucy Ann Lobdell — Female Hunter of Long Eddy"; and Soden, "The Oral History of Irma Kimble Simons."
6. Riki Anne Wilchins, *Queer Theory, Gender Theory* (Los Angeles: Alyson Books, 2004), 8.
7. Jennifer Ladd Nelson, "Dress Reform and the Bloomer," *Journal of American and Comparative Cultures* 23, no. 1 (2000): 21.
8. Fischer, *Pantaloons and Power*, 24.
9. Nelson, "Dress Reform and the Bloomer," 23.
10. Fischer, *Pantaloons and Power*, 5.
11. Robert E. Riegel, "Women's Clothes and Women's Rights," *American Quarterly* 15, no. 3 (Autumn 1963): 393.
12. Barker-Benfield, *The Horrors of the Half-Known Life*, 85.
13. Fischer, *Pantaloons and Power*, 83.
14. Smith-Rosenberg, *Disorderly Conduct*, 46.
15. Mosse, "Nationalism and Respectability," 228.
16. See Butler, "Introduction to Bodies That Matter."
17. For more on the performative nature of gender, see Judith Butler's "Introduction to Bodies That Matter."
18. Nelson, "Dress Reform and the Bloomer," 24.

19. See "Lucy Ann Lobdell Dead," *Stamford Mirror*.
20. See Woodward, "Lucy Ann Lobdell — Female Hunter of Long Eddy."
21. See Soden, "Oral History of Irma Kimble Simons."
22. Halberstam, *In a Queer Time and Place*, 77.
23. "Lucy Ann Lobdell — The Wayne County Female Hunter Dead," *Wayne County Herald*, July 2, 1885.
24. See Woodward account.
25. Peter Boag, "Thinking Like Mount Rushmore: Sexuality and Gender in the Republican Landscape," in *Seeing Nature Through Gender*, ed. Virginia J. Scharff (Lawrence: University Press of Kansas, 2003), 46.
26. Two male authorities, Smith and Wise, do actually speak to Lobdell in a legal interviewing process, but both present their interpretation of Lobdell's words along with their assumptions.
27. For discussion of the dangers that bachelors presented to society by not marrying and living within established marital and familial structures, see Barker-Benfield, *The Horrors of the Half-Known Life* (9–14). He also includes Catherine Beecher's beliefs that women had the civilizing power to inhibit the destructive tendencies of male pursuit of autonomy and her prediction that foregoing marriage would lead to uncontrolled anti-social behavior and masturbation (49), which would lead directly to a state of imbecility and feebleness, destroying a man's mental, physical, and moral powers forever (180).
28. The U.S. Census of June 14, 1855, for Delaware County, Hancock, New York, Household #69, Visitation #72, does not list Lucy Ann Slater as living in her father's house, or any other residence in Long Eddy, a village listed under the town of Hancock, New York. Lobdell's daughter, Helen Slater, is listed as living with her grandparents, James and Sarah Lobdell.
29. Lobdell's adventure in Minnesota was unknown to the East Coast until Mindy Desens, fascinated with an account she found of Lobdell in *History of Meeker County* by A. C. Smith in her local historical library of Litchfield, Minnesota, contacted Edith Lobdell of Deposit, New York, seeking any other information on Lucy/La-Roi. Thus were the two halves of Lobdell's recorded life fused.
30. A. C. Smith, "A Wild Woman's History — The Slayer of Hundreds of Bears and Wildcats," in *History of Meeker County: A Historical Sketch of Meeker County, Minnesota from Its First Settlement to July 4th, 1876* (Litchfield, MN: Belfoy & Joubert, 1877), 101.
31. The 1857 Territorial Pioneers Census lists Louis Lobdell, twenty-two, male, as living in household #118 in Swede Grove Township, Meeker County, Minnesota. Smith seems unaware of this name and those involved in this narrative only know Lobdell as La-Roi. In light of the name change after life in Bethany, I can only speculate that some similar trouble in St. Paul necessitated another name change.
32. A. C. Smith, "A Wild Woman's History," 102.
33. Ibid.
34. When the original owner of the property did not return, ownership moved to Lobdell, who could legally claim it by writing out a quit-claim deed.
35. A. C. Smith, "A Wild Woman's History," 103.
36. Ibid.
37. Ibid., 104–5.
38. The reference to Satan is vague, except for its connection to original sin, commonly understood to be sex, so its meaning is hard to decipher exactly. One other similar trial that mentions Satan as the cause of deviancy was that of Catherina Margaretha Linck who dressed as a man and married a woman. The wife complained to her mother about her husband, and Linck's mother-in-law and a neighbor attacked Linck with a sword, cut her pants off to examine her, and learned that she was a woman. Linck was tried for sodomy and executed in 1721. In her defense, Linck claimed she had been deluded by Satan. See Theo van der Meer, "Tribades on Trial: Female Same-Sex Offenders in Late Eighteenth-Century Amsterdam," *Journal of the History of Sexuality* 1 (January 1991): 424–45.

39. A. C. Smith, "A Wild Woman's History," 105–6. The "blue code of Connecticut" stated that any person, man or woman, found to be wearing elaborate clothing with lace, gold, silk, slashed sleeves, cutwork or embroidery who could be judged as "uncomely or prejudiciall to the common good, and the party offending reforme not the same upon notice given to him, that then the nexte Assistant, being informed thereof, shall have power to bind the party soe offending to answer it at the nexte Courte, if the case so requires" (www.quinnipiac.edu/other/abl/etext/trueblue/bluelaws.html).

40. Judith Butler, *Gender Trouble: Feminism and the Subversion of Identity* (New York: Routledge, 1999), 48.

41. Sharon W. Tiffany and Kathleen J. Adams, *The Wild Woman: An Inquiry into the Anthropology of an Idea* (Cambridge, MA: Schekman, 1985), 62.

42. A. C. Smith, "A Wild Woman's History," 102–3.

43. Ibid., 103.

44. Riki Anne Wilchins, *Read My Lips: Sexual Subversion and the End of Gender* (Ithaca, NY: Firebrand Books, 1997), 154.

45. A. C. Smith, "A Wild Woman's History," 105.

46. Lisa Duggan, *Sapphic Slashers: Sex, Violence, and American Modernity* (Durham, NC: Duke University Press, 2000), 144.

47. Butler, "Introduction to Bodies That Matter," 373.

48. A. C. Smith, "A Wild Woman's History," 106.

49. Ibid., 105–6. Ironically, the same summer La-Roi was being tried for impersonating a man, a similar case was "pending before the civil Tribune of Castelsarrazin, near Toulouse" in Minnesota. A woman who had been married for thirteen years had brought "action against her husband to have the marriage declared null and void, on the ground that he is not a man but a woman!" "Extraordinary Affair," *St. Paul Daily Times*, September 15, 1858.

50. Judith Halberstam, *Female Masculinity* (Durham, NC, and London: Duke University Press, 1998), 62.

51. Duggan, *Sapphic Slashers:*, 63.

52. A. C. Smith, "A Wild Woman's History," 106.

53. Ibid.

54. Ibid.

55. Halberstam, *Female Masculinity*, 1.

56. Ibid.

57. Kate Bornstein, *Gender Outlaw: On Men, Women, and the Rest of Us* (New York: Vintage Books, 1994), 74.

58. A. C. Smith, "A Wild Woman's History," 105.

59. Ibid.

60. Ibid., 104.

61. Ibid., 98. This information was copied from an article from the *Port Jervis Evening Gazette*, "A Wild Woman's History: The Slayer of Hundreds of Bears and Wildcats," July 27, 1876.

62. A. C. Smith, "A Wild Woman's History," 98.

63. "Romantic Paupers: The Strange History of Two Penniless Women," *Stamford Mirror*, September 5, 1871; "The Female Hunter," *Wayne Citizen*; "Lucy Ann Lobdell Dead," *Stamford Mirror*; "Lucy Ann Lobdell — The Wayne County Female Hunter Dead," *Wayne County Herald*.

64. "Extraordinary Narrative: Singular Experiences of Two Women — They Voluntarily Assume a Wild Life — Peculiar Chain of Remarkable Circumstances — The Slater Mystery Solved," *New York Times*, August 25, 1871: 5.

65. Halberstam, *Female Masculinity*, 49.

66. A. C. Smith, "A Wild Woman's History," 100.

67. Merle Potter, "Meeker County's 'Wild Woman,'" in *101 Best Stories of Minnesota* (Minneapolis: n.p., 1931), 119.

68. For an even less accurate telling of Lucy's hunting prowess and portrayal of her as a

failed-marksman-turned-bride, see Frank Lamson's *Condensed History of Meeker County: 1855–1939* (Litchfield, MN: Brown, 1939) or Ethelyn Pearson's " Early Female Impersonator Was Scandal of Minnesota!" in *It Really Happened Here!* (Fargo, ND: McCleary & Sons, 2000).

69. A. C. Smith, "A Wild Woman's History," 107.
70. Halberstam, *Female Masculinity*, 2.
71. Ibid., 15.
72. See "Extraordinary Narrative," *New York Times*, August 25, 1871. This information also appeared in the *Stamford Mirror* on September 5, 1871.
73. According to the federal census on July 18, 1860, for Hancock, Delaware County, New York, Lucy Ann Lobdell was living with her parents, James and Sarah Lobdell, along with daughter Helen Slater, at this date. So Lobdell must have entered the poorhouse after this time.
74. Michael Katz, *In the Shadow of the Poorhouse: A Social History of Welfare in America* (New York: Basic Books, 1996), 6.
75. For a complete discussion of poorhouses, see Katz, *In the Shadow of the Poorhouse*.
76. Nineteenth-century newspaper sources claim Perry entered the area in 1868, but the New York State census for June 1865 lists Lucy Ann Lobdell and Maria Perry, aged 32, living in Delaware County with James and Sarah Lobdell.
77. Details of Marie's entry into Lobdell's life can be found in the following sources: "Romantic Paupers," *Stamford Mirror*; "Extraordinary Narrative," *New York Times*; "The Female Hunter," *Wayne Citizen*; "A Romance in Real Life," *Port Jervis Evening Gazette*, August 22, 1871; "Lucy Slater the Huntress," *Hancock Herald*, October 16, 1879; "Lucy Ann Lobdell Dead," *Stamford Mirror*.
78. The story of Marie's entrance into Lobdell's life is compiled from the following articles: "Lucy Slater the Huntress," *Hancock Herald*; "Two Strange Lives," *Galveston Daily News*, July 5, 1885; "A Queer Married Couple," *Warren Ledger*, November 9, 1883; "Extraordinary Narrative," *New York Times*; and "Romantic Paupers," *Stamford Mirror*.
79. "Lucy Ann Lobdell Dead," *Stamford Mirror*.

Chapter Three

1. Duggan, *Sapphic Slashers*, 115.
2. "Death of a Modern Diana: The Female Hunter of Long Eddy — The Strange History of Lucy Slater — Her Career as a Huntress, a Pauper, a Minister, and a Vagrant — Dressed in Men's Clothing She Wins a Girl's Love," New York Times, October 7, 1879: 2.
3. "Extraordinary Narrative," *New York Times*.
4. "A Mountain Romance: Strange Life of Unhappy Women — A Singular Family History — The Female Huntress of Long Eddy — Strange Love of Two Women — An Accomplished Boston Girl, A Voluntary Outcast — An Unfortunate Daughter," *New York Times*, April 8, 1877.
5. "Lucy Ann Lobdell Dead," *Stamford Mirror*.
6. See Woodward account.
7. See "A Curious Career: Remarkable Adventures of Lucy Ann Lobdell, an Eccentric Female Character Who Figured Successfully as Hermit, Music Teacher, Author and "Female Husband," *National Police Gazette*, October 25, 1879; "Lucy Slater the Huntress," *Hancock Herald*.
8. See July 18, 1860, federal census for Delaware County, New York. Lucy Ann Lobdell, age 30, is listed along with Helen Slater, age 7, as living with James and Sarah Lobdell.
9. "Mountain Romance," *New York Times*. This story is repeated in "Death of a Modern Diana," *New York Times*; "Lucy Slater the Huntress," *Hancock Herald*; "A Curious Career," *National Police Gazette*; and "Lucy Ann Lobdell — The Wayne County Female Hunter Dead," *Wayne County Herald*.
10. See "Lucy Ann Lobdell — The Wayne County Female Hunter Dead," *Wayne County*

Notes — Chapter Three

Herald; "Lucy Ann Lobdell Dead," *Stamford Mirror*; "A Queer Married Couple," *Warren Ledger*.

11. June 17, 1865 — the New York State Census, Hancock, Delaware County, New York, line 70, household #72, lists Lucy Ann Lobdell and Maria Perry, 32, as living with James and Sarah Lobdell.

12. For physical descriptions of Lobdell, see "The Man-Woman: Lucy Ann Lobdell in Town," *Port Jervis Evening Gazette*; "Extraordinary Narrative," *New York Times*; "The Female Hunter," *Wayne Citizen*; "Romantic Paupers," *Stamford Mirror*; "Lucy Ann Lobdell," *Wayne Citizen*; "Death of a Modern Diana," *New York Times*; "A Curious Career," *National Police Gazette*; and Woodward, "Lucy Ann Lobdell — Female Hunter of Long Eddy."

13. A. C. Smith, "A Wild Woman's History," 109.

14. "Who Are They?" *Jeffersonian*, August 10, 1871.

15. "A Queer Married Life," *Warren Ledger*, November 9, 1883.

16. Ibid.

17. "The Law of Vagrancy," *Wayne County Herald*, August 23, 1877. This same article continues, "It also provides for a commitment of such vagrants for not less than thirty days, nor more than six months with liability to labor under orders from the directors of the poor."

18. "Who Are They?" *Jeffersonian*.

19. "Joe Lobdell & Wife, Their History," *Jeffersonian*, August 17, 1871.

20. "Romantic Paupers," *Stamford Mirror*.

21. August 12, 1870: the U.S. Census of Hancock, Delaware County, New York, lists Lucy, age 46, as the housekeeper of the James and Sarah Lobdell household. Sarah is listed as insane.

22. "Extraordinary Narrative," *New York Times*.

23. "The Man-Woman: Lucy Ann Lobdell in Town," *Port Jervis Evening Gazette*.

24. "Lucy Ann Lobdell," *Wayne Citizen*, November 9, 1871.

25. See "The Female Hunter of Long Eddy a Raving Maniac," *Wayne County Herald*, November 2, 1871; and "Lucy Ann Lobdell," *Wayne Citizen*.

26. "Lucy Ann Lobdell," *Wayne Citizen*.

27. Visiting insane asylums and prisons in order to picnic and watch the inmates and residents was a common form of cheap entertainment for nineteenth-century families.

28. This article can be found in the Lobdell folder at the Wayne County Historical Society in Honesdale, Pennsylvania. It has no title or date recorded, but obviously concerns the same incident reported by others in November 1871.

29. This article, "The Lady in Pantaloons: She (Or He) Has Gone Away," *Wayne Citizen*, is found in the Lobdell file at the Wayne County Historical Society in Honesdale, Pennsylvania.

30. "Lucy Ann Lobdell," *Wayne Citizen*.

31. "A Wild Woman's History," *Port Jervis Evening Gazette*, July 27, 1876.

32. "Romantic Lunatics," *Port Jervis Evening Gazette*, September 21, 1876.

33. Ibid.

34. Duggan, *Sapphic Slashers*, 32.

35. Ibid., 60.

36. Michel Foucault, *The History of Sexuality: An Introduction* trans. Robert Hurely (New York: Vintage Books, 1990), 12.

37. "The Man-Woman: Lucy Ann Lobdell in Town," *Port Jervis Evening Gazette*. (This source can be found in the Lobdell file at the Wayne County Historical Society in Honesdale, Pennsylvania).

38. Lobdell file at the Wayne County Historical Society in Honesdale, Pennsylvania, November 2, 1871.

39. Lobdell file at the Wayne County Historical Society in Honesdale, Pennsylvania.

40. "Extraordinary Narrative," *New York Times*.

41. "The Man-Woman: Lucy Ann Lobdell in Town," *Port Jervis Evening Gazette*.

Notes — Chapter Three

42. Both articles are found in the Lobdell folder at the Wayne County Historical Society in Honesdale, Pennsylvania.
43. Carrol Smith-Rosenberg, "Discourses of Sexuality and Subjectivity: The New Woman, 1870–1936," in *Hidden from History: Reclaiming the Gay and Lesbian Past*, ed. Martin Bauml Duberman, Martha Vicinus, and George Chauncey, Jr. (Ontario, Canada: New American Library, 1989), 265.
44. See "Extraordinary Narrative," *New York Times*; "Death of a Modern Diana," *New York Times*; "Lucy Slater the Huntress," *Hancock Herald*; and "A Curious Career," *National Police Gazette*.
45. "The Spencer House" was a euphemism for the jail, which was under the authority of Sheriff Spencer at this time.
46. *Honesdale Citizen*, September 21, 1876.
47. "The Man-Woman: Lucy Ann Lobdell in Town," *Port Jervis Evening Gazette*.
48. "Extraordinary Narrative," *New York Times*.
49. "A Mountain Romance," *New York Times*.
50. Duggan, *Sapphic Slashers*, 71.
51. Ibid., 1.
52. Ibid., 42–43.
53. See histories by Woodward and Smith.
54. Halberstam, *A Queer Time and Place*, 10 and 15.
55. Smith-Rosenberg, *Disorderly Conduct*, 48.
56. Halberstam, *Female Masculinity*, 20.
57. Patricia Gagne, Richard Tewksbury, and Deanna McGaughey, "Coming Out and Crossing Over: Identity Formation and Proclamation in a Transgender Community," *Gender and Society* 11, no. 4 (August 1997): 492.
58. Butler, "Introduction to Bodies That Matter," 368.
59. Bornstein, *Gender Outlaw*, 94.
60. Smith-Rosenberg, *Disorderly Conduct*, 98.
61. Bornstein, *Gender Outlaw*, 89.
62. Ibid.
63. Smith-Rosenberg, "Discourses of Sexuality and Subjectivity," 277.
64. John Sloop, "Lucy Lobdell's Queer Circumstances," in *Queering Public Address: Sexualities in American Historical Discourse*, ed. Charles Morris III (Columbia: University of South Carolina Press, 2007).
65. Woodward, "Lucy Ann Lobdell — Female Hunter of Long Eddy."
66. "Romantic Paupers," *Stamford Mirror*; "Extraordinary Narrative," *New York Times*.
67. "Lucy Ann Lobdell Dead," *Stamford Mirror*.
68. "A Mountain Romance," *New York Times*.
69. Woodward, "Lucy Ann Lobdell — Female Hunter of Long Eddy."
70. "Lucy Ann Lobdell Dead," *Stamford Mirror*.
71. "Lucy Slater the Huntress," *Hancock Herald*.
72. "Extraordinary Narrative," *New York Times*.
73. Woodward. "Lucy Ann Lobdell — Female Hunter of Long Eddy."
74. "Lucy Ann Lobdell," *Wayne Citizen*.
75. A. C. Smith, "A Wild Woman's History," 109; "Lucy Slater the Huntress," *Hancock Herald*.
76. "A Mountain Romance," *New York Times*.
77. Woodward, "Lucy Ann Lobdell — Female Hunter of Long Eddy."
78. "A Mountain Romance," *New York Times*.
79. "Lucy Slater the Huntress," *Hancock Herald*.
80. Ibid.
81. "Lucy Ann Lobdell — The Wayne County Female Hunter Dead," *Wayne County Herald*.
82. Sidebar in the *Wayne County Herald*, May 18, 1882.

83. Woodward, "Lucy Ann Lobdell — Female Hunter of Long Eddy."
84. Halberstam, *In a Queer Time and Place*. 1.
85. Ibid.
86. Ibid., 10.
87. Ibid., 10.
88. Grantor-Seller Index; Sheriff's Sales, Book #50, pages 112–13, line 49. Deed was recorded on February 16, 1878. Lobdell purchased the parcel from August Yatto. This document is in the Wayne County Clerk's Office at the Courthouse in Honesdale, Pennsylvania.
89. In the column "Hereabouts and Thereabouts," *Wayne County Herald*, February 21, 1878.
90. See John Lobdell's addendum in his sworn statements, included in Lobdell's lunacy testimonials.
91. Sidebar article, *Wayne Independent*, March 28, 1878: "Lucy Ann Lobdell, the female huntress and woman's rights actress of the wild woods, after years of wanderings, has at last settled down into a peaceful life."
92. Smith-Rosenberg, "Discourses of Sexuality and Subjectivity," 278.
93. *Forest and Stream: A Journal of Outdoor Life, Travel, Nature Study, and Shooting* 13, no. 12 (October 23, 1879): 751.
94. Wise, "A Case of Sexual Perversion," 89.
95. Lobdell's life on the farm actually lasted just a matter of months before he was moved into a house owned by his brother, John.
96. Guinnip, personal letter to Friend Woodward.
97. While Marie intended this letter to be a private communication to Mr. Ham, he felt it "so well expresses her views on matters of public interest" that he published it in the *Wayne County Herald*, on June 15, 1882, under the title "The Problem of Life — What the 'Apparent Widow' of the Female Hunter Has to Say About It."
98. "The Hunters of Long Eddy," from an undated article attached to the doctor's clipboard. Footnoted in Katz's *Gay American History: Lesbians and Gay Men in the U.S.A.* (New York: Thomas Y. Crowell, 1976), 601.
99. "Lucy Ann Lobdell — The Wayne County Female Hunter Dead," *Wayne County Herald*.
100. See Walter Peak's testimony in Lobdell's lunacy inquisition.
101. Lobdell lunacy testimonials.
102. Ibid.
103. This "Certificate of Insanity," now in the Willard archives in Albany, New York, was signed on October 9, 1880, by Delaware County Judge Maynard and Dr. Isaacs of Delhi.
104. Wise's psychiatric treatment of Lobdell will be dealt with in more detail in the next chapter.
105. Judith Lorber, *Paradoxes of Gender* (New Haven, CT: Yale University Press, 1994), 96.

Chapter Four

1. In a phone conversation, Susan Bartoletti used the word "genderful" to mean a selection of gender expression and identity that runs the gamut of various blends of masculinity and femininity.
2. Wise, "A Case of Sexual Perversion," 87.
3. Smith-Rosenberg, *Disorderly Conduct*, 46.
4. Nikki Sullivan, *A Critical Introduction to Queer Theory* (New York: New York University Press, 2003), 4–6.
5. Ibid., 10–11.
6. Esther Newton, "The Mythic Mannish Lesbian: Radclyffe Hall and the New Woman," *Signs* 9, no. 4, *The Lesbian Issue* (Summer 1984): 566–67.

7. George Chauncey, Jr., "From Sexual Inversion to Homosexuality: Medicine and the Changing Conceptualization of Female Desire," *Salmagundi*, no. 58/59 (Winter 1982–1983): 118.

8. See Richard von Krafft-Ebbing, *Psychopathia Sexualis* 1886), reprinted in English translation (New York: Samuel Login, 1908).

9. Smith-Rosenberg, "Discourses of Sexuality and Subjectivity," 268. Note that Smith-Rosenberg refers to a classification developed to define the second generation of New Woman in the 1930s, which challenged traditional gender relations and distribution of power; however, Krafft-Ebbing's ideas were commonly known in sexological circles of the late nineteenth century when Wise was exploring the subject.

10. Duggan, *Sapphic Slashers*, 26.

11. For discussion of early sexology, see Carrol Smith-Rosenberg's *Disorderly Conduct*, Havelock Ellis's *Psychology of Sex*, and Richard von Krafft-Ebbing's *Psychopathia Sexualis*.

12. Duggan, *Sapphic Slashers*, 25.

13. Smith-Rosenberg, "Discourses of Sexuality and Subjectivity," 268–69.

14. Wise, "A Case of Sexual Perversion," 87.

15. Ibid.

16. Chauncey, "From Sexual Inversion to Homosexuality," 119.

17. Duggan, *Sapphic Slashers*, 49.

18. Wise, "A Case of Sexual Perversion," 88.

19. See U.S. census records for Hancock, Delaware County, New York, in 1860 and 1870.

20. Wise, "A Case of Sexual Perversion," 88

21. Ibid.

22. Foucault, *The History of Sexuality*, 61–62.

23. Wise, "A Case of Sexual Perversion," 88

24. Foucault, *The History of Sexuality*, 67.

25. Wise, "A Case of Sexual Perversion," 89.

26. Ibid.

27. Ibid., 89–90, emphasis mine.

28. Smith-Rosenberg, "Discourses of Sexuality and Subjectivity," 273.

29. Wise, "A Case of Sexual Perversion," 89.

30. Ibid., 87.

31. Newton, "The Mythic Mannish Lesbian," 561.

32. Duggan, *Sapphic Slashers*, 106.

33. Wise, "A Case of Sexual Perversion," 90.

34. Ibid., 87.

35. Ibid., 88.

36. Tasmin Spargo, *Foucault and Queer Theory* (New York: Totem Books, 1999), 16.

37. Eve K. Sedgwick, *Epistemology of the Closet* (Berkeley: University of California Press, 1990), 4.

38. Ibid., 11.

39. Ibid., 7.

40. Wise, "A Case of Sexual Perversion," 91.

41. Ibid., 91.

42. James Kiernan, "Perverted Sexual Instincts: Notes on a Paper Read by J. C. Kiernan, M.D.," *Chicago Medical Journal and Examiner* XLVIII (1884): 264.

43. Havelock Ellis, "Sexual Inversion in Women," *Alienist and Neurologist: A Quarterly Journal of Scientific, Clinical and Forensic Psychiatry and Neurology* 16 (1895): 142.

44. Ibid., 147–148.

45. Ibid., 154.

46. Ibid., 153.

47. Foucault, *The History of Sexuality*, 84.

48. Butler, *Gender Trouble*, xx.

49. See "Lucy Ann Lobdell Dead," in the *Stamford Mirror*, June 23, 1885, and the *Wayne County Herald*, June 2, 1885.

50. James Kiernan, "Psychological Aspects of the Sexual Appetite," *Alienist and Neurologist: A Quarterly Journal of Scientific, Clinical and Forensic Psychiatry and Neurology* (April 1891): 200–204; "Perverted Sexual Instincts"; "Original Communications: Insanity. Lecture XXVI — Sexual Perversion," *Detroit Lancet* 7, no. 11 (May 1884): 481–83.

51. Kiernan, "Psychological Aspects of the Sexual Appetite," 203.

52. See Katz's *Gay American History*, the source for numerous articles about Lobdell.

53. This two-year space of time is a tantalizing mystery, as I have found no documented evidence of where Lobdell was or what he was doing during that time. He is noticeably absent from newspapers though, which suggests strict incarceration somewhere, possibly in the home of some family member.

54. A transcript of death, held at the Bureau of Vital Statistics in Binghamton, New York, states Lobdell died on May 28, 1912, of chronic endocarditis — manic depression psychosis. (This information was obtained through Dorothy Ceesay, senior medical records clerk at Binghamton Psychiatric Center, in response to a personal request.)

55. The role of administrator for Lobdell's estate changed four times over the thirty-two years of Lobdell's incarceration, for he outlived all of those who had worked to have him institutionalized. When he died in 1912, he left the considerable sum of $3,500 to two grandsons, sons of Helen Crawson, who had also died before this time. A July 17, 1912, document from Surrogate's Court, Delaware County, lists Bruce Crawson as the executor for Lobdell's estate.

56. Personal conversation with Susan Crawson Shields, great-great-granddaughter of Lucy Ann Lobdell.

57. Butler, "Introductions to Bodies That Matter," 371.

58. Ernest C. James, *Ancestors and Descendants of the James Family: Narrative and Publications Relating to Lucy Ann Lobdell, the Female Hunter of Delaware and Sullivan Counties, New York* (Sacramento, CA: Self-published, 1996), 2.

59. Susan Crawson Shields, "Lucy Ann, 'the Female Hunter,'" *The Echo* 7, no. 5 (Spring 1989): 4.

60. Desens, "The Wild Woman of Manannah."

61. Dwyer, *Homes for the Mad*, xiii.

62. Halberstam, *Female Masculinity*, 50.

63. Katz, *Gay American History*, 209.

64. Ibid., 225.

65. Katz, *Gay/Lesbian Almanac*, 155.

66. Jonathan Katz, "Making Sexual History," *CLAGSnews* XIII, no. 1 (Winter 2003).

67. See "She Even Chewed Tobacco: A Pictorial Narrative of Passing Women in America," by the San Francisco Lesbian and Gay History Project, found in *Hidden from History: Reclaiming the Gay and Lesbian Past*.

68. Halberstam, *In a Queer Time and Place*, 72.

69. See http://findarticles.com/p/articles/mi_km4448/is_200510/ai_n16261076.

70. This same entry in Faderman's 2005 encyclopedia gives Lobdell's death as "1891?" A simple search on the Internet would have provided her with the actual year of death as I posted it on Swade's Tribal Chant History website, www.swade.net/lesbian/tribal_chant/les_hist.html, in 1999. The information listed for Lucy Ann Lobdell has been copied, often word for word, by many other websites.

71. Lillian Faderman, *Odd Girls and Twilight Lovers: A History of Lesbian Life in Twentieth-Century America* (New York: Penguin, 1991), 5.

72. Smith-Rosenberg, *Disorderly Conduct*, 272.

73. See www.miaminewtimes.com/issues/1996-01-04/columns2_2.htm, www.oah.org/pubs/nl/2004aug/freedman.html, www.swade.net/lesbian/tribal_chant/les_hist.html, http://niftynats.tripod.com/lesbians/, www.jtsears.com/histime.htm, www.infopt.demon.co.uk/lesbians.htm. Note: this is just a partial listing.

74. GLBT Terminology, November 2006, www.awsd.com/burgdorf/terminology.htm.
75. Gordene Olga Mackenzie, *Transgender Nation* (Bowling Green, KY: Bowling Green State University Press, 1994), 13–14.
76. Wise, "A Case of Sexual Perversion," 88.
77. Halberstam, *In a Queer Time and Place*, 56.
78. See "A Female Hunter," August 31, 1871, edition of the *Jeffersonian* about Miss Jennie Rucker, a 60-year-old widow with short hair who "kills deer, bear and other game with the skill of forty years' experience."
79. Richard Tewksbury and Patricia Gagne, "Transgenderists: Products of Non-normative Intersections of Sex, Gender, and Sexuality," *Journal of Men's Studies* 5, no. 2 (November 1996): 7.
80. Susan Stryker, "My Words to Victor Frankenstein Above the Village of Chamounix: Performing Transgender Rage," *GLQ* 1 (1994): 251.
81. Wise, "A Case of Sexual Perversion." 88.
82. Ibid., 90.
83. Ki Namaste, "The Politics of Inside/Out: Queer Theory, Poststructuralism, and a Sociological Approach to Sexuality," *Sociological Theory* 12, no. 2 (July 1994): 229.
84. Pat Califia, *Sex Changes: The Politics of Transgenderism* (San Francisco: Cleis Press, 1997), 216.
85. Sloop, "Lucy Lobdell's Queer Circumstance," 27.
86. See entry in Maria Leach, ed., *Funk and Wagnall's Standard Dictionary of Folklore, Mythology, and Legend* (San Francisco: Harper & Row, 1984).
87. Stryker, "My Words to Victor Frankenstein," 240.
88. Califia, *Sex Changes*, 162.
89. Namaste, "The Politics of Inside/Out," 220.
90. Mackenzie, *Transgender Nation*, 2.
91. Ibid., 14.
92. Sullivan, *A Critical Introduction to Queer Theory*, 39.
93. Halberstam, *Female Masculinity*, 173.
94. Sedgwick, *Epistemology of the Closet*, 8.
95. Bornstein, *Gender Outlaw*, 53.
96. Mackenzie, *Transgender Nation*, 6.
97. Bornstein, *Gender Outlaw*, 141.
98. Ibid., 121.
99. Butler, "Introduction to Bodies That Matter," 369.
100. Foucault, *The History of Sexuality*, 7.

Appendix C

1. "Onanistic practices" was the terminology used for masturbation.
2. Karl Westphal was a German physician whose theories of effeminate male and masculine female same-sex attractions were published in *Archiv für Psychiatrie und Nervenkrankheiten* in 1869. His theory that homosexuality was a congenital form of insanity greatly influenced the field of sexology.

Bibliography

Barker-Benfield, G. J. *The Horrors of the Half-Known Life: Male Attitudes Toward Women and Sexuality in Nineteenth-Century America*. New York: Harper & Row, 1976.
Boag, Peter. "Thinking Like Mount Rushmore: Sexuality and Gender in the Republican Landscape." In *Seeing Nature Through Gender*, edited by Virginia J. Scharff. Lawrence: University Press of Kansas, 2003.
Bornstein, Kate. *Gender Outlaw: On Men, Women, and the Rest of Us*. New York: Vintage Books, 1994.
Butler, Judith. *Gender Trouble: Feminism and the Subversion of Identity*. New York: Routledge, 1999.
———. "Introduction to Bodies That Matter." In *Women, Autobiography, Theory*, edited by Sidonie Smith and Julia Watson. Madison: University of Wisconsin Press, 1998, 367–79.
Califia, Pat. *Sex Changes: The Politics of Transgenderism*. San Francisco: Cleis Press, 1997.
"Certificate of Insanity." October 11, 1880. Archives of the Willard Psychiatric Institute, Albany, New York.
Chauncey, George, Jr. "From Sexual Inversion to Homosexuality: Medicine and the Changing Conceptualization of Female Desire." *Salmagundi*, no. 58/59 (Winter 1982–1983): 114–45.
"A Curious Career: Remarkable Adventures of Lucy Ann Lobdell, an Eccentric Female Character Who Figured Successfully as Hermit, Hunter, Music Teacher, Author and 'Female' Husband." *National Police Gazette*. October 25, 1879: 7.
"Death of a Modern Diana: The Female Hunter of Long Eddy — The Strange History of Lucy Slater — Her Career as a Huntress, a Pauper, a Minister, and a Vagrant — Dressed in Men's Clothing She Wins a Girl's Love." New York Times. October 7, 1879: 2.
Desens, Mindy. "The Wild Woman of Manannah." www.manannah.com/wildwoman.htm.
Duggan, Lisa. *Sapphic Slashers: Sex, Violence, and American Modernity*. Durham, NC: Duke University Press, 2000.
Dwyer, Ellen. *Homes for the Mad: Life Inside Two Nineteenth-Century Asylums*. New Brunswick, NJ: Rutgers University Press, 1987.
Ellis, Havelock. "Sexual Inversion in Women." *Alienist and Neurologist: A Quarterly Journal of Scientific, Clinical and Forensic Psychiatry and Neurology* 16 (1895): 141–58.

"Extraordinary Affair." St. Paul Daily Times. September 15, 1858.
"Extraordinary Narrative: Singular Experiences of Two Women — They Voluntarily Assume a Wild Life — Peculiar Chain of Remarkable Circumstances — The Slater Mystery Solved." New York Times. August 25, 1871: 5.
Faderman, Lillian. "Lobdell, Lucy Ann (b. 1829; d. 1890/1891?). hunter, writer." *Encyclopedia of Lesbian, Gay, Bisexual and Transgender History in America*. Ed. Marc Stein. New York: Thomson-Gale, 2004.
_____. *Odd Girls and Twilight Lovers: A History of Lesbian Life in Twentieth-Century America*. New York: Penguin, 1991.
_____. *Surpassing the Love of Men: Romantic Friendship and Love Between Women from the Renaissance to the Present*. New York: Quality Paperback Book Club, 1981.
Feinberg, Leslie. *Transgender Warrior: Making History from Joan of Arc to Dennis Rodman*. Boston: Beacon Press, 1996.
"A Female Hunter." *Jeffersonian*. August 31, 1871.
"The Female Hunter." *Wayne Citizen*. August 24, 1871.
"The Female Hunter of Long Eddy a Raving Maniac." *Wayne County Herald*. November 2, 1871.
Fischer, Gayle V. *Pantaloons and Power: A Nineteenth-Century Dress Reform in the United States*. Kent, OH: Kent State University Press, 2001.
Forest and Stream: A Journal of Outdoor Life, Travel, Nature Study, and Shooting 13, no. 12 (October 23, 1879): 751.
Forman-Brunell, Miriam. *Girlhood in America, an Encyclopedia*, volume 1. Santa Barbara, CA: ABC-CLIO, 2001.
Foucault, Michel. *The History of Sexuality: An Introduction*. Translated by Robert Hurely. New York: Vintage Books, 1990.
GLBT Terminology (website). November 2006. www.awsd.com/burgdorf/terminology.htm.
Gabrial, Brian. "A Woman's Place: Defiance and Obedience — Newspaper Stories About Women During the Trial of John Brown." *Journalism* 25, no. 1 (Winter 2008): 7–29.
Gagne, Patricia, Richard Tewksbury, and Deanna McGaughey. "Coming Out and Crossing Over: Identity Formation and Proclamation in a Transgender Community." *Gender and Society* 11, no. 4 (August 1997): 478–508.
Guinnip, W. B. Personal letter to Friend Woodward. From "Spooking Around Memory's Garret." Republished October 19, 1928. In Lobdell file at the Wayne County Historical Society in Honesdale, Pennsylvania.
Halberstam, Judith. *Female Masculinity*. Durham, NC, and London: Duke University Press, 1998.
_____. *In a Queer Time and Place: Transgender Bodies, Subcultural Lives*. New York and London: New York University Press, 2005.
"Hereabouts and Therabouts" (column). *Wayne County Herald*. February 21, 1878.
Hurner, Sheryl. "Discursive Identity Formation of Suffrage Women: Reframing the 'Cult of True Womanhood' Through Song." *Western Journal of Communication* 70, no. 3 (July 2006): 234–60.
James, Ernest C. *Ancestors and Descendants of the James Family: Narrative and Publications Relating to Lucy Ann Lobdell, the Female Hunter of Delaware and Sullivan Counties, New York*. Sacramento, CA: Self-published, 1996.
"Joe Lobdell & Wife, Their History." *Jeffersonian*. August 17, 1871.
Katz, Jonathan. *Gay American History: Lesbians and Gay Men in the U.S.A.* New York: Thomas Y. Crowell, 1976.
_____. *Gay/Lesbian Almanac: A New Documentary*. New York: Carroll & Graf, 1983.

———. "Making Sexual History: Obsessions of a Quarter Century." *CLAGSnews* XIII, no. 1 (Winter 2003).

Katz, Michael B. *In the Shadow of the Poorhouse: A Social History of Welfare in America.* New York: Basic Books, 1996.

Kiernan, James. "Original Communications: Lectures XXVI — Sexual Perversion." *Detroit Lancet* 7, no. 11 (May 1884): 481–83.

———. "Perverted Sexual Instincts: Notes on a Paper Read by J. C. Kiernan, M.D." *Chicago Medical Journal and Examiner* XLVIII (1884): 263–65.

———. "Psychological Aspects of the Sexual Appetite." *Alienist and Neurologist: A Quarterly Journal of Scientific, Clinical and Forensic Psychiatry and Neurology* (April 1891): 202–4.

Krafft-Ebbing, Richard von. *Psychopathia Sexualis.* Reprinted in English translation. New York: Samuel Login, 1908.

"The Lady in Pantaloons: She (or He) Has Gone Away." *Wayne Citizen.* November 9, 1871.

LaValley, Leslie D. *Basket Letters: A History of That Mountainous Region of the Upper Delaware That Was Once Known as the South Woods and the Wilds of the Basket.* Walton, NY: Reporter in cooperation with the Basket Historical Society of the Upper Delaware Valley, 1990.

"The Law of Vagrancy." *Wayne County Herald.* August 23, 1877.

Leach, Maria, ed. *Funk and Wagnall's Standard Dictionary of Folklore, Mythology, and Legend.* San Francisco: Harper & Row, 1984.

Lobdell, Doug, Sr. Personal interview. June 14, 1999.

Lobdell, Lucy Ann. *The Narrative of the Female Hunter of Delaware and Sullivan Counties.* New York: Published for the author, 1855.

Lorber, Judith. *Paradoxes of Gender.* New Haven, CT: Yale University Press, 1994.

"Lucy Ann Lobdell." *Wayne Citizen.* November 9, 1871.

"Lucy Ann Lobdell Dead." *Stamford Mirror.* June 23, 1885: 1.

"Lucy Ann Lobdell — The Wayne County Female Hunter Dead." *Wayne County Herald.* July 2, 1885.

"Lucy Slater the Huntress." *Hancock Herald.* October 16, 1879: 1.

Lunacy testimonials on Lucy Ann Lobdell Slater, kept in Delhi, New York, Delaware County seat.

Mackenzie, Gordene Olga. *Transgender Nation.* Bowling Green, KY: Bowling Green State University Press, 1994.

"The Man-Woman: Lucy Ann Lobdell in Town." *Port Jervis Evening Gazette.* August 10, 1876.

Mosse, George L. "Nationalism and Respectability: Normal and Abnormal Sexuality in the Nineteenth Century." *Journal of Contemporary History*, 17, no. 2 *Sexuality in History* (April 1982): 221–46.

"A Mountain Romance: Strange Life of Unhappy Women, a Singular Family History — The Female Huntress of Long Eddy — Strange Love of Two Women — An Accomplished Boston Girl a Voluntary Outcast — An Unfortunate Daughter." *New York Times.* April 8, 1877: 7.

Namaste, Ki. "The Politics of Inside/Out: Queer Theory, Poststructuralism, and a Sociological Approach to Sexuality." *Sociological Theory* 12, no. 2 (July 1994): 220–31.

Nelson, Jennifer Ladd. "Dress Reform and the Bloomer." *Journal of American and Comparative Cultures* 23, no. 1 (2000): 21–25.

Newton, Esther. "The Mythic Mannish Lesbian: Radclyffe Hall and the New Woman." *Signs* 9, no. 4, *The Lesbian Issue* (Summer 1984): 557–75.

Bibliography

Potter, Merle. "Meeker County's 'Wild Woman.'" *101 Best Stories of Minnesota*. Minneapolis: n.p., 1931, 118–21.
"The Problem of Life — What the 'Apparent Widow' of the Female Hunter Has to Say About It." *Wayne County Herald*. June 15, 1882. "A Queer Married Couple." *Warren Ledger*. November 9, 1883.
Riegel, Robert E. "Women's Clothes and Women's Rights." *American Quarterly* 15, no. 3 (Autumn 1963): 390–401.
Roberts, Helene E. "The Exquisite Slave: The Role of Clothes in the Making of the Victorian Woman." *Signs: Journal of Women in Culture and Society* 2, no. 3 (1977): 554–69.
"A Romance in Real Life." *Port Jervis Evening Gazette*. August 22, 1871.
"Romantic Lunatics." *Port Jervis Evening Gazette*. September 21, 1876.
"Romantic Paupers: The Strange History of Two Penniless Women." *Stamford Mirror*. September 5, 1871.
Sedgwick, Eve K. *Epistemology of the Closet*. Berkeley: University of California Press, 1990.
"She Even Chewed Tobacco: A Pictorial Narrative of Passing Women in America." In *Hidden from History: Reclaiming the Gay and Lesbian Past*, edited by Martin Bauml Duberman, Martha Vicinus, and George Chauncey, Jr. Ontario, Canada: New American Library, 1989.
Shields, Susan Crawson. "Lucy Ann, 'the Female Hunter.'" *The Echo* 7, no. 5 (Spring 1989): 1–4.
_____. Personal interview. May 2000.
Sidebar (no title). *Wayne County Herald*. May 18, 1882.
Sidebar (no title). *Wayne Independent*. March 28, 1878.
Sloop, John M. "Lucy Lobdell's Queer Circumstances." In *Queering Public Address: Sexualities in American Historical Discourse*, edited by Charles Morris III. Columbia: University of South Carolina Press, 2007.
Smith, A.C. "A Wild Woman's History — The Slayer of Hundreds of Bears and Wildcats." *History of Meeker County: A Historical Sketch of Meeker County, Minnesota from Its First Settlement to July 4th, 1876*. Litchfield, MN: Belfoy & Joubert, 1877, 98–111.
Smith, Sidonie. "The Autobiographical Manifesto: Identities, Temporalities, Politics." In *Autobiography and Questions of Gender*, edited by Shirley Neuman. London: Frank Cass, 1991, 186–94.
Smith-Rosenberg, Carrol. "Discourses of Sexuality and Subjectivity: The New Woman, 1870–1936." In *Hidden from History: Reclaiming the Gay and Lesbian Past*, edited by Martin Bauml Duberman, Martha Vicinus, and George Chauncey, Jr. Ontario, Canada: New American Library, 1989, 264–80.
_____. *Disorderly Conduct: Visions of Gender in Victorian America*. New York: Oxford University Press, 1985.
_____. "The Female Animal: Medical and Biological Views of Woman and Her Role in Nineteenth-Century America." *Journal of American History* 60, no. 2 (September 1973): 332–56.
Soden, Sally. "Oral History of Irma Kimble Simons." August 15, 2005. In the Wayne County Historical Society in Honesdale, Pennsylvania.
Spargo, Tasmin. *Foucault and Queer Theory*. New York: Totem Books, 1999.
Stryker, Susan. "My Words to Victor Frankenstein Above the Village of Chamounix: Performing Transgender Rage." *GLQ* 1 (1994): 237–54.
Sullivan, Nikki. *A Critical Introduction to Queer Theory*. New York: New York University Press, 2003.

Territorial Pioneers Census (Minnesota), 1857.
Tewksbury, Richard, and Patricia Gagne. "Transgenderists: Products of Non-normative Intersections of Sex, Gender, and Sexuality." *Journal of Men's Studies* 5, no. 2 (November 1996): 105–25.
Tiffany, Sharon W., and Kathleen J. Adams. *The Wild Woman: An Inquiry into the Anthropology of an Idea*. Cambridge, MA: Schekman, 1985.
"Two Strange Lives." *Galveston Daily News*. July 5, 1885.
U.S. Census Bureau. *Federal Census: Westerlo, Albany County, New York*. October 3, 1850.
U.S. Census Bureau. *Federal Census: Hancock, Delaware County, New York*. July 1860.
U.S. Census Bureau. *New York State Census: Hancock, Delaware County*. June 14, 1855.
U.S. Census Bureau. *New York State Census: Hancock, Delaware County*. June 1865.
U.S. Census Bureau. *New York State Census: Hancock, Delaware County*. August 12, 1870.
van der Meer, Theo. "Tribades on Trial: Female Same-Sex Offenders in Late Eighteenth-Century Amsterdam." *Journal of the History of Sexuality* 1 (January 1991): 424–45.
Weitz, Rose. "A History of Women's Bodies." In *The Politics of Women's Bodies: Sexuality, Appearance, and Behavior*, edited by Rose Weitz. New York: Oxford University Press, 2003, 3–25.
Welter, Barbara. "The Cult of True Womanhood: 1820–1860." *American Quarterly* 18, no. 2, part 1 (Summer 1966): 151–74.
"Who Are They?" *Jeffersonian*. August 10, 1871.
Wilchins, Riki Anne. *Queer Theory, Gender Theory*. Los Angeles: Alyson Books, 2004.
_____. *Read My Lips: Sexual Subversion and the End of Gender*. Ithaca, NY: Firebrand Books, 1997.
"A Wild Woman's History." *Port Jervis Evening Gazette*. July 27, 1876.
Wise, P. M. "A Case of Sexual Perversion." *Alienist and Neurologist: A Quarterly Journal of Scientific, Clinical and Forensic Psychiatry and Neurology* 4 (January 1883): 87–91.
Woodward, Frank P. "Lucy Ann Lobdell — Female Hunter of Long Eddy." From "Spooking Around Memory's Garret." Republished October 19, 1928. In Lobdell file at Wayne County Historical Society in Honesdale, Pennsylvania.

Index

Albany County 7
Alienist and Neurologist 9, 124, 131, 137, 199
Allen, Edwin 35–36, 164–165
Archiv für Psychiatrie und Nervenkrankheiten 128
Arrests 75, 97, 98, 99, 100–101, 103, 104, 201, 203
Atkinson, J.B. 207

Barker-Benfield, G.J. 26
The Basket Historical Society 140
Bethany, Pennsylvania 7, 17, 18, 58, 87; singing teacher 9–68, 104
Biedekapp, John 193, 194
Binghamton Insane Asylum 9, 139
Blackstone, Sir William 44
Bornstein, Kate 23, 152
Bridgeport, Conn. 176
Butler, Judith 109, 139, 151

Cagwin, John 189, 190
Calicoon Depot 180
Califia, Pat 152
Canadensis, Pennsylvania 96
A Case of Sexual Perversion 9, 57, 124
Certificate of insanity 122
Chandler, John 167, 169, 178
Chauncey, George, Jr. 132
CLAGSnews 143
Clark, Amasa 193, 194
Coxsackie, New York 33, 160, 161, 171, 172
Crawford, John 192, 193
Crawson, Helen 121, 187, 189, 194
Crawson Shields, Susan 1, 140
Cult of True Womanhood 16, 28, 37–40, 44, 47–48, 50
Cultural stories 2, 5, 8, 14, 15, 20, 66, 140

Darwin 11
Delaware County Poorhouse at Delhi 18, 87, 89, 96, 97, 101, 205, 209
Delhi, New York 121
Desens, Mindy 140–141
Dictionary of Psychological Medicine 132
Duggan, Lisa 74, 130, 135, 145, 148
Dwyer, Ellen 9, 141

The Echo 140
Ellis, Havelock 137
Encyclopedia of Lesbian, Gay, Bisexual and Transgender History in America 144
Escoffier, Jeffrey 152

F2M 22
Faderman, Lillian 9, 144–145, 148
Feinberg, Leslie 23
Female hunter of Delaware County 6, 7
Female Masculinity 85
Forest and Stream 118
Foucault, Michel 11, 15, 104, 138, 152

Gagne, Patricia 109
Galveston Daily News 8
Gearse, John 169
Gelerama 53
Gender: biologically determined 27–28, 29, 63–64; confusion 98, 73, 105–106, 131–132; as language 26–27; restriction of clothing 48–49, 51–52, 55, 60–64, 97–98; as social construct 48, 63, 65, 66, 77–78, 79–80, 86; as social organizing principle 27, 28–29, 39, 45, 51, 54, 57, 62
Gould, John 185, 186, 188, 189, 190
Grant, Rauson 189
Gribble, Edwin 70, 72, 205–206
Guinnip, W.B. 54

229

230 Index

Hacker, John 98
Haight, Oscar 193, 194
Halberstam, Judith 17, 65–66, 85, 92, 108, 115, 116, 141, 152
Hale, Dr. 36, 38, 163, 164
Hallock, David 197
Halsey, Evelyn 53
Hancock, New York 88, 96, 184, 186, 189, 195
The History of Meeker County 70, 78
The History of Sexuality 11
Honesdale, Pennsylvania 8, 19, 70, 98, 138

Industrial Revolution 16, 27
Ingals, T. 170–171
Inman, John 194
Insane asylum 8
Inverts 11, 129, 131, 137–138

Justinian 76

Katz, Jonathan 9, 142–144, 148
Kerberry, Karl Maria 128
Kiernan, James 131, 139
Koon, H.W.M. 190
Krafft-Ebbing, Richard von 129, 131, 132, 137, 202

LaValley, Helen 166, 167, 168
LaValley, Leslie D. 53
LaValley, Mr. 164, 165
LaValley, Roderick 166
"Lesbian" etiology 145
"Lesbian love" 9, 12, 124, 134, 144
Lesbian-transgender conflation 15, 21–22, 125–126, 138, 141–142, 145–146, 148
Lesbianism 13, 15, 68
Lobdell, Eadie 1
Lobdell, James 155
Lobdell, John 121, 122, 184, 185, 187, 188, 189, 190, 192, 193, 195, 197
Lobdell, La-Roi 3, 14, 70–76
Lobdell, Lucy Ann: birth 7, 156; buys a farm 117; death 9, 123, 139; declared insane 8, 107, 122; forced to wear women's clothes 81, 97–98, 102, 147, 203; hunting 173–176; learning to shoot 31, 40, 81–82, 94, 172–173, 203–204; living in the woods 8, 19, 96, 98, 115, 117, 204, 207; marriage myth 83–84
Lobdell, Mary 174
Lobdell, Sarah 155
Lobdell, Sidney 184, 185, 186, 189, 190, 192, 193, 194
Long, Eddy 7, 58, 203

MacCormack, Carol 71
Mackenzie, Gordene Olga 152
Mains, William W. 193, 194, 196

Manannah, Minnesota 7, 17, 18, 71, 72, 73, 87, 206
Marble, Ken, J. 194
Maynard, Judge Isaac H. 121, 184, 188, 191, 198
McGaughey, Deanna 109
Meeker County's Wild Woman 83
Milk, David 193, 194
Milk, George 194
More, Arthur 188, 190, 191, 192, 193, 194, 195, 196, 197, 198

The Narrative of Lucy Ann Lobdell, Female Hunter of Delaware and Sullivan Counties, N.Y. 7, 30, 56
Narrative technologies 6, 12, 15, 66, 67–68, 78–80, 90, 91, 93–96, 102–103, 104–108
Narrowsburg, New York 99, 180
National Police Gazette 118
New York Times 8, 87, 112, 118, 147, 207
Newton, John 186, 187

Odd Girls and Twilight Lovers: A History of Lesbian Life in Twentieth-Century America 144
O'Meara, Ellen 53

Passing Woman 9–10, 13, 21
Peak, Walter 184, 186
Perry, Marie Louise 7, 8, 9, 11, 13, 15, 18, 19, 21, 88–89, 140, 208; composition 111–113; feminine 110–111; relationship with Joe 90–93, 101–102, 112–114; trans-erotic desire 20, 22, 126–128, 133–134, 148–149; as widow 119–120; writes petition 101, 113, 201
Pettingill, Dr. Ed L. 122, 195–196
Phifer, Henry 193, 194
Pierce, Capt. A.D. 85, 207
Poorhouse 88, 95
Potter, Merle 83
Psychopathia Sexualis 129

Queer, defined 20, 91
Queer theory 20, 92
Queer Time 17, 66, 73, 92, 108, 115

Robson, John, Esq. J.P. 75, 207
Rock Valley 54
Rubin, Gayle 152
Ryden, Stephen 193, 194
Ryder, Inid 196–197

St. John, Mr. 158
Sapphic Slashers 145
Sedgwick, Eve 152
Sexology 10, 11, 13, 128, 130, 132
Shifer, Henry 193
Slater, George Washington 7, 8, 9, 32–37,

Index

39–40, 43, 121, 133, 158–161, 162–165, 167–168, 169, 173, 178–179, 185, 197, 204
Sloop, John M. 149–150
Smith, A.C. 70, 78–79, 81, 84, 207
Smith, Buell 167
Smith, Peter 168, 169
Smith, Thomas 169
Smith, William 156–158, 166, 168, 172
Smith-Rosenberg, Carrol 110, 129, 131, 149
Spearbeck, Ebenezer 166, 192, 193, 194
Spenser, Sheriff 81
Stephens, Edson 193, 194, 196
Strathern, Marilyn 71
Stroudsburg, Pennsylvania 97, 98, 146
Surpassing the Love of Men 144

Talmage the peddler 41–43, 77, 176–178
Tewksbury, Richard 109
Third space 19–20, 23, 93, 108, 109, 115, 152
Transgender defined 12, 14

Truman, John 193
Tuke, D. Hack 132

Ulrichs, Karl Heinrich 128
Utica asylum 164

Walsh, George 197
Walsh, Harry 54, 121, 191, 197–198
Waymart, Pennsylvania 113
Wayne Citizen 99
Wayne County Herald 67, 117
Westerloo, New York 30, 155, 168, 170, 178
Westphal, Karl 128, 137, 201
Wheeler, F.O. 192, 193
Wilchins, Riki Anne 73
A Wild Woman's History 80
Willard Insane Asylum 21, 57, 122, 139, 141, 199, 201
Willie, U.S. 207
Wise, Dr. P.M. 8–9, 11, 12, 13, 21, 34, 57, 119, 122, 124, 126, 131, 132–137, 146, 148, 199
Woodward, Frank 67–68, 139

www.ingramcontent.com/pod-product-compliance
Ingram Content Group UK Ltd.
Pitfield, Milton Keynes, MK11 3LW, UK
UKHW041944140426
5217IPUK00014B/648